SOCIAL
EXPERIMENTS

SOCIAL
EXPERIMENTS

Evaluating

Public

Programs

With

Experimental

Methods

LARRY L. ORR

SAGE Publications
International Educational and Professional Publisher
Thousand Oaks London New Delhi

For information:

SAGE Publications, Inc.
2455 Teller Road
Thousand Oaks, California 91320
E-mail: order@sagepub.com

SAGE Publications Ltd.
6 Bonhill Street
London EC2A 4PU
United Kingdom

SAGE Publications India Pvt. Ltd.
M-32 Market
Greater Kailash I
New Delhi 110 048 India

Printed in the United States of America

Library of Congress Cataloging-in-Publication Data

Library of Congress Cataloging-in-Publication Data

Orr, Larry L.
    Social experiments: Evaluating public programs with
experimental methods / by Larry L. Orr.
        p. cm.
    Includes bibliographical references and index.
    ISBN 0-7619-1294-0 (cloth : acid-free paper)
    ISBN 0-7619-1295-9 (pbk. : acid-free paper)
    1. Social sciences--Experiments. 2. Experimental design. 3.
Social sciences--Research. I. Title.
    H62 .O755 1998
    300'.7'2--ddc21   98-25337

This book is printed on acid-free paper.

99 00 01 02 03 04 05 10 9 8 7 6 5 4 3 2 1

Acquiring Editor:	C. Deborah Laughton
Editorial Assistant:	Eileen Carr
Production Editor:	Wendy Westgate
Production Assistant:	Nevair Kabakain
Typesetter/Designer:	Rose Tylak
Cover Designer:	Candice Harman

Contents

Preface

As a young economist, I had two seminal experiences that have had a profound effect on my view of research throughout my professional career. First, I wrote a dissertation. In the course of this effort, I learned that, using standard econometric techniques, I could obtain almost any result I wanted through the simple expedient of "fishing"—estimating alternative "structural models," no one of which had any greater claim to validity than any other. In doing so, I was trading on correlations in the data that may or may not have represented causal relationships (and, in the process, wreaking havoc with the tests of statistical significance that should have been my protection against erroneous inferences). As a result of this experience, I was deeply impressed with the extreme difficulty of ever knowing with any confidence what causes what in the real world on the basis of statistical analysis of data.

The second seminal experience of my young career was my involvement, first at the Institute for Research on Poverty and then at the Office of Economic Opportunity, in the design of the income maintenance experiments, which were among the first major "social experiments." I was struck by the power of this novel technique to cut through the clouds of confusing correlations that make the inference of causality so hazardous in the data that economists normally analyze. With experimental data, one could state with measurable confidence whether a particular public policy affected a particular outcome. I have never quite lost my sense of wonder at this amazing fact.

In the 30 years since my introduction to experimentation, the method has become widely accepted as the "gold standard" of program evaluation.

Equally important, a body of relatively standard experimental methods has emerged from the large number of experiments that have been conducted during this period. Until very recently, however, this body of knowledge was largely buried in technical reports or carried around in the heads of practitioners, inaccessible to the uninitiated. Little of it was published in academic journals, much less textbooks. The only available text resembling a comprehensive treatment of the application of experimental design to public policy was Campbell and Stanley's classic *Experimental and Quasi-Experimental Designs for Research,* which was last revised in 1963.[1] Although Campbell and Stanley's book remains a lucid exposition of the principles of experimental design, it does not capture the richness of 30 years of experience using the method. This book attempts to codify some of this knowledge.

To make the book accessible to as wide an audience as possible, I tried to minimize reliance on mathematics and statistics. I am firmly convinced that most of the fundamental principles of experimentation can be stated in plain English, and that when they are stated in English, they are more understandable to most readers. Experimental design, however, is an exercise in applied statistics; indeed, social experimentation owes its power to the amazing ability of statistical methods to control for the random noise and chance associations that pervade human affairs. Therefore, an understanding of some basic statistical concepts is necessary if one is truly to understand social experiments and correctly interpret their results. I have tried to develop these concepts from first principles in the text, although I admit that for the reader with no statistical training some sections may be difficult. Sections of Chapter 6 assume a knowledge of multiple regression analysis; the nontechnical reader may want to skip these parts, although I strongly recommend that even (especially?) nontechnical readers read the sections of Chapter 6 that deal with the dangers of misinterpreting subgroup analyses.

This is a "how-to" book. It is intended to provide a basic understanding not only of how to design and implement social experiments but also of how to interpret their results once they are completed. Thus, it should be useful not only to those who plan to conduct experiments but also to the much larger group who will, at one time or another, want to understand the results of experimental evaluations. This latter group includes students of public policy, government research managers, legislators and their staffs, and program operators. Although there is little in this book that is not widely known by professional evaluators with experience conducting social experiments, I hope that even this group can learn something from a systematic treatment of experimental principles. I know that I certainly learned a great deal from a careful review of the foundations of the craft I have practiced for many years.

For most of its history, social experimentation has not been taught in graduate schools. Practitioners of experimental evaluation, including myself, have learned most of what we know about the method through on-the-job training. Much of the contents of this book I learned by working on a number of experiments with some extraordinarily gifted colleagues. First and foremost, I owe an enormous intellectual debt to Joe Newhouse, who opened my eyes to the possibilities of the method with his masterful design of the Health Insurance Experiment. Later, I was privileged to work with, and learn from, Steve Bell on the Aid to Families with Dependent Children Homemaker-Home Health Aide Demonstrations and the National Job Training Partnership Act (JTPA) Study and with Howard Bloom on the National JTPA Study.

This book was made possible by financial support from the U.S. Department of Health and Human Services (DHHS). I am indebted to David Ellwood and Wendell Primus, former Assistant Secretary and former Deputy Assistant Secretary for Planning and Evaluation, respectively, for their belief in the value of this undertaking and their willingness to support it. I am also indebted to Wendell Knox, President of Abt Associates and my boss, for allowing me the time and support required to complete the final chapters of the book and to revise it for publication. I thank Howard Rolston, Peter Germanis, Steve Bell, and the participants in a series of seminars for DHHS staff for their helpful comments on early drafts of portions of this book, as well as the anonymous reviewers for Sage Publications, who provided valuable input to the final revisions. Erik Beecroft and Lu Nguyen provided assistance in developing some of the exhibits and Chris Treston of the DHHS graphics department created the graphics.

Note

1. While this book was in preparation, an excellent treatise on social experimentation, *Randomized Experiments for Planning and Evaluation* by Robert Boruch (1997), was published by Sage.

References

Boruch, R. (1997). *Randomized experiments for planning and evaluation.* Thousand Oaks, CA: Sage.

Campbell, D. T., & Stanley, J. C. (1963). *Experimental and quasi-experimental designs for research.* Chicago: Rand McNally.

In memory of my mother, Margery Orr,
who taught me the importance
of doing the job right.

Chapter ❶

Why Experiment?
The Rationale and History
of Social Experiments

In 1966, a graduate student in economics at the Massachusetts Institute of Technology approached the Office of Economic Opportunity (OEO), President Lyndon Johnson's antipoverty agency, with an unusual proposal. Heather Ross (1966) suggested that OEO test the negative income tax (NIT) concept that was then being discussed among academic economists by actually giving money to working poor families and monitoring their behavior. The test would focus on whether the NIT would cause poor families to quit working, as its critics alleged.

What made Ross's proposal different from the many demonstration projects that were funded by OEO as part of the War on Poverty was the suggestion that the test be structured as a classical statistical experiment, with random assignment of families to a "treatment" group, which would be eligible to receive NIT payments, or a "control" group, which would not. The difference in outcomes between the two groups would provide a measure of the effect of the NIT program.

The project that ultimately resulted from Ross's proposal—the New Jersey Income Maintenance Experiment—is generally regarded as the first large-scale "social experiment."[1] During 1968 and 1969, 1,300 low-income families in five cities were randomly assigned to treatment or control status, and the treatment group received negative income tax payments for the next 3 years. The effects of the experimental program on family members' employment and earnings, educational attainment, marital stability, and other behavioral outcomes were measured by the difference in subsequent outcomes for the two groups.

As will be discussed later, the New Jersey Experiment was not entirely unprecedented. Whether or not it was the first social experiment, however, it certainly sparked widespread interest in the application of experimental methods to a broad range of public programs and policies that had rarely, if ever, been subjected to such rigorous evaluation techniques.

In this chapter, I discuss the rationale for using experimental methods to evaluate public programs and the limitations of the experimental approach. Then, I examine the ethical issues that are sometimes raised with regard to experiments. This chapter concludes with a brief review of the history of the use of experimental methods for program evaluation, both before and since the New Jersey Experiment.

Why Experiment?

In popular parlance, implementing a program on an experimental basis is usually taken to mean "trying out" a new program on a small scale to see if it "works." If the program is truly new, then only by setting up a pilot test can we obtain any empirical evidence of its effects. So one rationale for social experiments is to create a working model of the program so that we can evaluate it. Determining whether the program works, however, requires much more than simply observing it in action. To understand why, we must consider what is meant when a program is said to either work or not work and the alternative means of making this determination. As will be shown, the evaluation of ongoing programs raises many of the same issues as the testing of new programs.

We take the question of whether a program works to mean whether it is effective in achieving its goals. For most social programs, these goals concern the effects of the program on its participants. The goal of a job training program, for example, is to raise participants' earnings. If the program is targeted at welfare recipients, it might have the further objective of getting them off welfare, or at least reducing their welfare benefits. The goals of a teen parenting program might be to induce teen parents to remain in or return to school, make them better parents, reduce future childbirth, or all three. A remedial education program might have the objective of raising students' math skills or reading comprehension. These behaviors and circumstances of the participants after they enter the program are termed *outcomes*.[2] To determine whether the program is "working," we must determine whether it was successful in changing the outcomes it is intended to affect.

One can, of course, observe the outcomes of interest—employment, receipt of welfare, school attendance, and so on—simply by following participants after they leave the program. One cannot, however, on the basis of participant behavior alone know what portion of the observed postprogram outcomes should be attributed to the program. The *impact* of the program is defined as the difference between the observed outcomes of participants (e.g., their postprogram earnings) and what those outcomes would have been in the absence of the program.

Suppose, for example, that 80% of the graduates of a job training program obtain jobs when they leave the program. Does that mean that the program is achieving its objective of increasing the employment and earnings of its participants? Not necessarily. Some of the participants would have gotten jobs even if they had not gone through the training program. If only 20% would have found jobs in the absence of the program, then the program has increased participants' employment rate by 60 percentage points. If 80% of the participants would have gotten jobs without the program's help, however, the program has had zero impact on participants' employment rate. (Of course, in this case, it may be helping them obtain better jobs or obtain jobs faster, so we would need to examine outcomes such as earnings and hours of work in addition to employment rates.)

Similar reasoning applies to most social programs. Some individuals would have gotten off welfare, returned to school, or improved their educational performance even without special assistance. We can only attribute behavioral changes over and above that base level to the program. The fundamental problem of program evaluation, then, is to determine what would have happened in the absence of the program. Measuring the actual outcomes of participants is relatively straightforward; not surprisingly, measuring what participants would have done in the absence of the program is much more difficult. Like the White Knight's green whiskers, what would have happened to the participants in the absence of the program is forever hidden from view.

There are, however, a number of different ways to attempt to estimate what would have happened to the participants in the absence of the program. To understand why experimental methods are the preferred approach, it is useful to understand the shortcomings of other approaches. I therefore discuss the two principal alternatives to experimental designs: pre-post designs (sometimes called "reflexive" designs) and comparison group designs. The discussion here and elsewhere in this book focuses on programs in which the principal effects of interest to the evaluator are on individual program participants rather than on institutions or the broader community. The discussion encompasses both the evaluation of ongoing programs and the testing of new programs in special demonstrations.

Pre-Post Designs

A particularly simple way to attempt to determine what would have happened in the absence of a program is to use the behavior of the participants before they came into the program. In the case of a job training program, for example, we might use the earnings of the participants in the year before they applied to the program. In a remedial education program for high school students, we might use the students' grades from the previous school year. We would then measure the impact of the program by the change in earnings or grades between the year prior to program participation and the year after. This design has the advantage of requiring only data on participants.

Pre-post designs are not always feasible. The institutional setting may preclude collection of the relevant data before the intervention begins, or the outcome of interest may not be defined in the preprogram period. Suppose, for example, that we are evaluating a program of prenatal care and the principal outcomes of interest are measures of the health of the baby; these measures are not defined in the preprogram period.

Even when preprogram data can be collected, however, for several reasons behavior in the period prior to program entry may not be a good predictor of what would have happened later in the absence of the program. *Factors external to the program* may change during the same time period. In the case of the training program, for example, an improvement in the local economy might result in increased earnings, quite aside from any effect of the program. A pre-post impact measure would erroneously attribute this

Participants' outcomes may also change over time because of natural *maturation processes*. Suppose, for example, that we wish to measure the effect of a preschool program on the social skills of children. Even without a special program, children's social skills can be expected to improve over time. Thus, a pre-post impact measure would overstate the effects of the program by including gains in social skills that would have occurred anyway. Much the same type of maturation effects are likely to affect the employment and earnings of teenagers entering the job market; pre-post measures are therefore likely to overstate the impact of job training programs on young workers.

Even when there are no pronounced secular trends in the outcome measure for the population at large or maturation effects, pre-post designs will yield misleading conclusions if, on average, the preprogram period was atypical for participants. For example, individuals usually apply to job training programs when they are unemployed. Even without the program's assistance, however, some of the participants would eventually find work on their own. Thus, in the absence of the program, job training participants would show a rising earnings trend from the period before program entry to the period after. Statisticians refer to this as *"regression to the mean."*

This phenomenon of individuals participating in public programs when their outcomes of interest are atypically low (or high) is not confined to job training programs. People naturally tend to apply to social programs when their need is greatest. Moreover, social programs often select participants on the basis of need—as measured by the same indicators that evaluators use to measure the impact of the program. To the extent that these needs would be only temporary even without the program's assistance, selection on need will result in regression to the mean, with need being greatest around the time of program entry and declining over time. In such cases, simple pre-post differences in outcomes will overstate the effect of the program by including the rebound from this temporary need for assistance that would have occurred even without the program's help.

Figure 1.1 shows how failure to take into account the temporary nature of the need for assistance can create a misleading impression of program effectiveness. The top of Figure 1.1 shows the time path of quarterly public assistance benefits to a sample of Aid to Families with Dependent Children recipients who were eligible for a program designed to help them become employed and leave the welfare rolls.

The steep downward trend in assistance payments would appear to indicate that the program was quite effective. This is in fact the type of "evidence" that is frequently used to demonstrate program effectiveness in the legislative

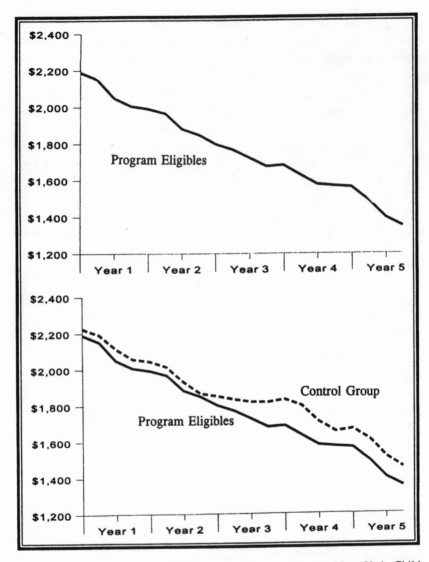

Figure 1.1. Average Quarterly Assistance Payments for the New York Child Assistance Program

process and in the popular media. As shown in the bottom panel of Figure 1.1, however, the decline in benefits was nearly as steep for a control group of program eligibles who were excluded from the program as part of a social experiment. This comparison demonstrates that most of the decline in benefits experienced by the participant group was the result of normal turnover of the welfare rolls as recipients' circumstances improved and they were able to leave welfare. Attributing the effects of this turnover to the program greatly overstates its effectiveness.

Comparison Group Designs

As the previous example suggests, one way to avoid some of the hazards of pre-post designs is through the use of a comparison group. This approach involves selecting a group of individuals who are as similar as possible to the participants, except that they do not participate in the program, and monitoring their outcomes. The pre-post change in outcomes of the comparison group is used to represent what would have happened to the participants in the absence of the program. Ideally, the pre-post change in earnings of the comparison group will reflect any general rise in earnings in the local labor market, natural maturation factors, or a rebound from a spell of unemployment. In the simplest case, subtracting the pre-post change in outcomes of the comparison group from the pre-post change in outcomes of the participants should yield a more accurate measure of the impact of the program.

Table 1.1 illustrates this approach for a hypothetical remedial education program. The outcome of interest, student grade point average (GPA), was measured during the semester before and the semester after the program for participants and for a comparison group of nonparticipants. The table shows that a simple pre-post measure of impact, using data for participants only, would indicate that the program increased GPA by 0.6 points. In the comparison group, however, GPA rose 0.2 points even without the assistance of the program. Under the assumption that participants would have experienced this same rise in GPA in the absence of the program, the comparison group approach estimates the impact of the program as 0.4 points—the change in GPA from pre- to postprogram for the participant group less the pre-post change for the comparison group.

The comparison group design thus avoids the erroneous attribution of the full increase in GPA to the program that would occur with a simple pre-post measure of impact. It is, however, still potentially subject to bias associated with the way the treatment group and comparison group were selected. Because the pervasiveness of "selection bias" in nonexperimental comparison group designs is one of the most important reasons for preferring experimental methods, we examine this phenomenon in detail in the following section.

TABLE 1.1 Illustrative Comparison Group Design

Group	Preprogram GPA	Postprogram GPA	Pre-Post Change
Participants	2.0	2.6	0.6
Comparison group	2.2	2.4	0.2
Estimated impact			0.4

Selection Bias

The comparison group design is based on the assumption that program participants would have experienced the same change in outcomes as members of the comparison group had they not gone through the program. Estimates based on comparison group designs are only as valid as this assumption. Ultimately, one can never be sure how valid this assumption is because it is a statement about something that is inherently unobservable—the experience of the program participants if they had not entered the program.

What we do know is that the participants were either self-selected or selected by somebody else (e.g., a teacher or a welfare caseworker) to enter the program, whereas the comparison group members were not. Unless those selection decisions were totally random, this means that the two groups differ in some way. If the difference(s) that led one group to be selected for the program and the other not to be selected also leads to differences in the outcomes of interest, the comparison group design will erroneously attribute the differences in outcomes to the impact of the program. Such errors in attribution are termed *selection bias*.

Suppose, for example, that the hypothetical remedial education program discussed previously was open, on a voluntary basis, to all students with GPAs below 2.5 and that the comparison group was composed of all students who were eligible but did not volunteer to participate. The fact that the participants volunteered for the program may suggest that they are more motivated than the students in the comparison group, who did not, and this may indicate that their improvement in grades would have been greater than that of the comparison group even without the program's help.

Table 1.2 illustrates how this would lead to bias in the estimate of program impact. The first three rows simply reproduce the information in Table 1.1. The fourth row shows the (unobservable) pre-post change in participants'

TABLE 1.2 Illustrative Comparison Group Design, Relative to True Impact

Group	Preprogram GPA	Postprogram GPA	Pre-Post Change
Participants, with program	2.0	2.6	0.6
Comparison group	2.2	2.4	0.2
Estimated impact	—	—	0.4
Participants, without program	2.0	2.5	0.5
True impact	—	—	0.1

GPA that would have occurred in the absence of the program—here assumed to be more than that of the comparison group because the participants are assumed to be more motivated. The true impact of the program is the difference between the observed pre-post change in participants' GPA minus the change that would have occurred in the absence of the program. In this case, the true impact is 0.1. The estimate based on the comparison group (0.4) overstates the true impact by the difference between the pre-post change in the comparison group and the true without-program pre-post change for the participants.[3]

Alternatively, suppose the participants were selected by their teachers. If the teachers selected those who were least likely to do well without the program's assistance, the comparison group's grade gains might well overstate the change in grades that could be expected for participants in the absence of the program. In this case, the estimate based on the comparison group would understate the effect of the program—that is, it would be biased downward.

Selection bias encompasses any differences between the program participants and the comparison group that affect the outcomes of interest. Suppose, for example, that a comparison group for the participants in a job training program is selected from communities in which the program is not conducted. Differences between the labor markets in the program communities and the comparison communities may cause the employment and earnings of the comparison group either to overstate or to understate what would have happened to the program participants in the absence of the program.

One can, of course, attempt to match the comparison group to the participants in terms of such personal characteristics as age, race, gender, prior employment experience or grades (depending on the nature of the experiment), environmental characteristics such as the local unemployment rate or rural versus urban setting, or all these. Comparison groups are sometimes drawn from national survey databases, such as the Current Population Survey or the decennial census, using such matching techniques. One can match only on measured characteristics, however. If the two groups differ in unmeasured characteristics, such as motivation or native ability, their outcomes may differ for reasons that have nothing to do with the program.

Experimental Designs

As noted previously, the main problem in measuring the impact of a program is that we cannot observe what the participants' outcomes would have been in the absence of the program. We can try to represent those outcomes with those of a comparison group, but if there are systematic differences between the comparison group and the participants that affect the outcomes of interest, impact estimates based on the comparison group will be biased.

Random assignment offers a way to create a comparison group that is not systematically different from the participants—that is, one that is not subject to selection bias. If assignment to the program or to the comparison group is completely random, selection into one group or the other is by definition unrelated to any characteristic of the individual and therefore to the individual's subsequent outcomes. Thus, any systematic differences in postrandom assignment outcomes between the two groups can confidently be attributed to the experimental program.[4]

The defining characteristic of a *social experiment* is random assignment of some pool of individuals to two or more groups that are subject to different policy regimes. One of these groups is a *control group* that is subject to the existing policy environment—that is, it is excluded from the experimental program.[5] In addition, one or more *treatment groups* consist of individuals assigned to one or more variants of the program being evaluated. Data on the relevant outcomes of each group are then measured over some follow-up period and the impact of the program is estimated as the difference between treatment and control group outcomes.

By *random assignment*, I mean assignment of individuals to groups on the basis of a random event such that each individual has a specified probability of being assigned to each group.[6] The random event can be as simple as the flip of a coin: If the coin is heads, the individual is assigned to the treatment group, whereas if it is tails, he or she is assigned to the control group. In this case, each individual would have a 50% chance of assignment to each group and, if large numbers of applicants are randomly assigned, the total sample will be divided approximately evenly between the two groups. In practice, random assignment is usually based on specially designed tables of random numbers or computer algorithms that generate random numbers.[7] No matter which method is employed, it is important that each individual have a specified probability of being assigned to each group and that the assignment itself be made by chance alone.

Suppose, for example, that we wish to evaluate a new job training program. We begin by setting the program up on a pilot basis and recruiting applicants. Those judged eligible (and still interested after learning more about the program) would then be randomly assigned to a treatment group, which is allowed to enter the program, or to a control group, which is not. Because the primary objective of a training program is to raise participants' earnings, we would collect data on the earnings of individuals in both groups following random assignment. The impact of the program on participants' earnings would be measured by the difference in mean earnings between the treatment and control groups during the follow-up period. Because the two groups were well matched at the point of entry into the program, it is not essential to compare the changes in the two groups' earnings during the follow-up period, as we did in the comparison group design. The simple treatment-control difference in postrandom assignment earnings will, on average, give the same answer as the treatment-control difference in changes in earnings because there was no systematic difference between the two groups at the point of random assignment. (As will be shown in Chapter 6, however, accounting for the preprogram value of the outcome variable will improve the precision of the impact estimates.)

Although this simple example illustrates the fundamental elements of a social experiment, the range of possible variations on this basic theme is enormous. For example, instead of evaluating a single program, one might wish to compare several different program models or estimate the effects of specific program components. Instead of studying the effects of the program on applicants who voluntarily apply to the program, one might wish to study its effects on the entire population eligible for the program or a subset of eligibles. The program to be evaluated need not be a new one; it could be an ongoing program. Also, policymakers may be interested in the effects of the program on a range of participant outcomes, including some that are difficult to quantify, and not just a single, easily quantified outcome such as earnings. In subsequent chapters, we will explore the design variations that will allow the experimenter to address these and other evaluation objectives.

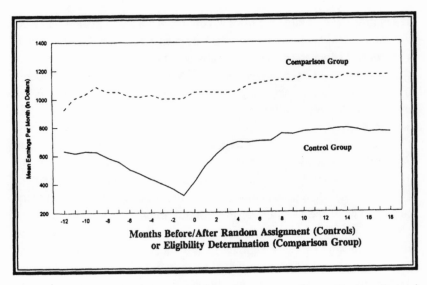

Figure 1.2. Mean Earnings, Experimental Control Group Versus Nonexperimental Comparison Group, National JTPA Study

Experimental Versus Nonexperimental Impact Estimates: An Empirical Example

The difference between nonexperimental comparison groups and randomly assigned control groups—and therefore the potential for selection bias in impact estimates based on comparison groups—can be quite striking. Figure 1.2 compares the time path of earnings for an experimental control group of job training applicants with that of a comparison group of individuals who were eligible for the program but did not apply.[8] As shown in the figure, controls' earnings fell sharply in the months prior to application to the program and then rebounded after they applied to the Job Training Partnership Act (JTPA) program. In contrast, the time path of earnings of the eligible nonparticipant comparison group shows only a slight upward trend during this 2.5-year time period.

This stark difference in earnings paths reflects the difference in the two groups' situations at the time they were selected. Controls were selected at a point in time when many of them had just experienced a period of unemployment, leading them to apply to JTPA.[9] In contrast, the comparison group members were selected solely on the basis of their eligibility for JTPA, without regard to their recent work history. Because JTPA eligibility is determined primarily by family income, this selection procedure ensures that the comparison group members will have relatively low earnings. Because selection into the comparison group was not keyed to any particular event in the individuals' lives, however, the average earnings of the group is stable over time.

To determine how these differences in earnings paths can lead to biased impact estimates, consider Table 1.3, which presents alternative estimates of program impact based on data in Figure 1.2 and data on the earnings of program participants. As can be seen in Table 1.3, an impact estimate based on the comparison group of eligible nonapplicants erroneously attributes a large share of the change in participants' earnings from preprogram to postprogram to the impact of the program (compare rows 1 and 3) because there was very little change in comparison group earnings over time (row 2). In contrast, the earnings path of the control group shows that almost all the change would have occurred even in the absence of the program. The comparison group-based estimate, therefore, substantially overstates the impact of the program.

It must be noted that there are statistical methods that can be used to attempt to adjust nonexperimental impact estimates for differences between the comparison group and the participants (Heckman & Robb, 1985). These methods, however, rely on assumptions about the behavior of the two groups that are generally impossible to verify. Thus, one cannot be certain whether the method successfully adjusted for all the relevant differences between the two groups. The multiplicity of the nonexperimental estimators available compounds the uncertainty; because different nonexperimental methods generally give different answers, it is unclear which method one should apply.

Detailed discussion of these methods is beyond the scope of this book. Fortunately, it is also unnecessary. The great methodological advantage of experimental methods over nonexperimental estimators does not lie in the technical details of either approach. It lies in the fact that, unlike any nonexperimental method, properly implemented random assignment guarantees impact estimates that, aside from sampling error, reflect only the effects of the experimental treatment. Nonexperimental methods may be equally reliable in any given application; we simply cannot know a priori that they are reliable, as we can with experimental methods.

TABLE 1.3 Comparison Group-Based Impact Estimate Versus Experimental Estimate of JTPA Impact on Annual Earnings

Group	Preprogram Earnings ($)	Postprogram Earnings ($)	Pre-Post Change ($)
Participants	6,300	8,900	+2,600
Comparison group	12,000	13,200	+1,200
Estimated impact	—	—	+1,400
Experimental control group	6,300	8,800	+2,500
Experimental impact estimate	—	—	+100

Internal Validity and External Validity of Experimental Estimates

Evaluation methods that provide unbiased estimates of the impact of the specific program tested on the population to which it was applied are termed *internally valid*. Unlike nonexperimental methods, properly implemented social experiments are guaranteed to provide internally valid impact estimates. To be useful for policy purposes, however, impact estimates must have both internal validity and external validity. *Externally valid* estimators provide unbiased estimates of the impact of the program of interest for policy purposes on the population to which it is to be applied. That is, only if the experiment faithfully replicates the program of interest to policymakers and applies it to a sample that is representative of the policy-relevant population will it have external validity and provide a reliable guide for policy decisions.

The external validity of the experiment can be compromised in a number of ways. For example, because experiments take time to conduct, the policy of interest often evolves and changes while the experiment is under way so that when the results become available they represent a somewhat different intervention than the one under consideration at that time. Also, for reasons of cost and logistics, experimental samples are usually clustered in a small number of localities; this makes it difficult to draw a sample that is truly representative of the entire U.S. population.

In subsequent chapters, I consider ways to protect against these and other threats to external validity in the implementation of the experiment. True external validity, however, is an ideal that is almost impossible to attain, if only because the continually evolving policy process represents such a moving target. Nevertheless, it is an important ideal to strive for, and in assessing the strengths and weaknesses of alternative evaluation methods or results, it is important to gauge their external validity as well as their internal validity.

Some Limitations of the Experimental Method

In addition to the internal and external validity of the estimates, certain inherent limitations of the experimental method must be borne in mind in designing and interpreting experimental studies. These circumscribe the kinds of information that can be derived from experiments and, therefore, the kinds of intervention that can appropriately be evaluated with experimental methods.

One such limitation is the fact that experiments focus on the behavior of individual program participants or their families or both. Random assignment of program participants cannot provide estimates of program effects on broader aggregations of individuals, such as neighborhoods or entire cities. An example of a program that might cause such *"community effects"* is a rent subsidy program that is expected to substantially increase the demand for housing within the local housing market. Random assignment of families to a program group that receives the subsidy or to an unsubsidized control group will allow estimation of the effects of the subsidy on the behavior of individual families. The broader effects on the housing market (e.g., any resulting increase in market rent levels) cannot be captured by such an experiment, however, for several reasons. First, because the experimental sample is unlikely to include all eligible families in the local housing market and, in any case, the control group will not receive the subsidy, the change in aggregate demand induced by the experiment will be less than would be expected in a real program. Second, estimation of aggregate effects would require random assignment of housing markets rather than individuals or families. That is, we would want to compare a sample of housing markets in which the program was implemented (at full scale) with a statistically equivalent sample of housing markets without the subsidy. Although such a design is conceptually possible, in practice it would be very difficult to implement the experiment in a large enough sample of housing markets to allow accurate estimation of the market effects of the subsidy. In Chapter 4, I discuss such designs in more detail. In the remainder of this book, however, we focus on programs that are expected to affect primarily the behavior of program participants.

A second limitation on the types of intervention that can be evaluated experimentally arises from the need to exclude the control group from the experimental treatment. For some interventions, this would not be possible. For example, one could not use experimental methods to measure the impact of a public information campaign conducted through the mass media because the control group could not be excluded from receiving the treatment.

Another important limitation of social experiments is that, because they monitor the behavioral responses to the treatment in real time, experiments take a significant amount of time to complete. Often, the responses to the experimental intervention extend over several years; in addition, typically several years are needed to design and field the experiment and analyze its results. This means that the experimental estimates will usually not be available until at least 3 to 5 years after the decision to launch the experiment. In some cases, the lag can be as much as 10 to 15 years. As discussed in subsequent chapters, this places a premium on selecting for experimental analysis only those interventions and policies that are likely to still be of interest to policymakers 5 years later.

Because experiments usually require direct contact with program participants to administer the treatment and collect data, experimental samples tend to be clustered within a small number of geographic areas to keep costs manageable. As noted previously, this may raise issues of the external validity of the experimental results. I address these issues in Chapter 4.

Another inherent limitation is that experiments estimate the average impact of the program on groups of participants. They cannot measure the impact of the program on specific individuals. One can estimate, however, average impacts for subgroups of the participant population, and one can analyze how impacts vary with participant or site characteristics. I discuss these analytic approaches and their limitations in Chapters 3 and 6.

Finally, it is important to recognize that the experimental impact estimates represent the effects of the specific intervention implemented on the specific population who participated. For the results to be useful in the policy process, it is imperative that the nature of the program and the characteristics of its participants be carefully documented. This means that virtually every experiment should be accompanied by a *process analysis* that describes the experimental intervention in sufficient detail so that it is clear what was tested, and also that descriptive data on the participant population should be collected. It will also be important to know whether the treatment was implemented as intended; frequently, the reason experimental programs do not have their intended effects is not necessarily because the treatment is ineffective but rather because it was poorly implemented. Therefore, experimental studies should also include an ***implementation analysis*** to document how the program was implemented in the field. This will also provide useful guidance to others who may wish to replicate the program elsewhere.

More generally, the limitations of the experimental method discussed in this section are less a reason not to field experiments than a reason to supplement experiments with other types of evaluation research. Part of the art of evaluation lies in combining all the tools in the evaluator's tool kit to take maximum advantage of the strengths of each. For instance, in the housing subsidy example, one approach would be to combine an experiment focused on the effects of subsidies on the behavior of families with a ***saturation demonstration*** in which subsidies would be offered to all eligible families in several cities to test the market effects of the intervention. This latter demonstration would be evaluated with pre-post, comparison site methods. This is in fact the strategy that the U.S. Department of Housing and Urban Development followed in the early 1970s when it began testing housing allowances as an alternative to public housing (Friedman & Weinberg, 1985).

Detailed discussion of nonexperimental evaluation methods is beyond the scope of this book. This does not imply that I do not view these methods as useful: On the contrary, I believe that experimental and nonexperimental methods are complementary, not competitive. This book focuses on experimental methods because this is the area least covered by the existing literature.

Is Experimentation Ethical?

Because they are the only known design to offer confidence in avoiding the risk of selection bias, experimental designs have become the preferred method of program evaluation among most of the policy research community and among a growing number of policymakers. Such designs, however, are also subject to a widespread concern, especially among program practitioners: Do they violate ethical standards by denying program services to the control group?

It should be noted that posing the question this way presumes that the program services are beneficial. This is not necessarily the case. Job training programs have been known to reduce the earnings of their participants, and the offer of wage subsidies to employers as an inducement to hire welfare recipients has been shown to reduce their employment rate.[10] In fact, the very existence of the evaluation is evidence that the agency that funded it is uncertain about the value of the service. Thus, the fact that the control group is denied program services does not automatically mean that it is disadvantaged by the study.

Nevertheless, it is important to know whether controls are in fact "denied" services in any meaningful sense. To answer this question, we must consider the following distinct experimental contexts:

♦ Special demonstration programs set up explicitly to study the effects of a new program
♦ Ongoing programs that can accommodate only a limited number of participants
♦ Ongoing programs that accept all eligible applicants (so-called "entitlement" programs)

Demonstration Programs

There is little disagreement that random assignment to a control group is ethical when it occurs in the context of a special, small-scale demonstration to test a new program. In this context, denial of program services or benefits to members of the control group simply leaves them in the same position they would have been in if the demonstration had never occurred. It is not so much that such demonstrations deny benefits to controls as that they do not provide them to everybody. In this context, random assignment can be viewed simply as a way to ration limited program resources among those who apply to the demonstration.

To argue that such a demonstration should not be conducted because it does not provide benefits to everybody who wants or needs them is to argue that programs should never be tested on a pilot basis before full-scale implementation. Clearly, from the standpoint of society as a whole, it is more ethical to conduct a small-scale test of a new program before opening it to the entire target population because it could have harmful effects or, if not actually harmful, could be an ineffective waste of resources. Also, if we are to test new programs, we should use the most accurate, reliable evaluation methods available to do so.

Ongoing Programs With Limited Enrollments

The same argument applies to ongoing programs that serve less than their entire eligible population. Many programs are in this category; each year Congress appropriates fixed amounts for job training programs, housing subsidies, and child care assistance that are far less than what would be required to provide services or benefits to all individuals who are eligible for them. Program administrators respond to this shortfall in a number of ways. In some programs, excess demand is rationed by waiting lists, on a first-come, first-served basis or on the basis of service priorities. In other programs, the flow of applications is controlled by varying the amount of program outreach and recruiting activity. Some programs simply turn away those applicants who, in the judgment of program staff, are least likely to benefit from the program.

In this context, random assignment need not reduce the total number of individuals served by the program. If there is excess demand for program services or benefits, random assignment may simply reallocate program services or benefits to a different set of participants. The ethical issue then becomes whether random assignment is a more ethical way to ration scarce resources than the rationing device the program would otherwise have used.

Suppose, for example, that there are 150 applicants to a housing subsidy program, but that the program's budget will only accommodate 100 families. One solution would be to give subsidies to the first 100 families that apply and turn away the remaining 50. Another solution might be for program staff to exercise their judgment and provide the subsidies to the 100 most "deserving" applicants. Alternatively, one could randomly assign 100 families to receive subsidies and 50 families to a control group. Because it gives each family an equal chance of receiving a subsidy, random assignment is arguably a fairer way to allocate the scarce subsidy funds than either a first-come, first-served policy or staff judgment. In addition, it has the added social benefit of generating knowledge about the effects of the program; this knowledge can then be used to improve the program to the benefit of these and other similar families.

Ongoing Entitlement Programs

In an ongoing program that provides services or benefits to all eligible individuals (or all that apply), random assignment to a no-service control group would constitute denial of services, even in the aggregate. To decide whether an experiment would be ethical in this situation, one must weigh the harm done by that denial of service against the social benefits of the knowledge to be gained from the experiment. To date, evaluators and policymakers have taken the position that it is not permissible to deny entitlements for research purposes; this does not mean, however, that there are no instances in which such denial would be justified.

The ethical problems raised by denial of entitlements argue strongly for thorough testing of programs on a small-scale before they are applied to the population at large. Once a service or benefit has become an entitlement, further testing of its effects becomes extremely problematic, if not impossible. This means that we might never know if an entitlement is actually harmful, or simply ineffective, and the harm, or waste of resources, might be perpetuated indefinitely.

There are, however, ways in which at least some entitlement programs might be ethically evaluated with experimental methods. One method is to compare the effects of the existing program with those of an alternative program that provides comparable benefits. For example, it might be deemed unethical to deny food stamps to a control group to test the effects of food stamps on the nutrition of low-income families. Most observers would agree, however, that it is ethical to replace food stamps with a cash equivalent for a randomly assigned control group to measure the nutritional effects of earmarking the subsidy for food. Such an experiment would not, of course, reveal any effects—positive or negative—that are common to both modes of subsidy.

More generally, it is sometimes possible to compensate subjects for any loss of benefits they may suffer as a result of participating in the experiment. In the Health Insurance Experiment, families were asked to give up their existing health insurance policies and accept specially designed policies provided by the study. Some of the experimental policies contained "cost-sharing" provisions that required the family to pay a portion of the cost of the care they consumed to allow the researchers to estimate the effect of the net price of medical care (i.e., its cost to the family) on the use of medical care. In those cases in which the family's existing policy covered a larger fraction of the cost of care than the experimental policy, a lump-sum cash payment was made to the family to make up the difference.[11]

As this example suggests, however, in compensating experimental subjects for loss of benefits, one must be careful not to change the experimental treatment or the treatment-control contrast.[12] It might be argued that the lump-sum payments in the Health Insurance Experiment offset the cost-sharing provisions of the experimental plans. Because they were unrestricted cash payments that could be used for any purpose and were unrelated to the amount of medical care used by the family, however, the lump-sum payments did not affect the price of medical care of the family; at most, the payments may have had a small income effect on the family's consumption of care.

Other Ethical Considerations

In considering whether experiments are ethical, it is important not to focus too exclusively on the issue of denial of services to controls. Other members of society have a stake in whether the experiment is performed. In particular, failure to obtain reliable estimates of the efficacy of an ongoing program can entail substantial costs to the taxpayers who support it. An ineffective program can waste millions or billions of the taxpayers' dollars year after year.

Moreover, failure to detect ineffective programs imposes costs on the intended beneficiaries of those programs. Not only do such programs waste participants' time and create false expectations but also they consume resources that might otherwise be devoted to more effective solutions to the problems the programs were intended to address. Thus, "protecting" program beneficiaries from experiments is not necessarily in their best interest.

Similar considerations apply in the case of demonstrations of new programs. In the absence of reliable knowledge about program effectiveness, ineffective solutions are likely to be legislated, with the same attendant waste of tax resources, disappointed expectations, and displacement of more effective programs.

These considerations do not imply that experiments are always ethically sound. They do suggest, however, that well-designed experiments addressing important policy issues can have great social value, and that this value must be weighed against any loss to the experimental subjects in deciding whether a particular experiment is ethical.

Informed Consent[13]

One approach that is often suggested, and frequently used, to attempt to protect experimental subjects is to require that experimenters obtain the subjects' informed consent. This involves giving subjects a complete description of the experimental procedures, including any risks to the subject, and obtaining their voluntary consent to participate in the experiment.

Informed consent was developed by medical researchers to protect patients from unwittingly being subjected to experimental medical procedures that might actually be harmful to them. Properly implemented, it is an effective device for this purpose, and I strongly recommend that it be employed in any experiment in which the treatment entails any risk of harm to the subject.

More generally, in the context of a demonstration to test a new program, informed consent ensures that each sample member views participation in the experiment as beneficial to him or her. In this case, refusal to consent—and therefore exclusion from the demonstration—leaves the individual no worse off than he or she would have been in the absence of the experiment. Thus, the individual will only consent to participate if, in his or her judgment, the experiment conveys positive net benefits.

In the case of an ongoing program, however, the informed consent of the applicant cannot be taken to mean that he or she expects the experiment to convey net positive benefits relative to his or her situation in the absence of the experiment. In this case, the applicant may have received program services in the absence of the experiment. Therefore, refusal to consent, resulting in exclusion from the program, leaves the applicant worse off than he or she would have been in the absence of the experiment.[14] Thus, consent implies only that the applicant prefers some chance of receiving program services to no chance at all. To ascertain whether the typical applicant is worse off than he or she would have been in the absence of the experiment, one must determine whether the experiment reduces the total number of applicants accepted into the program and therefore the probability of acceptance, as discussed earlier.

Even in this case, informed consent ensures that potential experimental subjects receive a thorough explanation of the experimental treatment and procedures, including any attendant risks. Also, it is useful to ask the subject to sign a form outlining these procedures to document that he or she has been so informed. It is important to recognize, however, that, unlike the case of a special demonstration, in an ongoing program informed consent does not deal with the issue of denial of services to controls.

A Brief History of Social Experimentation

As noted previously, the New Jersey Income Maintenance Experiment of the late 1960s marked the beginning of sustained interest in the use of experimental methods to evaluate social policies. In this section, I briefly review the intellectual history of social experiments, their growing use and widespread acceptance, and the influence they have had on policy.

The Origins of the Experimental Method in the Social Sciences

Social experimentation has a superficial resemblance to the laboratory experiments that have been well-established in the physical and biological sciences for more than 300 years. In both cases, the outcomes of different "treatments" are carefully measured and differences in those outcomes are attributed to the difference in treatment.

Social experiments differ from laboratory experiments in one very crucial respect. Laboratory researchers attempt to isolate the effects of treatment by directly controlling the research environment so that the materials or animals to which the alternative treatments are applied, and the conditions under which they are applied, are identical and the only difference lies in the treatment itself. In social programs, direct control of all the factors that might influence the outcomes of interest (i.e., the behavior of the people who make up the sample) is unattainable. Instead, the social experimenter uses random assignment to ensure the statistical equivalence of the different treatment groups—that is, to ensure that they do not differ systematically in ways that could affect the outcomes. The experimenter then applies statistical tests to the outcomes to distinguish the effects of the treatment from the chance variation produced by random assignment.

The power of random assignment to eliminate bias by establishing comparable groups was recognized by educational researchers as early as the 1920s. Campbell and Stanley (1963) credit W. A. McCall with having this insight in his 1923 book *How to Experiment in Education*. Lindquist (1953) cites an experimental study published by Hurlock in 1925. The great statistician R. A. Fisher laid the statistical foundations of experimentation with random assignment in his seminal books *Statistical Methods for Research Workers* (1925) and *The Design of Experiments* (1935).

Since the 1930s, random assignment has been used routinely in educational and psychological research, usually with small groups of students exposed to different teaching methods or psychological stimuli. By the 1950s, statistical procedures for the design and analysis of relatively complex experiments were firmly established in psychology and education (Cochran & Cox, 1950; Lindquist, 1953). Campbell and Stanley's own 1963 classic, *Experimental and Quasi-Experimental Designs for Research*, clearly laid out all the issues discussed so far in this book in the context of educational research. During the same period, random assignment became one of the dominant modes of medical research, with patients randomly assigned to receive experimental drugs or medical procedures for comparison with control groups receiving standard treatments or placebos.

Application of Experimental Methods to Social Programs

By the 1960s, the use of the experimental model was sufficiently widespread in education, psychology, and medicine that it was quite natural to apply it to social programs and policies outside these fields. From 1961 to 1964, for example, the Manhattan Bail Bond project used random assignment to test the proposition that many individuals could successfully be released without bail prior to trial (Botein, 1965). Other experimental tests of law-related programs and procedures undertaken in the 1960s included studies of a variety of approaches to the prevention and treatment of juvenile delinquency, the use of legal counsel in juvenile court, the effects of pretrial conferences, low-stress versus high-stress training for police, alternative penalties for drunk driving, and vocational, surgical, and social rehabilitation for former prisoners (see Riecken & Boruch, 1974, for more detailed descriptions of these and other early experiments).

These early applications to social policy received little attention outside the immediate circles of the researchers and funding agencies involved, however. Therefore, in 1967, when the proposal was made to use random assignment to evaluate the NIT concept, it was viewed as a totally novel idea. In many ways, it was. The New Jersey Income Maintenance Experiment marked the first use of experimental methods to test a proposed social policy in the field on a large scale. The sample of 1,300 families randomly assigned in the New Jersey Experiment was larger than the samples in previous experiments. More important, the experiment involved administering care-fully controlled treatments to, and observing the behavior of, this large sample of individuals in the course of their daily lives, not in a classroom, hospital, or other institutional setting. In addition, the question addressed by the experiment—whether receipt of welfare would cause poor families to stop working—was a highly visible, politically charged issue.

The New Jersey Experiment represented the marriage of the statistical tradition described previously with the demonstration programs that flour-ished in the Great Society era of the mid-1960s.[15] Funded by a number of federal agencies, but most notably by the new antipoverty agency, the OEO, these demonstrations were intended as pilot tests of service delivery models that their designers hoped would ultimately be implemented on a national scale. The typical demonstration program was designed more to mobilize political support for the program than to measure its effects; few involved careful data collection and, prior to 1967, none involved a rigorous research design. The New Jersey Experiment imposed statistical rigor on this nor-mally chaotic field enterprise.

The New Jersey Experiment was designed to address an issue that had stymied advocates of the negative income tax concept: Would cash transfers to the working poor cause them to substantially reduce their work effort, as critics of the policy alleged? Previous efforts to address this question with existing data had yielded very inconclusive results. Because large-scale cash transfers to this population had never been implemented, nonexperimental studies of this question, using survey data on the national population of working poor families, essentially compared the labor supply of low-income individuals who received such "unearned income" as unemployment com-pensation, veterans' benefits, and workman's compensation with that of individuals with no such income. Such comparisons are subject to severe selection bias because eligibility for these forms of income is determined in part by the individual's past and current work effort. As a result, different nonexperimental methods yielded widely varying estimates. The experiment was intended to resolve this crucial political issue.

OEO's decision to launch the New Jersey Experiment triggered several more large-scale social experiments. In 1968, in recognition that a large portion of the poverty population resided in rural areas, OEO initiated the Rural Income Maintenance Experiment in Iowa and North Carolina. The following year, the Department of Health, Education, and Welfare (HEW) funded income maintenance experiments in Gary, Indiana, and Seattle, Washington, to test whether the addition of day care subsidies (in Gary) or

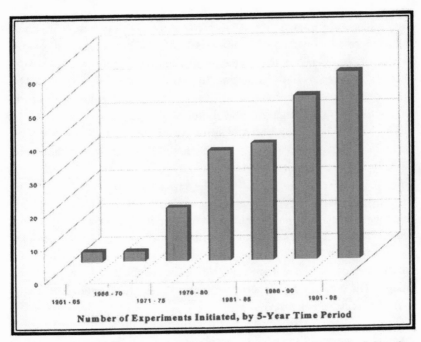

Figure 1.3. Social Experiments Initiated, 1961-1995 (Source: Greenberg & Shroder, 1997)

vocational counseling or training or both (in Seattle) would offset any tendency of cash transfers to cause reductions in work effort. Approximately 5,000 families were randomly assigned in the largest of these four experiments, which ultimately became the Seattle-Denver Income Maintenance Experiment.

These highly visible studies of a politically controversial issue prompted other federal agencies to adopt this novel technique in the early 1970s. Large-scale experimental tests of housing vouchers, by the Department of Housing and Urban Development, and alternative health insurance plans, by HEW, were explicitly patterned on the income maintenance experiments. In the mid- to late 1970s, a number of experiments were conducted by the U.S. Department of Labor (DOL) and other funding agencies to test alternative employment and training services for unemployed workers, welfare recipients, disadvantaged youths, the mentally impaired, ex-offenders, and substance abusers. Figure 1.3 shows the growth in the number of social experiments initiated during the period 1961 to 1995. By 1980, 55 social experiments had been initiated; by 1995, 195 experimental studies had begun, according to Greenberg and Shroder (1997).[16]

The growth in acceptance and use of experimental methods to measure the effects of public programs was primarily attributable to two factors: frustration with the failure of nonexperimental methods to yield unequivocal estimates of these effects and the conceptual appeal of the experimental approach. As noted previously, much of the motivation for the income maintenance experiments was the inability of researchers to obtain consistent estimates of the effects of cash transfers on work effort from existing data. A similar experience with the evaluation of job training programs led to reliance on experimental methods in this area.

In the late 1970s, the DOL spent large sums of money on two major evaluation efforts. The first was a series of evaluations of its major job training program for disadvantaged workers, the Comprehensive Employment and Training Act (CETA) program. These evaluations were based on data from a follow-up survey of CETA participants, the Continuous Longitudinal Manpower Survey, in conjunction with comparison groups drawn from the Current Population Surveys. During the same period, the DOL also funded more than 400 demonstrations of employment and training programs for youth under the Youth Employment Demonstration Program Act (YEDPA). Most of these demonstrations involved nonexperimental evaluations.

The CETA evaluations produced widely divergent estimates of the impact of the program on participants' earnings, even though they were all based on essentially the same data (Barnow, 1987). These differences in results were apparently due to differences in the assumptions underlying different nonexperimental methods. Also, because these assumptions could not be tested or verified, there was no way to know which estimates were most reliable. Moreover, when researchers applied the same set of nonexperimental methods to data drawn from a social experiment, in which the experimental estimate provided an unbiased benchmark, they obtained a similar dispersion of estimates (LaLonde, 1986; Maynard & Fraker, 1987). This experience led an expert panel convened to advise the DOL on the evaluation of JTPA, the program that succeeded CETA, to recommend strongly that JTPA be evaluated with experimental methods (Stromsdorfer et al., 1985).

Similarly, a National Academy of Sciences committee (Betsey, Hollister, & Papageorgiou, 1985) formed to review the YEDPA demonstrations of the late 1970s concluded that "despite the magnitude of the resources ostensibly devoted to the objectives of research and demonstration, there is little reliable information on the effectiveness of the programs in solving youth employment problems" (p. 22) and that "it is evident that if random assignment had been consistently used, much more could have been learned" (p. 18). These recommendations led to the National JTPA Study, in which more than 20,000 JTPA applicants in 16 local programs throughout the United States were randomly assigned to the program or to a control group that was excluded from the program.

On the basis of experiences such as these, a consensus has emerged within the professional evaluation community that random assignment is the method of choice for evaluating public programs. This consensus among the technical experts has led policymakers to accept experimental designs not only as a technical matter but also as a way to avoid the methodological debates that often accompany the presentation of nonexperimental results, detracting from their credibility and deflecting the policy discussion from substance to method.

Experimental methods are also conceptually appealing to policymakers. In contrast to the arcane statistical sophistication of many nonexperimental methods, the experimental method is relatively simple and intuitively understandable. Even very nontechnical policymakers can appreciate the logic of the experimental contrast between one group exposed to the program and another, which differs from the first only by chance, that is not exposed to the program. This makes experimental studies more accessible and credible to laypersons in the policy process.

For these reasons, not only has the number of social experiments funded and conducted increased enormously during the past two decades but also, on a number of occasions, random assignment evaluations have been mandated by Congress. This was the case for the evaluation of the Family Support Act of 1988 and for demonstrations of job training for welfare recipients, self-employment assistance for unemployed workers, and job search assistance for unemployment insurance claimants. The landmark welfare reform act passed in 1996 directed the Secretary of Health and Human Services to evaluate the programs funded under the act and "to the maximum extent feasible, use random assignment as an evaluation methodology" (Public Law 104-193, § 413(b)(2)).

Impact of Social Experiments on Policy

Research of any kind is seldom the determining factor in shaping public policy. Experimentation is no exception to this rule. Nevertheless, in part because of their intuitive appeal and credibility, experimental studies have sometimes had decisive effects on policy.

A notable example is the Perry Preschool Project, conducted in the 1960s, in which a sample of 3- and 4-year-old children were randomly assigned either to intensive educational and social services or to a control group that received no special services. A long-term follow-up study of the sample revealed large treatment-control differences in such outcomes as educational attainment at age 19 (Schweinhart, Barnes, & Weikart, 1993). This study has had a crucial effect on support for intensive early childhood interventions such as Head Start (Barnett & Boocock, 1998).

Another early experiment that had a direct effect on policy was the Manhattan Bail Bond project. Its finding that pretrial release without bail did not increase the incidence of failure to appear for trial led to the incorporation of many of the features of the experimental treatment into the 1966 Bail Reform Act.

The Work-Welfare Experiments, a set of experimental evaluations of state training and job search programs for welfare recipients perfomed in the early 1980s, are frequently cited as a major factor in the passage of the Family Support Act of 1988, which established similar programs as national policy (see Gueron & Pauly, 1991, for a description of these experiments). Similarly, the Unemployment Insurance Self-Employment Demonstrations led directly to national legislation enabling states to provide technical and financial assistance to help unemployed workers become self-employed (Orr, Wandner, Lah, & Benus, 1994).

Recently, the results of the National JTPA Study have been influential in decisions by both the Democratic administration and the Republican Congress with respect to funding for JTPA. This study's finding that the program had little or no effect on the earnings of youth was the basis for a substantial reduction in the budget of the youth component and initiation of a systematic search for more effective program models for youth. At the same time, in an era of across-the-board cuts in social programs, funding for the adult component was left intact, largely because the experimental study showed that it was cost-effective.[17]

In these instances, the effects of experimental evaluations have been very clear and direct. More often, such studies have a more subtle influence on the policy process. The income maintenance experiments, for example, added greatly to our knowledge of the labor supply behavior of the low-income population and therefore conditioned the way income-transfer policy was viewed, without leading directly to acceptance or rejection of any specific policy.[18] Similarly, the Health Insurance Experiment produced an enormous amount of valuable information about the relationship between health insurance and the demand for medical services, which has helped inform the national debate on health policy, but was not a decisive factor in the enactment of any specific legislation.

One should not expect that evaluations will determine policy in all cases. Even the best research is only one of many influences in the policy process, and behavioral impacts are only one of many possible legislative objectives. Evaluators will have made a significant contribution to improving the policy process if they provide accurate information on important policy questions in a form that policymakers can understand. In the remainder of this book, I discuss how experiments can be designed, implemented, and analyzed to achieve this goal.

Notes

1. The formal name of the project was the Graduated Work Incentives Experiment. It was originally implemented in four cities in New Jersey—hence the popular name "New Jersey Experiment"—and subsequently expanded to include families in Scranton, Pennsylvania. See Watts and Rees (1977) for a complete description of the project.

2. Because some program effects can occur almost immediately, while the participant is still in the program, I define outcomes to include everything that happens after program entry, not just what happens after the participant leaves the program.

3. In this and other examples presented in this section, for simplicity and clarity of exposition I abstract from the sampling variability of the estimates. Determining empirically whether a particular impact estimate is biased is an extremely complex matter once sampling variability is taken into account (see Bell, Orr, Blomquist, & Cain, 1995, for a discussion of this issue).

4. By "systematic" differences, I mean any differences that are larger than might be expected on the basis of sampling error. In Chapter 2, I discuss how one can test whether the treatment-control difference could be due to sampling error.

5. Although experimental control groups are a type of comparison group, for the sake of clarity I generally use the term *comparison group* to mean a nonexperimental comparison group. The term *control group* always denotes random assignment. In rare instances, in which the principal policy interest is in comparison of alternative new policies, the experiment may not include a control group subject to current policy.

6. It is important to recognize that random assignment does not simply mean haphazard or arbitrary assignment. In practice, great care must be taken to ensure that each individual assigned has the prescribed probability of assignment to each group. I discuss this topic in Chapter 5.

7. In Chapter 5, procedures for implementing random assignment are discussed in detail.

8. Figure 1.2 is based on data from the National JTPA Study (unpublished tabulations). The comparison group shown here is composed of a representative sample of JTPA eligibles at four

study sites who were identified through a screening survey of randomly selected households. Both the control group and the comparison group are composed of adult men.

9. In the employment and training literature, the decline in earnings prior to program entry is known as the "preprogram dip."

10. See Orr et al. (1996) for an example of the former and Burtless (1985) for an example of the latter.

11. To ensure that no family could be made worse off financially by participating in the experiment, the annual lump-sum payments were set equal to the maximum difference in medical costs that the family could experience during the year.

12. Alternatively, one can explicitly change the question under study to reflect the actual treatment-control contrast. The example of comparing the nutritional effects of food stamps (in the treatment group) with their cash equivalent (in the control group) can be viewed as a case of compensating controls for loss of benefits. In this case, we reformulated the question under study from, "What are the nutritional effects of food stamps compared to no assistance?" to "What are the nutritional effects of earmarking assistance for food compared with cash assistance?" In general, however, the question to be studied should be determined by the policy issues that prompted the study and not by the feasibility of the experimental design.

13. For a more in-depth discussion of informed consent in the context of social experiments, see Gramlich and Orr (1975).

14. In experimental evaluations of ongoing programs, applicants who refuse to consent to random assignment must be excluded from the program. Otherwise, all applicants would have an incentive to refuse to consent because refusal would increase their chances of getting into the program.

15. Two other notable developments in research methods were critical to the advent of large-scale field experiments: the development of sophisticated household survey techniques, beginning in the 1940s, and the development of high-speed computers in the 1950s and 1960s that were capable of processing large amounts of survey data quickly and efficiently.

16. The experiments summarized in Greenberg and Shroder (1997) are "field studies of social programs in which individuals or organizations are randomly assigned to two or more alternative treatments. The primary research objective of the experiments was the measurement of differences between the alternative treatments on market behavior (such as the receipt of earnings) and corresponding government fiscal outcomes (such as the receipt of transfer benefits)" (p. 4). Thus, they explicitly do not include in their survey experiments involving interventions such as drug treatment, medical care, or education programs, which are not intended to affect market behavior.

17. See Orr et al. (1996) for the results of the National JTPA Study and a discussion of its policy impacts.

18. Some analysts believe that the Seattle-Denver Experiment's finding that cash transfers may lead to marital breakup was responsible for persuading at least one key senator to withdraw his support of cash transfers to intact families, thereby effectively ending the political prospects for a universal negative income tax.

References

Barnett, W. S., & Boocock, S. S. (Eds.). (1998). *Early care and education for children in poverty: Promises, programs, and long-term results.* Albany: State University of New York Press.

Barnow, B. S. (1987, Spring). The impact of CETA programs on earnings: A review of the literature. *Journal of Human Resources, 22,* 157-193.

Bell, S. H., Orr, L. L., Blomquist, J. D., & Cain, G. G. (1995). *Program applicants as a comparison group in evaluating training programs.* Kalamazoo, MI: Upjohn Institute for Employment Research.

Betsey, C. L., Hollister, R. G., & Papageorgiou, M. R. (1985). *Youth Employment and Training Programs: The YEDPA years.* Washington, DC: National Academy Press.

Botein, B. (1965). The Manhattan Bail Project: Its impact in criminology and the criminal law process. *Texas Law Review, 43,* 319-331.

Burtless, G. (1985). Are targeted wage subsidies harmful? Evidence from a wage voucher experiment. *Industrial and Labor Relations Review, 39,* 105-114.

Campbell, D. T., & Stanley, J. C. (1963). *Experimental and quasi-experimental designs for research.* Chicago: Rand McNally.

Carroll, L. (1960). Through the looking glass. In M. Gardner (Ed.), *The annotated Alice.* Cleveland: World Publishing.

Cochran, W. G., & Cox, G. M. (1950). *Experimental designs.* New York: John Wiley.

Family Support Act of 1988, Pub. L. No. 104-193, § 413(b)(2) (1988).

Fisher, R. A. (1925). *Statistical methods for research workers.* London: Oliver & Boyd.

Fisher, R. A. (1935). *The design of experiments.* London: Oliver & Boyd.

Friedman, J., & Weinberg, D. (1985). Experimental Housing Allowance Program: History and overview. In L. H. Aiken & B. H. Kehrer (Eds.), *Evaluation studies review annual* (Vol. 10). Beverly Hills, CA: Sage.

Gramlich, E. M., & Orr, L. L. (1975). The ethics of large scale social experimentation. In *Ethical and legal issues of social experimentation.* Washington, DC: Brookings Institution.

Greenberg, D., & Shroder, M. (1997). *Digest of the social experiments.* Washington, DC: Urban Institute Press.

Gueron, J. M., & Pauly, E. (1991). *From welfare to work.* New York: Russell Sage.

Heckman, J. J., & Robb, R. (1985). Alternative methods for evaluating the impact of interventions: An overview. *Journal of Econometrics, 30,* 239-267.

Hurlock, E. B. (1925, March). An evaluation of certain incentives used in schoolwork. *Journal of Educational Psychology, 16,* 145-149.

LaLonde, R. J. (1986, September). Evaluating the econometric evaluations of training programs with experimental data. *American Economic Review, 76,* 604-620.

Lindquist, E. F. (1953). *Design and analysis of experiments in psychology and education.* Cambridge, MA: Houghton Mifflin.

Maynard, R., & Fraker, T. (1987, Spring). The adequacy of comparison group designs for evaluations of employment-related programs. *Journal of Human Resources, 22,* 194-227.

McCall, W. A. (1923). *How to experiment in education.* New York: Macmillan.

Orr, L. L., Bloom, H. S., Bell, S. H., Doolittle, F., Lin, W., & Cave, G. (1996). *Does job training for the disadvantaged work? Evidence from the National JTPA Study.* Washington, DC: Urban Institute Press.

Orr, L. L., Wandner, S. A., Lah, D., & Benus, J. M. (1994). *The use of evaluation results in employment and training policy: Two case studies.* Bethesda, MD: Abt.

Riecken, H. W., & Boruch, R. F. (Eds.). (1974). *Social experimentation: A method for planning and evaluating social intervention.* New York: Academic Press.

Ross, H. (1966). *A proposal for a demonstration of new techniques in income maintenance* [Mimeo]. Madison, WI: University of Wisconsin, Institute for Research on Poverty, Data Center Archives.

Schweinhart, L. J., Barnes, H. V., & Weikart, D. P. (1993). *Significant benefits: The High/Scope Perry Preschool Study through age 27.* Ypsilanti, MI: High/Scope Educational Research Foundation.

Stromsdorfer, E., Bloom, H., Boruch, R., Borus, M., Gueron, J., Gustman, A., Rossi, P., Scheuren, F., Smith, M., & Stafford, F. (1985). *Recommendations of the Job Training Longitudinal Survey Research Advisory Panel.* Washington, DC: U.S. Department of Labor, Employment and Training Administration.

Watts, H. W., & Rees, A. (Eds.). (1977). *The New Jersey Income Maintenance Experiment. Volume II: Labor-supply responses.* New York: Academic Press.

Chapter ❷

Basic Concepts and Principles of Social Experimentation

❝The beginning is the most important part of the work.❞
—*Plato*

In the previous chapter, I defined a social experiment as a comparison of the outcomes of two or more groups randomly assigned to different policy regimes. In this chapter, I explore in more detail the considerations involved in constructing this comparison and in interpreting the resultant differences in outcomes. I discuss the basic concepts and principles involved in

◆ Deciding whether to experiment
◆ Specifying the experimental treatment
◆ Specifying the outcomes of interest
◆ Interpreting the treatment-control service differential
◆ Interpreting treatment-control differences in outcomes

Deciding Whether to Experiment

A social experiment generally begins either with interest in some new program or a desire to determine whether an existing program is achieving its objectives. Unfortunately, given the limited resources available for program evaluation, not all new ideas and existing programs can be evaluated experimentally; sponsoring agencies must choose among competing uses of their evaluation budgets. The choice of policies or programs to be evaluated—and within this set, the ones to be evaluated experimentally—requires a careful assessment of the likely value of the information to be obtained through rigorous evaluation and the cost and feasibility of obtaining it. In this section, I discuss the questions that should be addressed in deciding which programs or policy issues to investigate experimentally.

What Does Society Stand to Gain From the Experiment?

A social experiment benefits society by providing better information on which to base public policy. Such information can improve policy in one of two ways: It can lead policymakers to adopt a program or policy that is found to have net social benefits (i.e., benefits to society that outweigh its costs), or it can lead to the termination of an existing program that is found to have net social costs (i.e., costs that outweigh its benefits to society).[1]

Of course, one cannot know before the fact whether any particular experiment will lead to a change in policy—this depends on the experimental findings and whether policymakers act on the findings. In deciding whether to conduct the experiment, then, one must act on the *expected value* of the experiment. This can be expressed as

Expected value of experiment = value of change in policy

$\times$ probability of change in policy

− cost of experiment

For a new program, the value of a change in policy due to the experiment is the net social benefit that will accrue if the experimental program is adopted. For an existing program, the value of a change in policy is its net social cost; this is a measure of the resource savings that will accrue if the program is terminated. These values can be quite large, such as those of the policy impacts of the National Job Training Partnership Act (JTPA) Study. This evaluation found that the out-of-school youth component of JTPA had essentially no impact on the earnings of youths who participated in it. As a direct result of this finding, funding for the out-of-school youth component of JTPA was reduced by more than $500 million per year. In just a few years, this savings of resources that would otherwise have been wasted on ineffective training services easily surpassed the cost of all the social experiments that have been conducted in the past 30 years.[2]

It is obviously difficult to predict either the value of a change in policy or the probability it will occur, but one can make statements about them that are useful in discriminating among potential experiments. First, other things being equal, the larger the program the larger its social benefit or cost are likely to be. Thus, social experiments focused on larger programs are likely to have higher social value. Second, in some cases previous research may allow one to make at least qualitative statements about the probability that a new program will be found to be effective or an existing program to be ineffective. The more credible nonexperimental evidence there is indicating that a new program may be effective or that an existing program may be ineffective—that is, that an experiment would indicate that a change in policy is warranted—the higher the expected value of the experiment is likely to be.[3]

The social value of an experiment depends not only on the inherent importance and validity of the information it provides but also on whether it is used to improve policy. An experiment is of no value to society if its results never influence policy. It is, of course, extremely difficult to predict a priori whether a particular set of evaluation results will be acted upon. Evaluation is only one of a number of forces impinging on the political process, and in many cases it is not the most important force. Still, one can identify certain factors that make it more or less likely that evaluation results will play a key role in policy deliberations. For example, the results are more likely to influence policy if the behavioral questions that evaluation can address are central to the policy debate than if policy decisions turn on philosophical or ideological issues. The following are extreme examples: Job training programs are based almost entirely on the premise that the services they provide will increase the employment and earnings of participants, a behavioral premise that can readily be tested experimentally, whereas Social Security benefits for the aged are justified primarily on equity grounds, without regard to any behavioral effects they may cause.

The likelihood that evaluation results will be acted upon will also be influenced by their timing, relative to the life span of the policy issue they address. Social experiments take time to plan, implement, and analyze. Often, the treatment itself lasts a year or more, and several more years may be required to observe the outcomes of interest and analyze the program's impact on them. The interval between the decision to mount an experiment and the availability of results is often 5 to 10 years. Only if an experiment addresses a relatively fundamental policy issue will its results still be relevant to the policy process after such a lag in time.

The income maintenance experiments and the Health Insurance Experiment are examples of social experiments that focused on fundamental policy issues that were still relevant many years after the experiments were completed. Rather than estimating the impact of a specific policy, these experiments were designed to estimate underlying behavioral parameters—the elasticity of supply of labor and the price elasticity of demand for medical care—that would be relevant to a wide range of policies. Although these experiments did not result in the adoption of any specific income maintenance or health insurance programs, their results have been used extensively in the analysis of a number of proposed programs and policies in these areas. Evaluations of ongoing programs are also highly likely to still be relevant when their results become available because the programs are likely to still be in place.

In contrast, novel program or policy proposals may have such a short life span that they are irrelevant to policy by the time an experimental test can be conducted. This is particularly true if the proposal initially has only limited support—for example, a proposal developed by a single government official without significant support from the rest of the executive branch or the legislature. Neither the official nor the proposal are likely to be present 5 years later.

Proposals that involve a complex package of programmatic components are particularly susceptible to shifts in policy interest away from the specific combination of program elements evaluated before the results become available, even though there may still be substantial interest in individual components. The experimental evaluations of state welfare reform demonstrations conducted in recent years illustrate the problem of experimenting with complex programs. Many of these demonstrations involved multiple policy interventions intended to reduce the dependence and increase the self-sufficiency of welfare recipients—for example, employment and training services, child care assistance, enhanced medical care, financial incentives to work, time limits on receipt of assistance, and elimination of benefit increases for additional children.[4] A demonstration evaluation designed only to estimate the impacts of the overall policy package will have only very limited policy applicability; its results apply only to that specific policy package. A much more powerful and versatile approach is to measure the impacts of the individual program components or alternative combinations of closely related components or both so that the impacts of other policy packages can be inferred. In a subsequent chapter, how experiments can be designed to do this is discussed.

What Would It Cost to Conduct an Experiment?

Against the potential value of an experiment must be weighed its expected costs. These include the costs of project planning, implementation and monitoring of random assignment, data collection, and analysis. The extent to which the costs of the experimental program itself represent a net cost to society depends on whether the experimental services generate social benefits, which in most cases cannot be known until the experiment has been conducted.[5] For planning purposes, it is probably prudent to treat these services, or some proportion of them, as a cost.

The costs of alternative experiments can differ enormously, depending on the sample sizes required to measure impacts with adequate precision and the method, frequency, and duration of data collection (these design issues are discussed in subsequent chapters). A typical social experiment costs $2 or 3 million, although it is quite possible to conduct one for substantially less, and some, such as the Seattle-Denver Income Maintenance Experiment and the Health Insurance Experiment, which involved intensive, long-term data collection, cost more than $80 million. In choosing among potential experiments, it is important to obtain accurate estimates of the costs of each. Fortunately, once a design has been specified, it is possible to predict the costs of an experiment fairly accurately.

What Are the Alternative Sources of Evaluation Information?

The benefits and costs of social experiments must be judged relative to those of the next best alternative source of information. If a reliable nonexperimental evaluation already exists, or could be conducted at little cost, an experiment may not add sufficient information to justify its cost. In a subsequent chapter, I discuss in more detail the relative strengths and weaknesses of experimental and nonexperimental analyses.

In deciding whether to rely on nonexperimental evidence, it is important to bear in mind the inherent risk of nonexperimental methods: Unlike experimental estimates, one can never be sure that nonexperimental estimates are unbiased. One must therefore examine carefully, and be prepared to accept, the assumptions on which any nonexperimental estimates are based. One should also apply several different nonexperimental methods to see if they yield similar estimates rather than simply accepting the results of a single method. Recall that it was the implausibility of the assumptions required to estimate the labor supply response to transfer payments nonexperimentally that led to the income maintenance experiments and the inconsistency of nonexperimental estimates of the impacts of training that led to the National JTPA Study.

Is an Experiment Ethically and Conceptually Feasible?

In Chapter 1, I discussed the ethical considerations involved in conducting an experiment. It is important that each prospective experiment be reviewed carefully with respect to these considerations to ensure that it can ethically be undertaken. As noted in that discussion, in some cases it may be possible to make an otherwise unethical experiment acceptable by changing the design or compensating the participants.

Potential experiments should also be reviewed for their conceptual feasibility. Some policy interventions are inherently inconsistent with random assignment at the individual level. For example, it is impossible to insulate a control group from the effects of a public education campaign conducted through the general media or one that attempts to change the educational philosophy of an entire school system. Although, as will be discussed in a subsequent chapter, it is conceptually possible to evaluate such interventions by randomly assigning groups of individuals, such as entire communities or school systems, this approach has severe limitations in many contexts.

Specifying the Experimental Treatment

The *experimental treatment* is the offer of services to, or the imposition of policies on, the treatment group that are not offered to or imposed on the control group. The treatment is usually synonymous with the program or policy being evaluated or considered for adoption on an ongoing basis. For example, in the National JTPA Study, the treatment group was offered entrance to JTPA, whereas the control group was barred from the program. In testing a new program, one would generally try to replicate as exactly as possible the features one would expect if the program were adopted as an ongoing program.

This means that in the case of a new program, specification of the treatment involves codification of a set of rules and procedures as detailed as the statutes and operating procedures that govern a regular program. In social experiments in which the treatment is administered by the research team, these procedures must be developed *de novo*; this can be a daunting task. The researchers who designed the income maintenance experiments, for example, developed rules for "countable" income, deductions from income, reporting requirements, filing unit composition, accounting periods, and appeals procedures as complex as those embodied in the Internal Revenue Service code.[6] The Health Insurance Experiment rules and procedures combined the complexity of a comprehensive health insurance policy with the income accounting and reporting rules required to administer income-conditioned insurance provisions.

Increasingly, experimental tests of new programs have relied on existing administrative agencies to deliver the treatment. For example, most of the welfare reform experiments of the 1980s and 1990s were carried out by local welfare agencies. This not only has the advantage of relieving the researchers of developing a voluminous procedures manual but also ensures that the program is administered more like an ongoing program would be administered. Reliance on existing administrative agencies should not, however, relieve the researchers of the responsibility of examining the practices, procedures, and philosophy of these agencies to ensure that they are consistent with those of the program being tested. For example, in one experimental test of employment and training services for women, it was belatedly discovered that one of the service providers routinely counseled women not to accept employment because they would lose their welfare grants.

It is important to recognize that the experimental treatment is defined as the offer of the program or the imposition of policy, not the actual receipt of program services or compliance with the experimental policy. It is the offer of service or the imposition of policy that automatically follows from random assignment and therefore definitively distinguishes the treatment group from the control group. The actual receipt of program services or compliance with the experimental policy is an experimental outcome that may or may not occur. The importance of this distinction is that the difference in outcomes between the treatment and control groups reflects the response of the entire treatment group to the offer of services or imposition of policy, whether they actually received those services or complied with the policy. How the impact of the receipt of services on program participants can sometimes be inferred from the impact of the offer of services on the entire treatment group is discussed later. This distinction also has important implications for the design of experiments (considered in a subsequent chapter).

As noted previously, the treatment is usually synonymous with the program or policy that is being considered for adoption on an ongoing basis. In certain instances, however, this is not the case. In the Manhattan Bail Bond Experiment, for example, the policy of interest was pretrial release without bail (Botein, 1965). The researchers, however, did not believe that they could persuade judges to agree to automatically release defendants without bail on the basis of random assignment to the treatment group. Therefore, the treatment in this experiment was a recommendation to the judge that the defendant be released without bail. Fortunately, the judges accepted a large enough proportion of these recommendations to produce a meaningful difference in release rates between the treatment and control groups. Nevertheless, in interpreting the results of this experiment, it must be borne in mind that not all the members of the treatment group were released before trial.

Experiments designed to estimate behavioral responses, rather than to test specific programs, are also cases in which the treatment may differ from the one that might be adopted on an ongoing basis. The Health Insurance Experiment, for example, was designed to estimate the price elasticity of demand for a broad range of medical services (Newhouse, 1993). To achieve this objective, the researchers deliberately designed the experimental insurance policies to include a much broader scope of benefits than was likely to be included in any governmental program. The cost-sharing provisions (deductibles and coinsurance) in the experimental policies were also much simpler than those likely to be included in a government program to allow direct estimation of demand elasticities. The intent of the study was that these elasticities could then be used to estimate the utilization of medical care under a wide range of health insurance policies.

Specifying the Outcomes of Interest

The fact that, at the point of random assignment, the treatment and control groups do not differ systematically in any way except eligibility for the experimental treatment means that any subsequent systematic difference in outcomes can be confidently attributed to the program. (By "outcome," I mean any behavior or events that occur after random assignment; later, I discuss what I mean by "systematic.") Only a limited number of outcomes can be measured, however, because data collection is costly. Thus, great care must be taken in choosing the outcomes to be measured. Three types of outcome data are usually collected in social experiments: those related to program participation, achievement of program objectives, and other benefits and costs of the experimental program.

Program Participation

As noted previously, the experimental treatment is the offer of services or the imposition of policy. It is important to measure the extent to which program services were actually received or the treatment group members complied with the experimental policy. This information will be critical in interpreting the impact estimates. It is sometimes the case, for example, that experimental programs had little or no impact because the services were not delivered as intended or because the treatment group did not comply with the experimental policy. More generally, it is important to document the services provided by the experiment so that policymakers know what intervention produced the estimated impacts.

Documentation of services received may also help indicate ways to deliver program services more efficiently or increase compliance with the experimental policy, and it may be helpful in planning for the implementation of the program or policy on an ongoing basis. A final use of data on program participation is in the procedure described later for inferring impacts on program participants when some treatment group members do not participate in the experimental program. This procedure requires individual-level data on service receipt.

The type of program participation data to be collected will obviously vary with the type of program being tested. In general, however, data on whether and when each sample member entered and left the program, the amount and type of services (or other benefits) received and when they were received, as well as narrative descriptions of the nature of the services and the service provider should be included.

When services similar to those provided by the experiment are available from nonexperimental sources, it is important to document receipt of nonexperimental services by both the treatment and the control groups. As shall be shown, the impact of the program will be determined by treatment-control differences in the combination of experimental and nonexperimental services.[7] Again, knowing the services received by the two groups can be critical to explaining the impact estimates. Suppose, for example, that an experimental employment program is found to have no impact, but the participation data show that the experimental services simply substituted for similar services that the treatment group would have received from other sources, such as the Employment Service. We conclude that the effectiveness of the experimental services had not really been tested because the experiment failed to create a treatment-control difference in total services. (Later, I discuss in more detail the interpretation of the impact estimates when services similar to those provided by the experiment are available elsewhere.)

Achievement of Program Objectives

Social programs are intended to address a problem afflicting individuals. The objectives of the program can usually be stated with reference to the problem. For example, training programs are intended to deal with the problems of unemployment and low earnings due to low skills. Their objectives, therefore, are to increase the employment and earnings of their participants. Prenatal nutrition programs are intended to address the problem of poor diet among low-income pregnant women that frequently results in unhealthy babies. The objectives of these programs are to improve the nutrition of expectant mothers and, therefore, the health of their babies.

To measure whether a program is achieving its stated objectives, an evaluation must define the objectives in terms of measurable outcomes, such as employment and earnings, the nutrition of expectant mothers, or the birth weight of infants. These are the outcomes on which program impacts will be estimated. As these examples suggest, programs may have multiple objectives. To provide a comprehensive evaluation of the program, it is important that the evaluation identify and specify measurable outcomes corresponding to as many of the program's objectives as possible. In doing so, it is essential that the researchers consult with policymakers and practitioners in the field, both to gain their insights regarding program objectives and to avoid the possibility that, after the experimental analysis has been completed, practitioners will point out a critical omission in the impacts measured by the experiment.

In some cases, it is useful to measure intermediate, as well as final, program objectives to elucidate the mechanisms through which the intervention has its effects or to determine why it failed to have an effect. Consider, for example, an experimental parenting program that is intended, among other things, to improve children's school performance. In such an experiment, it would be possible to measure the extent to which the parent understands the principles taught in the program, the extent to which he or she applies them, the extent to which they change his or her children's behavior, and the extent to which the children's altered behavior affects their school performance. Failure of the program to affect school performance could be the result of a breakdown of any of these linkages.

Remarkably, policymakers and program administrators sometimes cannot agree on the objectives of the programs they administer, or they may view delivery of the service as an end in itself. For example, some may view a child care program as aimed primarily at allowing mothers to work, others may see its objective as improving the child's social and cognitive skills, and yet others may view the delivery of "quality" child care as an end in itself. The evaluation need not resolve such disagreements, although prior discussion of program objectives is sometimes helpful in fostering agreement among those involved in the program. The evaluation's job is simply to measure all the outcomes that may be viewed as objectives of the program. Once program impacts on these outcomes have been estimated, the political process will decide whether the impacts justify the cost of the program.

Other Benefits and Costs of the Experimental Program

In designing a social experiment, it is important to attempt to anticipate all benefits and costs of the program, not just those that are directly related to the program's objectives. For example, interventions such as education and training or community service programs require a substantial investment of time on the part of their participants and may therefore divert participants from employment in the regular labor market. Thus, one impact of such programs may be to reduce the earnings of participants while they are in the program. It is important to measure such forgone earnings because they may be an important cost of the program.[8]

Of course, it is important to collect data on the cost of the experimental program itself, including any benefits to participants. As with the behavioral impacts of experimental programs, the guiding principle for measuring program costs is to include all costs, and only those costs, that would not have been incurred in the absence of the program.[9] As this implies, program costs are best measured as experimental impacts. For example, suppose that an educational program for welfare mothers causes them to stay on assistance longer than they would have otherwise. The cost of additional welfare benefits to participants can be measured as the difference in mean benefits between the treatment and control groups. Similarly, any savings in welfare benefits could be measured as treatment-control differences.

The responsibility for anticipating program impacts that are not directly related to program objectives—especially adverse impacts—nearly always falls entirely on the researchers designing the experiment. Policymakers and program managers tend to be advocates of the program and, therefore, to think only in terms of positive impacts. For example, in the design of one experiment, lengthy discussions with the managers of a set of community service programs generated a list of more than 20 outcomes representing objectives of the programs; the forgone earnings of participants during the 9 to 12 months they were in the programs were not mentioned as a possible effect of the programs.

Formal specification of a comprehensive benefit-cost framework before data collection plans are finalized is an essential step in ensuring that no important benefits or costs are overlooked. The role of benefit-cost analysis in social experiments is discussed in a subsequent chapter.

Interpreting the Treatment-Control Service Differential

The simplest type of experiment involves random assignment of program applicants to two groups—a treatment group that is allowed to enter the program and a control group that is not.[10] Treatment group members are allowed to receive all experimental program services as well as any services outside the experiment for which they would otherwise have been eligible. Controls are excluded from the experimental program but are otherwise free to do anything they wish, including receiving similar services from sources other than the experimental program. In this basic experimental design, the experience of the control group is intended to represent what would have happened to participants in the absence of the program—which is known as the *counterfactual*. The treatment-control difference in outcomes measures the impacts of the program tested relative to the policy environment faced by the control group. Interpretation of the impact estimates therefore requires an understanding of the policy environment faced by controls as well as the treatment received by the treatment group.

Of course, it is critical to ensure that the policy environment faced by the controls is in fact the desired counterfactual. Therefore, we must also consider the relationship between the difference in policy environments faced by treatment and control group members and the policy question the experiment is intended to inform.

The No-Service Counterfactual

In the simplest case, there are no services or benefits outside the experimental program similar to those offered to the treatment group. Thus, the experimental contrast is between a treatment group that receives the experimental services and a control group that receives no similar services. Suppose, for example, that an experimental training program provides 100 hours of training to the treatment group. Controls are excluded from the experimental program; if no nonexperimental training is available, controls will receive zero hours of training, and the treatment-control service differential will be 100 hours. Because the treatment-control difference in services received is identical to the full experimental treatment, treatment-control differences in outcomes can be interpreted as the full effect of the experimental treatment.

The Partial-Service Counterfactual

When services or benefits similar to those offered by the experiment are available outside the experimental program, the experimental services may displace some of the nonexperimental services that would have been received by the treatment group in the absence of the experiment. The treatment-control service differential, then, will be the net of the additional experimental services received by the treatment group and the reduction in the nonexperimental services the treatment group receives.

Table 2.1 illustrates this situation for a hypothetical experimental training program. Suppose that the experimental program provides 100 hours of training to the treatment group, that nonexperimental training is available in the community from existing programs (e.g., the Employment Service or community colleges), and that, although controls are excluded from the experimental program, neither treatment nor control group members are prohibited from receiving nonexperimental services.[11] In this illustration, the average treatment group member receives 100 hours of training in the experimental program and 25 hours of nonexperimental training, whereas the average control group member receives approximately 50 hours of

TABLE 2.1 Treatment-Control Service Differential: Partial Service Counterfactual

| | Hours of | | |
	Experimental Training	Nonexperimental Training	Total Hours of Training
Treatment group	100	25	125
Control group	0	50	50
Treatment-control difference	100	−25	75

nonexperimental training. Thus, the experimental program displaces 25 hours of nonexperimental training in the treatment group, and the overall treatment-control service differential is 75 hours rather than the full 100 hours of service provided by the experimental program. In this case, treatment-control differences in outcomes do not measure the full effect of the experimental treatment; they measure the ***incremental impact*** of an additional 75 hours of training.[12]

Relating Experimental Impacts to Policy Decisions

In the case of the no-service counterfactual, in which there are no similar nonexperimental services available, there is a clear correspondence between the experimental impact estimates and a policy decision with respect to the program. Adopting the experimental treatment as an ongoing program will result in a net increase in services equal to the amount of service provided by the program.[13] The experimental impact estimates, which measure the full effect of the program in this case, therefore represent the effects that could be expected if the program were adopted.

The relationship of the impact estimates to policy decisions is less straightforward in the case of the partial-service counterfactual. If adoption of the program would displace existing services to the same degree as did the experimental treatment, then the service differential created by the experiment (75 hours of training) will be a good measure of the service increment that would be created by an ongoing program, and the experimental impact estimates will be good estimates of the effects of adopting the program. There are several reasons, however, why the experimental service differential may not be a good measure of the incremental services provided by an ongoing program.

First, the experiment may cause control group members to receive a different level of services than they would have received in the absence of the experiment. For example, the outreach and recruiting activities of the experimental program may prompt some individuals who would not have sought services in the absence of the experiment to do so in its presence. When such individuals are assigned to the control group, they may seek out nonexperimental services that they would not have received in the absence of the experiment. Staff of the experimental program may also assist controls in finding nonexperimental services as a "consolation prize" for being denied experimental services. Alternatively, exclusion from the experimental program could discourage controls from seeking out sources of help that they would have found in the absence of the experiment. All these sources of **control group contamination** can cause the control level of services to differ from what it would have been in the absence of the experiment and, therefore, cause the treatment-control service differential to be different from that which would be created by adopting the program.

Second, adoption of the program may have **general equilibrium effects** that cause the resulting service increment to differ from the experimental treatment-control service differential. Suppose, for example, that adoption of the experimental treatment as an ongoing program would cause legislators to reduce funding for other programs providing similar services. In this case, the experimental service differential would not accurately represent the service increment that could be expected from adoption of the program. In the extreme case, in which the new program is entirely funded by transferring resources from other programs, there would be no increase in services in the aggregate but rather a relabeling and reallocation of services among the eligible population.[14]

In a subsequent chapter, the steps that can be taken in implementing the experiment to protect against control group contamination are discussed. Regardless of the precautions taken, however, one can never be certain that this risk has been entirely avoided. Moreover, general equilibrium effects are, almost by definition, virtually impossible to predict.[15] Therefore, caution must be exercised in the interpretation of the experimental impact estimates in cases in which similar services are available outside the experiment.

Even if one cannot confidently assert that the treatment-control service differential represents the service increment that would result from adoption of the program, the impact estimates based on that differential may still be quite useful for policy. Although these estimates may not correspond neatly to a policy action, such as adopting the program, they do provide valid estimates of the effects of a well-specified policy change—increasing the level of service by the amount of the treatment-control service differential.

In the training program example, for instance, we may not be able to determine that adoption of this program would lead to an increase of 75 hours of training per trainee. We could determine, however, that if an additional 75 hours of training of this type were provided, it would have the effects estimated by the experiment. These effects could then be compared to the costs of providing 75 additional hours of training to decide whether it would be worthwhile to provide this level of additional services. (The use of impact estimates in a benefit-cost analysis is discussed in a subsequent chapter.) Even if this level is not the level that would ultimately be provided through the policy process, such an analysis would provide a valuable benchmark for the likely social value of the program.

In practice, this may be the best that any type of study, experimental or nonexperimental, can achieve in predicting the effects of a new program. It will nearly always be impossible to predict the exact form that the final version of a piece of social legislation will take. Even legislation patterned explicitly on a successful demonstration is likely to depart significantly from the demonstration intervention as a result of the numerous other forces that impinge on the policy process. With an experiment, at least one can be confident that the impact estimates derived from the demonstration are unbiased measures of the effects of the service increment created by the demonstration.

Interpreting Treatment-Control
Differences in Outcomes

The fundamental rationale of social experiments is that random assignment creates two or more groups of individuals who do not differ systematically in any way except for the experimental treatment(s). Thus, any subsequent differences in their behavior that exceed the bounds of sampling error can confidently be attributed to the experimental treatment. In this section, I discuss the interpretation of the differences in outcomes (including what is meant by "the bounds of sampling error").

Admissible Comparisons

It is important to recognize that random assignment creates comparability between the entire treatment group and the entire control group; this fundamental strength of the experimental method does not necessarily apply to subgroups of the treatment and control groups.

Suppose, for example, that some individuals assigned to the treatment group fail to participate in the experimental program. One cannot simply drop them from the sample and compare the outcomes of the program participants with those of the controls. To do so would inject into the analysis the very selection bias that experiments are intended to avoid because treatment group members who choose to participate may well be systematically different from those who do not. Because there is no way to identify and exclude from the analysis the nonparticipants' counterparts in the control group, dropping the nonparticipants in the treatment group from the sample would create a fundamental mismatch between the two groups that could bias the impact estimates. (How impacts on members of the subgroup who participate can be estimated in certain circumstances is discussed later, but even this method requires that we first estimate the impact on all individuals randomly assigned.)

More generally, it is not possible to derive experimental estimates of the impact of the treatment on *"endogenously defined"* subgroups. By this, I mean groups defined on the basis of events or actions that occur after random assignment. Because such events or actions may be affected by the experimental treatment to which the individual was assigned, they may define subgroups of the treatment and control groups that are noncomparable. Also, as in the case of program participation, the event may be applicable only to one group or the other; in such cases, there is no way even to identify the corresponding subgroup in the other experimental group.

Therefore, it is sometimes not possible to estimate experimentally program impacts on subgroups in which there is strong policy interest. For example, policymakers are often interested in whether impact varies with treatment "dosage"; it is frequently suggested that this question can be analyzed by comparing impacts on those who leave the program early with those who stay in the program longer. Because the behavior that determines length of stay occurs after random assignment, one cannot analyze this issue experimentally. To compare self-selected (or program-selected) groups that received different levels of treatment would be analogous to studying the effects of medical care by comparing the health status of individuals who had short hospital stays with the health status of those who had long hospital stays.

Another common question that cannot be answered experimentally is the following: What were the impacts of the treatment after participants left the program, as distinct from those impacts that occurred while they were in the program? Because length of stay in the program typically varies within the treatment group and the concept "left the program" is not defined for the control group, there is no way to construct comparable time periods for treatment and control group members for analysis of this question.

Although the restrictions on the analysis of experimental subgroups may seem severe, one can often construct an experimental comparison—either ex ante or ex post—that either answers the question or provides an acceptable substitute. If there is strong interest in the effects of alternative treatment dosages, for example, the experiment can be designed to determine the effects by randomly assigning individuals to alternative levels of treatment. This will create two treatment groups that are comparable to one another and to the control group.

Also, although postprogram impacts cannot be precisely isolated, one can estimate impacts every month, quarter, or year after random assignment because time since random assignment is well-defined for both the treatment and the control groups and cannot be affected by experimental status (this analytical approach is discussed in more detail in a subsequent chapter). This allows one to estimate the impact of the program in the period when most, or all, of the participants have left the program.

One can also learn a great deal by analyzing subgroups that are not endogenously defined. In general, it is permissible to compare subgroups defined on the basis of events that occur, or characteristics that are measured, prior to random assignment. By definition, such events and characteristics cannot be affected by experimental status, which, under random assignment, is uncorrelated with all preexisting characteristics; moreover, such characteristics are well-defined for both the treatment and control groups. For example, the difference in mean outcomes between women in the treatment group and women in the control group is a valid measure of the impact of the program on women.

It is often of interest to estimate impacts for subgroups formed on the basis of demographic characteristics and baseline (i.e., pre-random assignment) values of the outcomes of interest. For example, suppose we are estimating the impacts of a training program on the earnings and welfare benefits of Aid to Families with Dependent Children recipients. It would be useful to estimate impacts for subgroups defined on the basis of age, education, ethnicity, length of time on welfare, or prior earnings or benefit level of the participant. This information would be useful in targeting the program to those recipients who could benefit most from it. Also, by identifying those recipients who were not benefiting from the program, it might also indicate ways to improve the program or at least target improvement efforts on the portion of the participant population in which they are most needed.

Protecting Against Chance Differences in Outcomes Between Treatment and Control Groups

Random assignment guarantees that the only systematic difference between the treatment and control group is access to the experimental treatment. Therefore, if one were to replicate the experiment many times, on average the difference in outcomes between the treatment and control groups would equal the true impact of access to the program. I define the *expected value* of an estimator as its average value over many replications. When the expected value of the estimator equals the true value of the parameter it estimates, the estimator is said to be *unbiased*. Experimental treatment-control differences are unbiased estimators of the true effect of the experimental treatment in the (entire) treatment group.

In practice, of course, experiments are generally performed only once. Thus, although the expected value of the treatment-control difference in outcomes equals the true impact of the experimental treatment, in any one application it may differ from that value due to *sampling error*—chance differences between the two groups that result when specific individuals are randomly assigned to each group in a particular replication. Fortunately, statistical procedures can be used to place bounds on the size of the difference that could reasonably be attributed to sampling error and, therefore, to determine whether the observed treatment-control difference is likely to reflect more than sampling error.

Suppose, for example, that we randomly assign students either to enter a remedial education program or to a control group that receives no remediation. One year later, we compute the difference in grade point averages (GPAs) between the two groups and find that the treatment group's grades are, on average, 0.6 points higher than those of the control group. Can we be sure that the program caused this difference? In addition to the effects of the program, grades will differ among students for any number of reasons that have nothing to do with the experimental program—for example, because of differences in native ability, motivation, health, or whether the student responds well to a particular teacher's pedagogical style.

It could be that, by the luck of the draw, more highly motivated students were randomly assigned to the treatment group than to the control group. If so, the treatment group's average GPA will be higher for this reason alone, and the treatment-control difference in grades will overstate the true impact of the intervention. Conversely, if those assigned to the treatment group were, on average, less motivated than the controls, the treatment-control difference will understate the true impact of the program.

How do we protect against mistakenly attributing these chance differences between the two groups to the program? The short answer is that we use information about the natural variation in the outcome variable (in this case, GPA) across the sample to estimate the probability that a difference as large as that observed could occur entirely by chance To understand how this is done, we must first review some basic statistical concepts.

Statistically, the variation of an outcome across individuals is measured by its variance. The variance of an outcome Y is defined in terms of the deviation of particular values of Y (e.g., each individual student's GPA) from the average value of Y in the population (which we denote μ_Y). Specifically,

$$V_Y = E\left[(Y - \mu_Y)^2\right] \qquad [1.1]$$

where $E\left[(Y - \mu_Y)^2\right]$ denotes expected value. Thus, the variance is the average of the squared deviations of Y around its mean.

The variance of Y measures how much individual Y values can be expected to vary around their mean. Suppose we draw a sample of individuals and compute their mean Y. The mean of Y can be expected to vary less from one sample to another than Y does from one individual to another because in the averaging process unusually high values and unusually low values offset each other. The variance of the sample mean of Y (denoted $\overline{Y}$) is the variance of Y divided by the number of observations in the sample, n:

$$V_{\overline{Y}} = \frac{V_Y}{n} \qquad [1.2]$$

Thus, the larger the sample, the less variable will be its mean.

The experimental impact estimate (I) is the difference between two means, the mean outcome of the treatment group ($\overline{Y}^T$) and the mean outcome of the control group ($\overline{Y}^C$):

$$I = \overline{Y}^T - \overline{Y}^C \qquad [1.3]$$

The variance of the difference between two independent means is the sum of their variances;[16] thus, the variance of the experimental estimator is given by the sum of the variances of the treatment and control group means:

$$V_I = \frac{V_Y}{n_T} + \frac{V_Y}{n_C} \qquad [1.4]$$

where n_T and n_C are the sample sizes of the treatment and control groups, respectively.[17]

This variance measures how much the experimental estimator would vary in repeated replications. As noted previously, if the experiment were repeated a large number of times, each replication would yield a somewhat different estimate of program impact because different sets of individuals would be assigned to the treatment and control groups in each replication. Taken together, the experimental estimates from many trials would form a pattern known as the **sampling distribution** of the experimental estimator. Figure 2.1 shows such a distribution. The height of the curve at any point along the horizontal axis represents the proportion of trials that will yield impact estimates with that value. The area under the curve within any interval along the horizontal axis measures the proportion of trials that would yield estimates within that range. This area may therefore be interpreted as the probability that, in a given replication of the experiment, the experimental impact estimate will fall within that interval. For example, the shaded area in Figure 2.1 measures the probability that, in a given replication, the estimate of program impact would be $>I_0$.

Because experimental estimates are unbiased (i.e., their average over many applications equals the true impact), we know that the sampling distribution of the experimental estimator is centered on I^*, the true impact. Its shape is that of a normal (bell-shaped) curve with variance equal to the variance of the experimental estimator. As can be seen from Equation 1.4, this variance

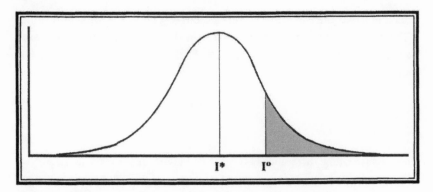

Figure 2.1. Sampling Distribution of the Experimental Estimator

depends on the variance of the outcome (V_Y) and the size of the experimental samples (n_T and n_C). The variance determines how flat or peaked the overall sampling distribution will be. The more highly variable the outcome of Y, the more widely will the sampling distribution be spread out along the horizontal axis. For any given variance of Y, the larger the sample sizes the more tightly clustered around I^* will be the distribution.

With the concept of the sampling distribution in hand, we return to our hypothetical remedial education experiment and ask the question, "How likely is it that we would obtain a treatment-control difference of 0.6 grade points or more by chance alone, when the true impact is zero?" To answer this question, we construct the sampling distribution that we would expect if the true impact of the program were zero. This distribution is centered on zero (the assumed true effect), with variance equal to the variance of the experimental impact estimate. The probability that an estimate of 0.6 or greater could have occurred by chance alone when the true impact is zero is given by the area under this distribution to the right of 0.6. This probability is the *p value* of the estimate. For example, a *p* value of .15 would indicate that, if the true impact is zero, we could expect an experimental impact estimate at least as large as 0.6 by chance alone 15% of the time.

The *p* value can be used to test the hypothesis that the true impact is ≤ 0—that is, that the experimental program did not have a positive effect on Y. We term this the *null hypothesis*; the *alternative hypothesis* is that the true impact is positive. In such a test, we reject the null hypothesis of no positive effect and accept the alternative hypothesis of a positive effect if the probability that a treatment-control difference at least as large as that observed in the experiment could have occurred by chance alone (the *p* value) is less than a prespecified *significance level*. If the *p* value exceeds this level, we cannot reject the null hypothesis. The significance levels usually used for this purpose are either 5% or 10%. That is, we require that the probability of obtaining an estimate as large as the observed result when the program truly has no positive effect be <1 in 20 (the 5% level) or 1 in 10 (the 10% level) before we accept the alternative hypothesis that the true impact is positive. Estimates that satisfy this criterion are said to be *statistically significantly greater than zero*.

Suppose, for example, that in the case of our hypothetical remedial education program the area under the sampling distribution to the right of 0.6 (the *p* value of our experimental impact estimate) is .07. This means that 7 times out of 100 an estimate of this size or larger would be produced by chance alone if there were no true effect. If the significance level we have chosen for the test is 10%, we would reject the null hypothesis that the true impact is zero because—if the impact were really zero—there is less than a 10% probability that an estimate as large as the one obtained would occur. Under the more stringent 5% significance level, however, we could not reject the null hypothesis and would have to entertain the possibility that the estimate differs from zero only because of sampling error.[18]

An equivalent test of the null hypothesis—and, in fact, the one that is usually used—is based on the *t statistic*. The *t* statistic is the impact estimate (*I*) divided by the square root of its variance, which is called the *standard error of estimate* (SEE*I*):

$$t = \frac{I}{\sqrt{V_I}} = \frac{I}{SEE_I} \qquad [1.5]$$

The *t* statistic measures the magnitude of the impact estimate in standard error units rather than in the natural units of the outcome variable (e.g., grade points). Thus, the sampling distribution of the *t* statistic is the same for all outcome variables under the null hypothesis of no effect. This means that, regardless of the outcome variable, one can test hypotheses using the same distribution of *t* values; this distribution is available in published tables. Like the sampling distribution of the impact estimate, the sampling distribution of the *t* statistic has the property that the area under the curve within a given range is the probability that the *t* statistic of the experimental impact estimate

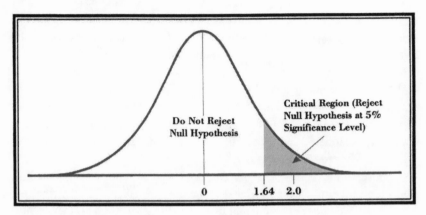

Figure 2.2. Sampling Distribution of the *t* Statistic

will fall within that range in any given application of the experiment, if the true impact is zero.

To test the null hypothesis of no program impact, one first establishes a *critical value* of the *t* statistic that corresponds to the significance level of the test. For the 5% significance level, for example, the critical value is the point on the horizontal axis beyond which lies 5% of the area under the curve under the null hypothesis. This value can be determined from published tables of the *t* distribution. The region outside the critical value is called the *critical region* (Figure 2.2). If the *t* statistic falls in the critical region, we reject the null hypothesis of no program effect because the probability of obtaining a *t* statistic this large (i.e., an impact estimate many standard errors from zero) by chance alone is less than our chosen significance level.

For example, for large samples 5% of the area under the sampling distribution of the *t* statistic lies to the right of 1.64.[19] (An impact estimate of 1.64 standard deviations above zero would produce a *t* value of this magnitude.) Thus, the critical value of the *t* statistic in a test for a positive impact at the 5% significance level is 1.64, and the critical region includes all values of $t > 1.64$. If the *t* statistic of the experimental estimate is >1.64, we reject the null hypothesis that the program had a zero or negative effect on the outcome and conclude that it had a positive impact.

Application of the *t* test is illustrated in Figure 2.2. In this example, the *t* statistic is 2.0; i.e., the impact estimate is twice its standard error. This means that the estimate lies 2 standard errors away from zero. As noted previously, the critical value for a test at the 5% significance level is 1.64;

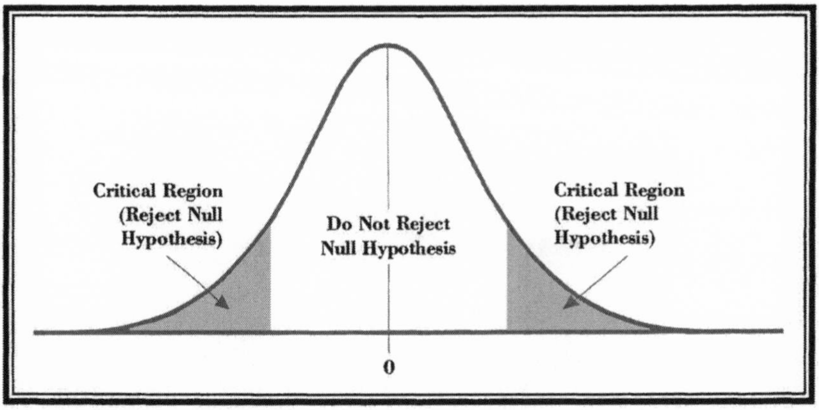

Figure 2.3. Two-Tailed *t* Test

thus, the impact estimate lies in the critical region, the shaded area to the right of the critical value. This means that the probability that an impact estimate this large would be observed when there is no true effect is < 5%, and we must reject the null hypothesis of zero impact at the 5% significance level.

We have so far considered only the possibility that the experimental impact estimate might be significantly different from zero in the positive direction. Thus, the critical region for the test was confined to the right-hand tail of the sampling distribution. Such a test is called a *one-tailed test*. One-tailed tests are appropriate when a finding of a negative impact would have the same policy implications as a finding of zero impact. Suppose, for example, that one is testing a new approach to drop-out prevention. A finding that the program actually encourages students to drop out would have the same policy implication as a finding of no impact—in either case, the approach should not be adopted. In such cases, we need only distinguish positive impacts from nonpositive impacts; a one-tailed test makes this distinction.[20]

In some cases, however, there will be policy interest in distinguishing among positive, negative, and zero impacts. In these cases, a *two-tailed test* is appropriate. In a two-tailed test, the critical region is divided (usually equally) between the two tails of the distribution. Figure 2.3 illustrates the critical region for a two-tailed test. If the *t* statistic falls in the critical region in either tail, we reject the null hypothesis of no effect. It should be noted that in a two-tailed test the sum of the areas in the critical region in the two tails is equal to the significance level. For example, for a test at the 10%

significance level, the area in the critical region in each tail would equal 5%. Thus, the two-tailed test is a more stringent test for positive outcomes than the one-tailed test at the same significance level (i.e., it is less likely to reject the null hypothesis).

Interpreting the Results
of Tests of Significance

In viewing the results of an experiment, it is important to understand what the results of tests of significance mean and what they do not mean. A finding that the impact is significantly different from zero means that we can be reasonably sure that the experimental program had a nonzero impact. In such cases, there is only a small chance that the estimated impact would be as large as the one actually obtained if the true impact were zero.

The fact that the estimate is significantly different from zero does not mean, however, that we know the size of the true impact exactly. There is still sampling error attached to the estimate. The most we can determine is that the true impact is likely to lie within a *confidence interval* around the estimate. The *k*% confidence interval is the range around the experimental estimate that has a *k*% chance of including the true impact. Confidence intervals are derived from the standard error of estimate, which measures the variability of the experimental impact estimate. The 95% confidence interval, for example, is the range 1.96 standard errors on either side of the experimental estimate. If the experiment were run repeatedly and this range calculated for each replication, 95% of these ranges would include the true impact.

Suppose, for example, that the estimated impact in our hypothetical remedial education program is 0.6, with a standard error estimate of 0.2. Its *t* statistic is 3.0 (= 0.6/0.2), which is well above the critical value for statistical significance at the 5% level. Therefore, we can be reasonably sure that the true impact is greater than zero. It may still be greater or less than 0.6, however. The standard error of estimate tells us that the probability is quite low—1 in 20 or less—that the true impact falls outside the range between 0.208 and 0.992 (= $0.6 \pm 1.96 \times 0.2$).

Just as rejection of the null hypothesis of zero effect does not mean that we know the experimental impact exactly, failure to reject the null hypothesis does not mean that we know that the program had zero effect. Again, the estimate is subject to sampling error; the best we can do is to place a confidence interval around the estimate. Suppose, for instance, that in the previous example the estimated impact of the remedial education program had been 0.2 grade points rather than 0.6. With a standard error of 0.2, the 95% confidence interval around this estimate would have been the range from –0.192 to 0.592 (= 0.2 ± 1.96 × 0.2). Because this range includes both positive and negative numbers, we cannot be 95% confident that the program had a positive effect on grade point averages.

Another way of stating the same point is that, although a statistical test can lead one to reject the null hypothesis of zero effect, it can never lead one to accept the null hypothesis—that is, one never concludes that the true impact is exactly zero. One simply "fails to reject" the hypothesis that the true effect is zero. Although this may seem like semantic hair-splitting, the difference between these two conclusions is enormous. The former indicates that we know the true effect exactly, whereas the latter indicates that we do not even know its direction! In policy terms, failure to reject the null hypothesis means that the evidence produced by the experiment was not strong enough to indicate whether the program tested was beneficial. This is far different from being convinced that it was not beneficial.

Even in this situation, however, the experiment may provide useful information about the size of the program effect. If the confidence interval around the estimated impact is so narrow that it includes only very small values on either side of zero, policymakers may not care whether the impact is positive or negative—even if there were a beneficial effect, it would have to be so small that it would not be sufficient to justify adopting the program. In contrast, if the confidence interval is so wide that it includes large beneficial values as well as zero effect, the program may still be worthwhile—the experiment has simply failed to prove that this is the case. In a subsequent chapter, I discuss ways to design the experiment to ensure that it has sufficient "power" to detect effects that are large enough to be important for policy, if they exist.

As this discussion suggests, statistical estimates—whether from an experiment or any other source—must be viewed in probabilistic terms. The true impact of a program can never be known with certainty. At best, we can place it within some range with a high degree of confidence. Although this may seem like a very limited objective, it is in fact an objective that is only attainable with experimental data. This is because experimental impact estimates are known to be unbiased and, therefore, depart from the true value only because of sampling error. Statistical tools are available to allow us to quantify the uncertainty attached to sampling error. Any nonexperimental estimation technique is subject not only to sampling error but also to an unknown degree of bias. Thus, one cannot place any bounds on the true impact with nonexperimental methods unless one is prepared to assume that the estimate is unbiased.

Finally, it is important to recognize that even experimental estimates are valid only for the population from which the research sample was drawn and the treatment to which they were subjected. Thus, in assessing the evaluation results, it is important to consider whether the experimental treatment and population studied are the relevant ones for the policy issue at hand.

Inferring Impacts on Program Participants When Some Treatment Group Members Do Not Participate

Random assignment ensures that the entire treatment group and the entire control group are comparable and that, therefore, the difference between their outcomes is an unbiased estimate of the average effect of the program on the treatment group as a whole. As pointed out earlier, this fundamental strength of the experimental method does not necessarily apply to subgroups defined by actions or events that occur after random assignment. A subgroup of particular importance is those treatment group members who participate in the program. If not all treatment group members participate, the average effect of the program on the overall treatment group is likely to be "diluted" by the inclusion of nonparticipants on whom the program had little or no effect and, therefore, to understate the effect on participants. Also, policy-makers are usually interested in the effect of the program on its participants, not on everyone who had the opportunity to participate.[21]

In social experiments, some degree of nonparticipation among treatment group members is almost unavoidable because program participation requires some action on the part of the sample member over which the experimenter has no control. In a typical experiment, individuals apply for services and go through an eligibility determination, and sometimes a needs assessment, before random assignment. Those found eligible and appropriate for the program are then randomly assigned, and those assigned to the treatment group are informed that they are eligible to participate. Inevitably, some treatment group members fail to show up for services or decide at the last minute that they are no longer interested in the program. In a voluntary program, there is nothing that the program or the experimenter can do about such "no-shows."

Unfortunately, it is impossible to identify the control counterparts of the subgroup of treatment group members who participate because controls do not have the option of participating in the program. Also, because participants are an endogenously defined subgroup, they will not necessarily be well-matched with the entire control group. Thus, one cannot obtain a direct experimental estimate of the impact of the program on participants. Fortunately, in some circumstances it is possible to infer this impact (the procedure described in the following paragraphs is from Bloom, 1984).

To see how this can be done, we first express the average impact on the entire treatment group as a weighted average of the impact on participants and the average impact on nonparticipants, where the weights reflect the relative proportions of the two subgroups. Letting I represent the overall impact, I_p and I_n the impacts on participants and nonparticipants, and r_p and r_n the proportions of participants and nonparticipants in the treatment group, we have

$$I = r_p I_p + r_n I_n \qquad [2.6]$$

In the special case in which the impact of the program on nonparticipants is zero ($I_n = 0$), the last term of this expression is zero and we have

$$I = r_p I_p \qquad [2.7]$$

Solving for I_p, we obtain

$$I_p = \frac{I}{r_p} \qquad [2.8]$$

That is, if the program had no effect on nonparticipants, the impact on participants is just the average impact on the overall treatment group divided by the proportion of the treatment group that participated (termed the *participation rate*).[22] Dividing by the participation rate to obtain the impact on participants is known as the *no-show adjustment*.

Suppose, for example, that the estimated impact of an experimental training program on the average annual earnings of the entire treatment group is $1,000, but that only 80% of the treatment group participated in the program.

The no-show-adjusted impact on the earnings of program participants would be $1,000/.80, or $1,250.

It is important to recognize that this derivation of the impact on participants makes no assumptions about the similarity or dissimilarity of participants and nonparticipants. The only assumption required is that the program has zero impact on nonparticipants. Under this assumption, the no-show adjustment will produce unbiased estimates of the impact on participants even when participants and nonparticipants are completely dissimilar and, therefore, participants are dissimilar to the control group. The adjustment simply averages the overall program effect across the participants rather than across the entire treatment group.

In most voluntary programs, we can probably safely assume that the behavior of individuals who did not participate in the program at all was unaffected by the program. This assumption, however, is not valid in all circumstances. For example, in a mandatory work program for welfare recipients, some recipients might go to work or leave the welfare rolls or both to avoid participating in the program. It must be recognized that the no-show adjustment is only as valid as this underlying assumption, and it should never be applied without careful consideration of the applicability of this assumption in the specific circumstances involved in the experiment.

A final point that should also be recognized in applying the no-show adjustment is that the resulting impact estimates apply only to the participants in the experimental program. Nothing can be determined regarding the impact the program would have had on nonparticipants had they participated; we simply did not observe the behavior they would have exhibited as program participants. Of course, if the same people would not have participated in an ongoing program, this is not a problem; in this case, the experimental participants represent the population of interest. This caveat is only important if the intake process in the experimental program is different from that which could be expected in a regular ongoing program so that one could expect a different subset of those accepted into the program to participate in a regular program. The potential for obtaining an experimental participant group that is nonrepresentative of what one would expect in an ongoing program is a strong argument for making the experimental intake process as similar as possible to the intake process that would be used in an ongoing program. In a subsequent chapter, I discuss ways in which this can be done.

Notes

1. The following argument is stated more formally in Burtless and Orr (1986). I discuss in a subsequent chapter how net social benefits and costs are estimated. In principle, experiments could also prevent the termination of an effective existing program or prevent the adoption of an ineffective new program. The former is analytically identical to the case in which the experiment leads to the adoption of an effective program, and the latter is identical to the case in which the experiment leads to the termination of an ineffective program.

2. See Greenberg and Shroder (1997) for a catalog of the social experiments that have been conducted and their cost. This result benefited not only the taxpayers but also the disadvantaged youths who were the intended beneficiaries of the program. Rather than perpetuating a program that wasted their time and raised false expectations, the government initiated a search for more effective ways to improve youths' earnings. Whether the search will be successful depends on the outcome of several experimental tests of youth training programs that are currently under way.

3. This presumes, of course, that the nonexperimental evidence is not sufficiently compelling to convince policymakers to make the change in policy without the benefit of an experiment. This may often be the case, however, because of the inherent risk that nonexperimental evidence may be contaminated by selection bias or the other threats to validity discussed in Chapter 1.

4. The 70 welfare reform demonstrations approved during the period 1989 to 1996 averaged approximately seven distinct policy interventions per demonstration, according to Wiseman (1996).

5. In the special case in which the experimental benefits take the form of cash or near-cash transfers (e.g., food stamps or housing subsidies), it can be assumed that the benefits to transfer recipients equal the cost to taxpayers so that the net cost to society is zero.

6. See Kershaw and Fair (1976) for a detailed description of the administrative procedures developed for the New Jersey Experiment.

7. This does not mean that we assume that experimental and nonexperimental services are equally effective. It simply means that any treatment-control difference in nonexperimental services can lead to differences in other outcomes, as can a treatment-control difference in experimental services. Thus, both must be measured.

8. In a subsequent chapter, I discuss measurement of the social benefits and costs of the program in a formal benefit-cost framework.

9. One must exclude, however, costs that are solely attributable to the research component of the experiment. If, for example, the program incurs additional costs for outreach and intake to recruit a control group, the added costs should be netted out.

10. For simplicity of exposition, the discussion in this chapter is framed in terms of randomly assigned individuals as the units of observation and analysis. In a subsequent chapter, I discuss random assignment of groups of individuals—for example, classes, caseloads, and communities.

11. For both ethical and logistical reasons, it is usually impossible to exclude either group from receiving existing nonexperimental services. As shall be shown, receipt of some existing services may also be the relevant counterfactual for policy purposes.

12. For illustrative purposes, this example treats experimental and nonexperimental training as interchangeable. The treatment-control differences in outcomes measure the effects of receiving 100 hours of experimental training and 25 hours of nonexperimental training versus receiving 50 hours of nonexperimental training. Only if 1 hour of experimental training and 1

hour of nonexperimental training can be assumed to have the same effects, we can net out the 50 hours of training received by the control group against the 125 total hours of training received by the treatment group and attribute the treatment-control difference in outcomes to the 75-hour difference.

13. This statement assumes that all treatment group members participate in the program. Later, I discuss the case in which some individuals assigned to the treatment group do not participate in the program.

14. In this case, the appropriate counterfactual would be the program the experimental treatment would displace, not the status-quo mix and level of nonexperimental services.

15. This same limitation applies, of course, to any nonexperimental analysis.

16. $\overline{Y}^T$ and $\overline{Y}^C$ are statistically independent because they are based on two separate samples.

17. For simplicity of exposition, we assume that the variance of Y in the treatment group equals the variance of Y in the control group. This need not be the case if the treatment affects the variance of the outcomes. If the variances differ, the formula would change slightly, but the principal conclusions presented here would remain the same.

18. Although the conventional practice is to apply tests of significance to the experimental estimate, an alternative approach is simply to compute the p value as a measure of the likelihood of an estimate at least as large as that obtained when the true impact is zero. Tests of statistical significance have the advantages that they yield a clear-cut yes or no decision on whether the experimental program had a real effect, and they force the researcher to establish a standard of evidence in advance. The advantage of p values is that they provide a more continuous, fine-grained measure of the risk that the estimate reflects only sampling error.

19. Because the variance of the impact estimate depends on sample size (see Equation 1.4), the sampling distribution of the t statistic also depends on sample size. For sample sizes more than approximately 30, however, the effect of sample size on the t distribution is negligible.

20. Of course, one can also construct a one-tailed test to distinguish negative impacts from zero or positive impacts.

21. Although it may seem a forgone conclusion that the only policy interest should be in program participants, this is not necessarily the case. In some programs, there may be policy interest in the average effects on the entire eligible population, as a measure of the program's effectiveness in addressing the broader problem that prompted interest in the program. For example, policymakers may want to know the effect of a training program for welfare recipients on the entire caseload and not just those who participate. In such cases, nonparticipation may be an important determinant of the program's effectiveness.

22. If we treat r_p as fixed (i.e., if we assume that it would be identical in repeated replications of the experiment), then the standard error of I_p is also $1/r_p$ times the standard error of I. Because both the estimate and its standard error have been multiplied by the same factor, the t statistic of the estimated impact on participants is identical to the t statistic of the estimated impact on the treatment group overall; tests of statistical significance on the two estimates therefore yield identical results.

References

Bloom, H. S. (1984, April). Accounting for no-shows in experimental evaluation designs. *Evaluation Review, 8,* 225-246.

Botein, B. (1965). The Manhattan Bail Project: Its impact in criminology and the criminal law process. *Texas Law Review, 43,* 319-331.

Burtless, G., & Orr, L. L. (1986, Fall). Are classical experiments needed for manpower policy? *Journal of Human Resources, 21,* 606-639.

Greenberg, D., & Shroder, M. (1997). *Digest of the social experiments.* Washington, DC: Urban Institute Press.

Kershaw, D., & Fair, J. (Eds.). (1976). *The New Jersey Income-Maintenance Experiment. Volume I: Operations, surveys, and administration.* New York: Academic Press.

Newhouse, J. P. (1993). *Free for all? Lessons from the RAND Health Insurance Experiment.* Cambridge, MA: Harvard University Press.

Wiseman, M. (1996, July). *State welfare reform demonstration projects* (Mimeo). Tables presented at the 1996 Annual Workshop of the National Association of Welfare Research and Statistics, San Francisco.

Chapter ❸

Alternative Random
Assignment Models

❝Everything should be made as simple as possible, but not simpler.❞
—*Albert Einstein, American Physicist*

I n Chapter 2, I discussed the fundamental principles of social experimentation in the context of simple two-group experiments. This chapter focuses on the design of more complex experiments to address a variety of policy questions. By *random assignment model,* I mean the way random assignment is integrated into the program intake process and the treatments to which individuals are assigned.

The way in which random assignment is integrated into the program intake process depends on the population of interest (e.g., participants or program eligibles) and the nature of the program—that is, whether it is voluntary or mandatory and whether it is an ongoing program or a special demonstration set up specifically for experimental purposes. This integration is critical to the design of the experiment because it determines the composition of the experimental sample and, therefore, the population to which the experimental estimates will apply. The treatments to which individuals are assigned will depend on the policy question to be addressed.

I first describe how random assignment is typically integrated into the intake process in simple two-group experiments designed to address the question, Does the program achieve its objectives? In the remainder of the chapter, I consider random assignment models that address other questions.

Integrating Random Assignment
Into the Intake Process

In this section, I examine the integration of random assignment into the program intake process in three different contexts: special demonstrations designed to estimate impacts on participants in voluntary programs, special demonstrations designed to estimate impacts on the entire population eligible for either voluntary or mandatory programs, and evaluations conducted in the context of ongoing programs. In a subsequent chapter, I discuss the implementation of these designs in the field. Here, I focus on the implications of the integration of random assignment into its programmatic context for the composition of the experimental sample.

Special Demonstrations Designed to Estimate
Impacts on Participants in Voluntary Programs

In voluntary programs, interest usually centers on the effects on program participants based on the presumption that nonparticipants are likely to be unaffected by the program. (This is not necessarily the case for mandatory programs, in which eligible individuals who do not participate face some penalty.) Figure 3.1 shows schematically the intake process, including random assignment, for a voluntary program.

As shown at the top of Figure 3.1, the intake process begins with program outreach to the target population to recruit applicants. Outreach can take any of a number of forms. For example, outreach for an employment program for welfare recipients might be conducted through telephone calls from caseworkers to selected recipients or notices sent with the monthly welfare check. Outreach for a home care program for the frail elderly might involve soliciting referrals from social agencies that serve the elderly, posting notices in adult day care centers, running ads in local newspapers, running announcements on television and radio, or all these.

Individuals who respond to program outreach (the "interested individuals" in Figure 3.1) are given more detailed information about the program and the evaluation to allow them to make a decision about whether to apply. This information may be provided through discussions with intake workers (either on the telephone or in person), written materials, or formal group orientation sessions. It includes a description of the services or benefits provided by the program, what program participation will entail for the individual, and the

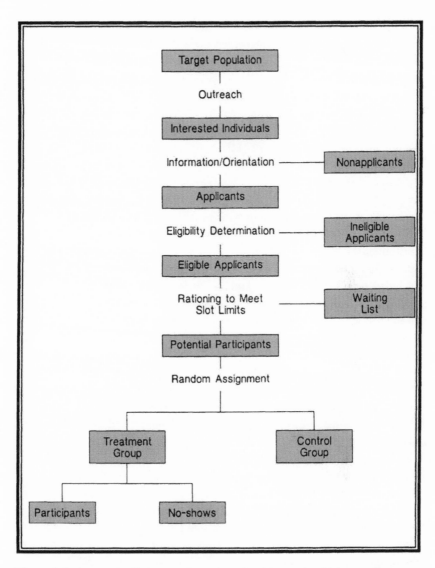

Figure 3.1. Design for Estimating Impacts on Participants in a Voluntary Program

random assignment process and its implications for the individual, as well as any data collection procedures that will impinge on sample members. Upon receiving this information, some individuals formally apply for program entry (the "applicants"), whereas others decide not to apply (the "nonapplicants").

Most social programs have some eligibility requirements. In some cases, there are relatively formal admission criteria, such as age, residence, family income, or receipt of welfare. For example, a community service program might be restricted to out-of-school youths between the ages of 18 and 25, and a home care program for the elderly might be restricted to individuals over the age of 65 who live alone. Information on these objective applicant characteristics is typically collected on the program application form or in documentation collected as part of the application. In other cases, eligibility criteria can be quite informal and judgmental, such as the intake worker's assessment of the individual's potential to benefit from the program. These judgments are usually formed on the basis of personal interviews with the applicant or with other social service providers who are familiar with the applicant (e.g., a social worker or health professional who has worked with the applicant). As shown in Figure 3.1, application of these criteria creates a set of "eligible applicants" and a set of "ineligible applicants," who are excluded from further consideration.

In a regular program or a nonexperimental demonstration, if the number of eligible applicants exceeds the number of participant slots in the program, program staff must apply further criteria to decide who will be admitted to the program. Because all eligible applicants are, by definition, eligible to participate, some criterion other than eligibility must be used. Eligible applicants might be admitted to the program on a first-come, first-served basis, with the remainder being placed on a waiting list. Program staff might also choose among eligible applicants on the basis of "deservingness" or need for program services. These choices produce a set of "potential participants" who are then offered admission to the program.

In an experiment, program staff use the same type of eligibility and selection criteria to choose a set of potential participants equal to the number of program slots to be filled plus the experimental control group. This group is then randomly assigned to one or more treatment groups, which are allowed to enter the program, or to a control group, which is excluded from the program. Under random assignment, both the treatment and the control groups are representative of the pool of individuals from which they are drawn. Thus, the experimental treatment and control groups represent the population of potential participants selected by program staff as being both eligible for the program and acceptable on the criteria (if any) intake staff would normally use to choose among eligible applicants when there are more than the program can accommodate.

Not all those randomly assigned to the treatment group will actually participate in the program, just as not all the potential participants accepted by the program would have participated in the absence of the experiment. Some will lose interest or change their minds at the last minute, or other events in their lives (illness, a family crisis, or finding a job on their own) will intervene and cause them to withdraw. These individuals are labeled "no-shows" in Figure 3.1; individuals who enter the program are labeled "participants."

Several important features of this intake and random assignment process should be noted. First, up to the point of random assignment, the process departs from the intake process that would be employed in a regular program in only two ways. The first difference is that potential applicants must be informed about the experiment. The second, less obvious, difference is that to provide for a control group, the program must recruit more applicants than it would normally. Suppose, for example, that the program is designed to serve 90 participants, and the expected no-show rate is 10%. In this case, 100 potential participants would have to be accepted into the program to fill the program's slots. If one-half of all eligible applicants are assigned to a control group, intake staff must identify 200 potential participants to generate a treatment group of 100.

With these two exceptions, program participants are chosen exactly the same way they would be chosen in the absence of the experiment—that is, using the same processes and criteria that would be used in a nonexperimental program. Therefore, as long as these two differences do not change the nature of the pool of potential participants, the treatment group will accurately represent the group that would be offered admission to the program in the absence of an experiment.

A second point to be noted is that random assignment could have taken place at any point in the intake process. For example, interested individuals (Figure 3.1), rather than potential participants, could have been randomly assigned to treatment and control groups. If that had been done, the treatment group would have advanced to the further steps in the intake process (application, eligibility determination, and selection of potential participants), whereas the control group would have been dropped from further consideration. This would have created comparable treatment and control groups composed of individuals who had expressed interest in the program, and experimental impact estimates could have been derived for this group. In most cases, it would also be possible to derive experimental estimates of program impact on participants under this design using the no-show adjustment described in Chapter 2.[1] As shall be shown in a subsequent chapter, the precision of these estimates would be much lower than that under a design that randomly assigned potential participants because of the larger number of nonparticipants in the interested individual population. When policy interest focuses on impacts on participants, it is preferable to position random assignment as late in the intake process as possible.

Special Demonstrations Designed to Estimate Impacts on the Eligible Population

In some cases, policy interest focuses on the impacts of the program on the entire population eligible for the program and not just on those who participate. When the impact on nonparticipants can safely be assumed to be zero, and the size of the eligible population is known, the impact on the eligible population can be inferred from the impact on participants through an adjustment procedure analogous to the no-show adjustment. Suppose, for example, that 25% of those eligible for a training program participate and that the program raises the average annual earnings of participants by $1,000. Then, the average impact on the eligible population would be $250 (= .25 × $1,000).

When the program may have nonzero impacts on nonparticipants, however, the experiment must be designed to measure impacts on the entire eligible population to capture all its effects. This would be the case, for example, with mandatory programs. Consider, for instance, a mandatory work program for welfare recipients with youngest children over the age of 2. Not all welfare recipients in the mandatory population will participate in the program, either because they refuse or are exempted or because the program may not be able to handle all those formally required to participate. Nonparticipants' behavior and circumstances, however, may still be affected by the program. Those who refuse to participate may be sanctioned, affecting their welfare benefits or, possibly, increasing their willingness to find work on their own. Those whom the program has not yet required to participate may also be motivated to find work on their own before they are required to participate in the program. Some recipients may find the requirement so onerous that they leave welfare altogether rather than participating. Even the behavior of those who are exempted from the requirement may be affected. In fact, recipients may change their behavior to be exempted—for example, by having another child or enrolling in an educational program. For all these reasons, the assumption of zero impacts on nonparticipants may be untenable in mandatory programs.

Even in the case of voluntary programs, it may not be appropriate to infer the impact on the entire eligible population from the impact on participants when random assignment is conducted as shown in Figure 3.1. This approach assumes that the participation rate among eligibles obtained in the experiment accurately represents the participation rate that would occur in an ongoing program. Suppose instead that we would expect virtually universal participation in an ongoing program, but that only a subset of eligibles would respond to outreach in a demonstration. For example, in the long run one would expect virtually all eligibles to participate in a publicly funded health insurance program but only a subset to participate in a demonstration program. Indeed, if outreach is conducted through general media advertising, it may not even be possible to compute a participation rate because we would not know how many eligible persons were exposed to outreach and therefore had the opportunity to participate. In such cases, a different sample intake strategy is indicated, even for voluntary programs. Figure 3.2 shows the appropriate intake process for an experiment designed to estimate the impacts of a voluntary program on the eligible population. Figure 3.3 shows the corresponding process for a mandatory program.

In both cases, the process begins with identification of a sample of eligible individuals within the general population. How this is done depends on the nature of the population. In the income maintenance experiments, for example, screening interviews were conducted with a random sample of households in the experimental sites; households with children and income below a specified level (adjusted for family size) were deemed eligible for the program. In mandatory work programs for welfare recipients, the eligible population within the existing caseload can usually be determined from data maintained in case records; eligibles among the new applicants to welfare can be identified as part of the regular welfare application process.

In voluntary programs, those identified as eligible are invited to participate in the program. At this stage, the information about the program and the experimental evaluation described in the previous section is conveyed to the potential applicants. Because eligibility for the program was determined at the outset, there is no need for an application process (although baseline data may be collected using a form similar to an application form).[2] All those who agree to participate (the "volunteers" in Figure 3.2) are randomly assigned to treatment or control status.[3]

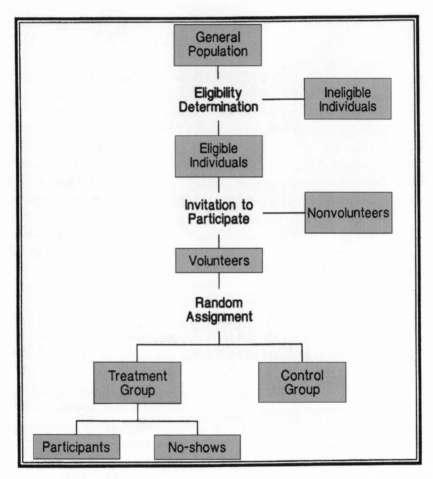

Figure 3.2. Design for Estimating Impacts on the Population Eligible for a Voluntary Program

If all those invited to participate agree to do so, the population randomly assigned—and therefore the experimental treatment and control groups—will accurately represent the eligible population.[4] Of course, this ideal is seldom attained because some of those invited to participate refuse. It will, however, at least be possible to describe the differences between the experimental sample and the eligible population using baseline data collected prior to the offer to participate.

In mandatory programs, it is important to include in the treatment group those who refuse to participate in the program because the program may

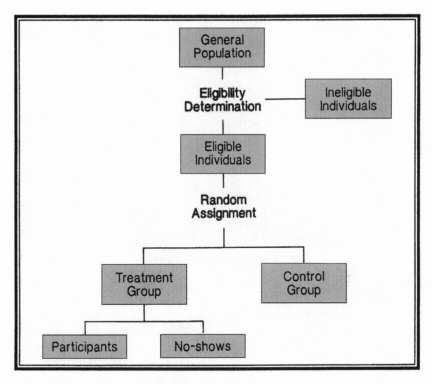

Figure 3.3. Design for Estimating Impacts on the Population Eligible for a Mandatory Program

affect their behavior and therefore the outcomes. Therefore, all those identified as eligible are randomly assigned. Those assigned to the treatment group are then informed of the program requirements (Figure 3.3). There is no need to contact the control group except to collect any baseline and follow-up data that may be needed. In this case, the experimental treatment and control groups accurately reflect the eligible population, and the experimental estimates will be unbiased estimates of program impact on that population.[5]

Evaluations in the Context of Ongoing Programs

Two types of experiment are carried out in the context of ongoing programs: those in which the ongoing program itself is being evaluated, and those in which a new treatment for participants in the ongoing program is being tested. An example of the latter is a test of a new employment and training program (the new treatment) for recipients of Aid to Families with Dependent Children (AFDC) (the ongoing program). The design of random assignment in evaluations in the context of ongoing programs will closely resemble the designs described previously for special demonstrations. Certain constraints apply to experiments undertaken within ongoing programs, however, that are not present in special demonstrations.

Perhaps the most important of these constraints is that the experimenter must work within the established program intake process. In a special demonstration, the intake process can be designed to facilitate the evaluation. In an ongoing program, changing the intake process risks changing the composition of the participant population. Even a simple change such as requiring an additional visit to the program office to meet with intake staff could serve to screen out individuals with transportation or child care problems. Moreover, the experimenter generally has little control over program staff and therefore often cannot convince them to change their established ways of doing things even if it would substantially improve the evaluation.

Although the intake processes described previously are quite general and apply to most ongoing programs as well as to special demonstrations, variations in the specific ways that the intake staff of existing programs interact with potential participants may make it difficult to inform potential applicants about the evaluation and perform random assignment in the manner that would be optimal from an evaluation standpoint.

For example, in an experimental evaluation of the California Conservation Corps (CCC), the population to be randomly assigned included potential participants in a residential program in one district of the state. Program outreach for the residential component of CCC is conducted by recruiters throughout the state, and potential participants are assigned to a particular district partly on the basis of the recruiter's recommendation. In this programmatic context, recruiters had an incentive to recommend that their applicants be assigned to districts other than the one in which the experiment was located to avoid having them assigned to the control group. Only by conducting random assignment after potential participants had been assigned to districts and doing so without the recruiters' prior knowledge could the experiment be designed to eliminate the possibility of recruiters "gaming" the random assignment process in this way. This approach to random assignment was deemed both unacceptable and infeasible. Instead, the experimenters met with the recruiters, explained the experimental objectives and procedures, and obtained their agreement to maintain the same pattern of recommendations they would have made in the absence of the experiment. Program staff at the state level then monitored geographic assignments to ensure an adequate flow of potential participants to the experimental district. Although there is no way to verify that the recruiters' recommendations were not influenced by the experiment, this was probably the best compromise that could be obtained in this programmatic context.

Designs to Address Alternative Policy Questions

So far, I have discussed random assignment models in which a single treatment group is compared with a single control group. Such designs address a relatively simple—though often important—factual question: Does the program in question achieve its objectives? The answer to this question bears on an equally simple policy question: Should the experimental program be adopted or (in the case of an ongoing program) continued?[6] More complex policy questions require more complex experimental designs. In this section, I discuss the designs required to address several other policy questions.

First, policy decisions frequently focus on choices among alternative program strategies rather than simply on whether or not to adopt (or continue) a particular program. In such situations, it is most useful to test several alternative program approaches in a single experiment to determine which is the most effective. When the alternatives being compared can be characterized as points along a continuum, the experiment can be designed to estimate underlying behavioral relationships. For example, the Health Insurance Experiment estimated the demand for medical care as a function of the net price to the consumer by providing a range of experimental insurance plans with different cost-sharing provisions.

A second type of policy question arises when the program of interest has multiple components and there is interest in the separate effects of the individual components. For example, a job training program may provide a number of different employment and training services; in deciding on the optimal mix of services, it is useful to know the impact of each on program participants. In this case, the design of the experiment will depend on whether the program of interest is a new program or an ongoing program.

In the following sections, I discuss the design of these more complex experiments, presenting detailed examples of each. Although these designs

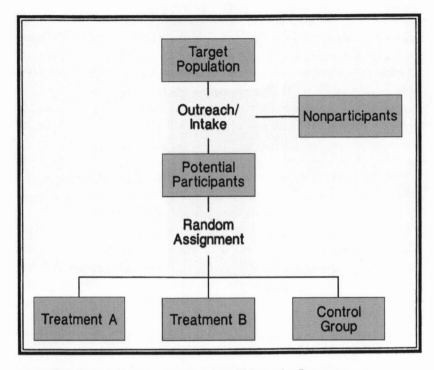

Figure 3.4. Design for Estimating Impacts of Alternative Programs

are similar in that each involves random assignment to multiple treatment groups, they are designed to answer very different policy questions. Therefore, it is essential that evaluators and sponsoring agencies be very clear about the policy question to be addressed before committing to a specific design.

Choosing Among Alternative Program Strategies

Figure 3.4 shows the intake and random assignment process for an experimental demonstration designed to compare two alternative program strategies. (For simplicity of exposition, the stages of outreach and intake leading up to selection of potential participants have been compressed into a single box.) In this design, potential participants are randomly assigned to three different groups: Treatment A, Treatment B, and a control group.

The impact of Treatment A is estimated by the difference in outcomes between those assigned to that treatment and the control group. Similarly, the impact of Treatment B is estimated by the difference in outcomes between those assigned to Treatment B and the control group. This design is thus essentially two experiments in one.

It might seem that one could dispense with the control group and simply compare the outcomes of those assigned to Treatment A with the outcomes of those assigned to Treatment B. This approach is not advisable for two reasons. First, using this approach one might learn whether Treatment A is preferred to Treatment B, but one would not learn whether either of these strategies is superior to the existing policy regime. Only by including a control group representing the status quo can one determine whether either of the new program strategies is a cost-effective improvement over existing programs.

A second reason for including a control group is that, without one, it may not even be possible to obtain a valid comparison of outcomes under Treatment A and those under Treatment B. This will be the case if policy interest focuses on impacts on participants and a nonnegligible number of treatment group members do not participate. Without a control group, impacts on participants cannot be estimated.[7]

An important feature of this design is that random assignment creates three groups that do not differ systematically except for experimental treatment. Thus, the experimental estimates of the impacts of Treatments A and B pertain to the same population—the potential participants who were randomly assigned. This means that the two impact estimates can be directly compared, and the more effective treatment for this population can be determined. (As will be shown, this is not true of all designs in which experimental impact estimates are derived for multiple treatments.) Estimates of the impact of different treatments on the same population are called *differential impact estimates*.

Illustrative Example: The Moving to Opportunity Demonstration

The federal government has traditionally provided two types of housing assistance for low-income families: public housing and rent vouchers. Public housing units are owned by local government agencies and rented to low-income families at below-market rates. Rent vouchers subsidize a portion of the cost of housing units rented by low-income families from landlords in the private housing market. Rent vouchers therefore avoid the concentration of large numbers of poor families in a small area that is typical of public housing projects. Nevertheless, families receiving rent vouchers tend to locate in high-poverty neighborhoods in part because of their family and social ties to these areas. The endemic social problems and limited employment and educational opportunities in these neighborhoods arguably perpetuate a cycle of poverty from one generation to the next.

The Moving to Opportunity (MTO) demonstration is designed to test one strategy for breaking this cycle of poverty: housing assistance that encourages poor families to move from high-poverty areas to low-poverty areas. The specific intervention used in the demonstration is rent vouchers that can be used only in low-poverty areas, coupled with intensive counseling and assistance in finding suitable, affordable units in those areas. This approach is patterned on programs in Chicago and other cities that were ordered by the courts as a way to reduce racial segregation. Nonexperimental evaluations of these programs had indicated substantial gains in earnings and educational attainment among participating families that moved from high-poverty to low-poverty areas (Rosenbaum, 1991). In 1994, the U.S. Department of Housing and Urban Development initiated an experimental demonstration to test whether the gains were attributable to the differences between the two environments rather than to selection effects among the families that chose to move to low-poverty areas. Geographically restricted vouchers were chosen as the experimental intervention, not because there was policy interest in such vouchers per se, but as a way to create comparable groups of families in the two environments. If the experiment demonstrates that a low-poverty environment has positive effects on the well-being of poor families, policies can then be devised to encourage dispersion of poor families to such areas.

In the MTO demonstration, families living in public housing projects are invited to apply for vouchers that allow them to move to private housing. Potential participants are randomly assigned to one of three groups:

◆ The *MTO voucher group*, which receives rent vouchers that can be used only in low-poverty areas, along with intensive counseling and assistance in finding suitable housing in those areas

◆ The *regular voucher group*, which receives traditional rent vouchers that can be used anywhere in the area

◆ A *control group*, which receives no vouchers but is allowed to continue to live in public housing

Demonstration intake is being conducted by local public housing authorities in five large cities (Baltimore, Boston, Chicago, Los Angeles, and New York). Counseling and relocation assistance are being provided by local nonprofit organizations to help families find private housing that meets minimum quality standards, with a landlord who is willing to accept the voucher. If they are unsuccessful in finding housing that meets these requirements, they are eligible to remain in public housing. Families in the experiment are guaranteed housing subsidies for 5 years.

The design calls for a total of approximately 4,400 families to be assigned to the three experimental groups.[8] Follow-up interviews with these families will be conducted over a 10-year period to allow estimation of long-term impacts on their employment, income, education, and social well-being. Long-term effects on the children in participating families will be of particular interest.

The impact analysis will compare the effects of the two different environments relative to public housing. That is, the difference in outcomes between the MTO voucher group and the control group provides an estimate of the effects of a low-poverty environment, relative to living in public housing in a high-poverty environment. Similarly, the difference in outcomes between those receiving traditional (unrestricted) vouchers and the control group is an estimate of the net effects of living in private housing in a high-poverty area, relative to living in public housing in the same type of area. These two impact estimates can be compared to determine the relative effects of living in low-poverty versus high-poverty areas compared to the common counterfactual of living in public housing.

Because the experimental design involved randomly assigning a common pool of potential participants to the three treatments, the groups assigned to MTO vouchers and regular vouchers are well matched; thus, the impacts of these two treatments on the entire treatment group are directly comparable. That is, we will be able to determine which approach had the larger effects (relative to public housing) on the entire group that was randomly assigned and given vouchers.

Not all the families in the two treatment groups that receive vouchers will be successful in finding private housing, however. Because the policy interest is in the relative effects of the two different environments, we would like to compare the impacts on those who actually move to low-poverty areas with those on families that remain in high-poverty areas. If we are willing to assume that the experiment has no impact on families that are unable to use the vouchers to obtain private housing, we can use the no-show correction discussed in Chapter 2 to estimate the impacts on the subgroups that are successful in using the vouchers to rent private housing and move out of public housing. Unfortunately, these subgroups are not necessarily comparable because the two voucher groups have different success rates: In the MTO voucher group, the success rate is approximately 60% to 70%, whereas in the regular voucher group, it is 80% to 90%. Therefore, in comparing the estimates of impact on successful families, it will be necessary to take into account any differences in the characteristics of these two populations.[9]

To the extent that participating families are successful in moving to, and remaining in, low-poverty areas, the MTO demonstration will provide for the first time reliable measures of the effects of the social and economic environment on the well-being of poor families and their children. It will compare the experiences of families living in poverty-stricken neighborhoods with those of families in the much richer social, economic, and educational environments of low-poverty areas. Only through an experimental design can one generate samples of comparable families living in these different environments to measure the effects of the environments themselves. Knowledge of these effects can be invaluable in assessing a wide range of public policies.

Estimating Behavioral Response Functions

A particularly powerful experimental design can be implemented when the program variants of interest can be characterized as points along a policy continuum. In such cases, one can estimate a behavioral response function, which shows how the effects of the program will change as its parameters change. For example, in the Housing Allowance Demand Experiment, families in different experimental groups received housing subsidies equal to 0%, 20%, 30%, 40%, 50%, or 60% of their rent.[10] The income maintenance experiments estimated the labor supply response of low-income families to a wide range of cash transfer programs that differed in the benefit provided a family with no other income (the "guarantee") and the rate at which that benefit was reduced as the family's earnings rose (the "tax rate").

Where feasible, estimation of behavioral response functions can provide policymakers with an extremely valuable tool for policy analysis. Not only do such functions allow the analyst to interpolate responses to parameter values between those tested or to extrapolate beyond the range of values tested but also the fundamental behavioral relationships underlying such functions may be applicable to policies that are entirely different from those originally tested. The labor supply parameters estimated in the income maintenance experiments were used to analyze not only a variety of negative income tax plans in the 1970s but also other policies that involved cash payments to low-income families with significant tax rates on earnings, such as the earned income tax credit. Similarly, the estimates of the price sensitivity of demand for medical care derived from the Health Insurance Experiment and the demand for housing from the Housing Allowance Demand Experiment are applicable to a wide range of policy analyses that involve consumption subsidies in these markets.

Unfortunately, the range of programs and policies that lend themselves to estimation of behavioral response functions may be fairly limited. The central features of most programs simply cannot be expressed as quantitative parameters that can be varied continuously. In a job training program, for example, the critical design features include the type of training provided (e.g., classroom training vs. on-the-job training), the content of the curriculum and occupation for which participants are trained, the skills and qualifications of the training staff, the nature of linkages to private employers, and other nonquantitative program characteristics. In such programs, the best one can do is to experiment with alternative combinations of these central features—for example, classroom training with and without close linkages to private employers or on-the-job training in alternative occupations or both. (Later, I discuss the design of experiments to estimate the effects of discrete program components.)

Illustrative Example: The Health Insurance Experiment[11]

The Health Insurance Experiment resulted from the debate in the early 1970s over proposals to provide universal health insurance, either through mandated employment-related coverage or through direct government provision.[12] Efforts to estimate the cost of these plans prompted a spirited debate about the effects that increased insurance coverage would have on the use of medical care. Economists pointed out that extension of health insurance to previously uncovered individuals constituted a substantial reduction in the net price of medical care to those individuals and could therefore be expected to result in an increase in the demand for care. To offset this increase in demand, which could be extremely expensive or inflationary or both, some analysts proposed that any such plan include "cost sharing" in the form of deductibles or coinsurance (an initial amount or a percentage of the bill to be paid by the beneficiary). Others argued that the use of medical care was not sensitive to monetary prices (Fein, 1971) or that cost-sharing provisions would deter individuals, especially the poor, from receiving needed care.

Efforts to estimate the price elasticity of demand for medical care nonexperimentally were hampered by lack of adequate data and faced a serious threat of selection bias. Individuals who expect to incur high medical expenses have a greater incentive to purchase health insurance than those who do not. Therefore, those with the highest expenditures may have the lowest prices (i.e., have the best insurance). Such "adverse selection" would create an upward bias in nonexperimental estimates of the effect of changes in the net price of medical care on consumption of care.

The Health Insurance Experiment estimated the price elasticity of demand for medical care by randomly assigning families to insurance plans with different cost-sharing provisions. Under the experimental plans, the family either received full reimbursement of all medical costs (the "free plan") or was required to pay 25%, 50%, or 95% of the cost of covered services, up to an annual limit that varied with family income but was capped at $1,000. Above this limit, the plan paid all medical costs.[13] The experimental policies covered a comprehensive range of inpatient and outpatient medical, dental, and mental health services.

A notable feature of the experiment was that it had no control group; all analyses were based on comparisons among the experimental plans. This reflects its fundamental objective of estimating the behavioral response to experimental variation in the price of care rather than estimating the impact of changing that price from the status quo to a different level.

Reflecting the policy interest in a national health insurance program with universal coverage, the experimental sample was drawn to represent the general population under the age of 65.[14] A random sample of the nonaged population at six sites was identified through screening surveys, assigned to the experimental treatments, and then invited to enroll in the experiment. Those who agreed to participate received coverage under the experimental insurance plans for either 3 or 5 years.[15] During the period 1974 to 1977, approximately 6,000 individuals were enrolled in the experiment.[16] The experimental plans were administered by a commercial claims processing firm under contract to the research organization that designed the experiment.

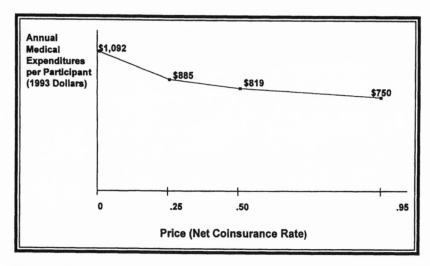

Figure 3.5. Demand for Medical Care: Estimates from the Health Insurance Experiment (Source: Newhouse, 1993)

Data on medical care costs and utilization were derived from the insurance claims submitted to the experiment. Baseline and follow-up data on physical, mental, and social health were collected through a combination of personal interviews and mail questionnaires; in addition, physical examinations were administered at baseline and at the end of the enrollment period.

The experimental results on the central issue of the price elasticity of demand were clear and striking. Overall medical expenditures were 45% higher under the free plan than under the 95% coinsurance plan; outpatient expenditures were 68% higher, whereas inpatient costs were 30% higher. Figure 3.5 shows the response function for total annual expenditures per participant, estimated from the experiment data.

The findings with respect to health status were equally striking: On the wide range of outcomes measured, the additional care induced by the free plan had little or no beneficial effect on health status.[17] The clear policy implication was that cost sharing is an effective way to contain health care costs and utilization, and that doing so will not have a deleterious effect on the health of covered individuals.

When the Health Insurance Experiment was begun in the early 1970s, the national policy debate concerned expanding access to medical care through a national health insurance program. By the time the experimental results became available in the 1980s, concern had switched to cost containment and limiting overutilization, although in the early 1990s there was a brief revival of interest in expanded coverage. By focusing on the fundamental issue of consumer response to the price incentives embodied in health insurance, the experiment was able to provide results that were highly relevant in both policy environments.[18]

Estimating the Effects of Discrete Program Components in Special Demonstrations

A third situation that calls for multiple treatment groups arises when the program of interest has multiple components and there is policy interest in their separate effects. This would be the case, for example, if policymakers were trying to decide what combination of provisions to include in a new program. In contrast to the case discussed in the previous section, in which the different treatments were viewed as alternatives, in this case the treatments are being considered for use in combination. The complication presented by this situation is that the effects of a given component may vary depending on the other components in the package. Thus, one must include in the experiment not only all the components but also all the feasible combinations of components.

Consider, for example, a welfare reform proposal consisting of employment and training services for current recipients and a guarantee of child care for a year after leaving the welfare rolls to take a job. Proponents of such a proposal might argue that employment and training services are ineffective in the absence of child care and that child care alone will not help recipients become employed, but that in combination the two can help recipients obtain and hold jobs. Others might contend that employment and training services alone would be sufficient and that, once they are provided, the child care guarantee would add little but additional cost. Still others might argue the reverse—that child care is the binding constraint and that once it is provided employment and training services are unnecessary. To determine which of these conflicting positions is correct, one must estimate not only the impacts of the overall proposal but also those of the two separate components considered by themselves.

Figure 3.6 shows the experimental design required to produce these estimates. In this design, potential participants are randomly assigned to four groups:

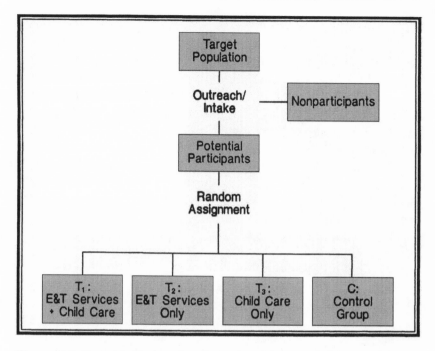

Figure 3.6. Factorial Design for Estimating Impacts of Discrete Program
Components

T_1: A treatment group that receives both employment and training services and the
child care guarantee.

T_2: A treatment group that receives only employment and training services.

T_3: A treatment group that receives only the child care guarantee.

C: A control group that receives no additional services.

Comparison of the outcomes of each of the treatment groups with those
of the control group provides experimental estimates of the impact of each
combination of services. These are differential impact estimates, which show
the impact of different policies on the same population. Thus, the impact
estimates allow us to choose the most effective combination of program
components for that population.

This design is an example of a *factorial* or *fully randomized* experimental design, in which all possible combinations of two or more treatments
are tested (see Campbell & Stanley, 1963, for a detailed discussion of
factorial designs). The need to test all possible combinations arises from the

possibility of interactions between the treatments—that is, the possibility that the combined effect of the two treatments is different from the sum of their individual effects. If there were no interactions, it would be possible to compute the effect of the combined treatment (T_1) by simply summing the effects of the two individual treatments (T_2 and T_3). The treatment group receiving both treatments would be unnecessary; this would allow the experiment to be conducted more cheaply or, alternatively, it would allow larger sample sizes in the experimental groups, thereby increasing the statistical precision of the estimates. Such efficiencies do have a cost, however: In adopting a design that assumes no interactions, we run the risk of seriously misestimating the combined effect of the two treatments if there really are interactions between the program components.

A better strategy is to adopt the complete factorial design and then, in the analysis, test for the presence of interactions. If the test shows that interactions are negligible, treatment T_1 can be combined with treatment T_2 in estimating the effects of the employment and training component and with treatment T_3 in estimating the effects of the child care component, thereby recouping the apparent loss of sample size in each treatment in the factorial design.[19]

Illustrative Example: The New Jersey Income Maintenance Experiment

Factorial designs arise quite naturally in the design of experiments to estimate behavioral response functions when the policy of interest is characterized by two or more parameters. The income maintenance experiments, for example, were designed to test the labor supply response to cash transfers in the form of a negative income tax. In its simplest form, the negative income tax is defined by two parameters: the *guarantee*, which is the amount of the transfer to a family with no other income, and the *tax rate*, which is the rate at which the transfer is reduced for each dollar of earnings. Because each of these parameters can be varied independently over a wide range, there was strong interest in determining the labor supply response to variations in each. Moreover, there were theoretical reasons to expect that the labor supply effects of a given guarantee depend on the level of the tax rate and vice versa—that is, interaction effects were expected. Therefore, factorial designs were adopted in all the income maintenance experiments.

TABLE 3.1 Experimental Treatments: New Jersey Income Maintenance
Experiment

Guarantee (% of Poverty Level)	Tax Rate (%)		
	30	*50*	*70*
50	X	X	
75	X	X	X
100		X	X

SOURCE: Kershaw and Fair (1976, p. 9). Used with permission.
NOTE: This is the original design of the New Jersey Experiment; an eighth experimental treatment with a guarantee at 125% of the poverty level and a 50% tax rate was subsequently added.

The New Jersey Income Maintenance Experiment, for example, was originally designed to test three tax rates (30, 50, and 70%) and three guarantee levels (50, 75, and 100% of the poverty line). As shown in Table 3.1, only seven of the nine possible combinations of these parameter values (indicated by Xs) were included in the design, however.[20] The combination of the highest guarantee and the lowest tax rate was deemed too generous and that of the lowest guarantee and highest tax rate was considered not generous enough to be relevant for policy. Thus, the design is an *incomplete factorial design*.

The experiment was fielded in four cities in New Jersey and one in Pennsylvania during the period 1968 to 1972.[21] Screening surveys were conducted in low-income areas in these cities to identify families headed by nonaged males with incomes below 150% of the poverty line; these families were then randomly assigned to treatment and control groups, and the treatment group members were invited to enroll in the experiment. Thus, the experimental sample was designed to be representative of the entire population of low-income, nonaged two-parent families in these areas.

During the 3-year enrollment period, the 725 families in the treatment groups filed monthly reports on their earnings and other income, on which their monthly negative income tax payments were based. The payments were administered by the research organizations running the experiment, according to rules and procedures designed especially for the experiment. The 632 control families received no negative income tax (NIT) payments but remained eligible for all other publicly provided payments or benefits.[22] Follow-up data on employment and earnings, expenditures, family composition, and a variety of other social, economic, and attitudinal outcomes were collected through personal interviews with family members.

Among male heads of family, the experiment found small reductions in labor supply that were not statistically significantly different from zero. Wives' labor supply responses were much larger, with reductions on the order of 20%. No consistent, statistically significant differences in impact on work effort were found among the NIT plans. This probably reflects the small samples enrolled in the different plans, the small overall response of male heads of family, and the small number of working wives in the sample. The most positive finding was that the experimental plans increased high school completion rates among children in the treatment group families by 25% to 50%.

The New Jersey Experiment was designed primarily to test whether extension of cash transfers to intact families (that had traditionally been excluded from AFDC) would cause them to work less—an issue that was central to academic discussions of the negative income tax and that was expected to be important in the national policy debate on welfare reform. The experimental results were relatively reassuring regarding this question; together with the results of three other similar income maintenance experiments, they probably played an important role in neutralizing the work effort issue in the national policy debate. Throughout the 1970s, however, all attempts to legislate such an extension were defeated by an unusual alliance of conservatives, who opposed extension of cash transfers to intact families on cost and equity grounds, and liberals, who viewed all politically viable plans as providing inadequate benefits. In 1981, the focus shifted to reducing the existing welfare rolls, and interest in cash transfers for intact families disappeared.

Although one cannot attribute any specific policy decision to the findings of the New Jersey Experiment, it and the other income maintenance experiments that were patterned after it provided valuable information on the labor market behavior of low-income families that has been used extensively in the analysis of a wide range of policy options. In particular, labor supply elasticities based on the larger samples available from the Seattle-Denver Income Maintenance Experiment were built into the simulation model that was used by the Department of Health, Education, and Welfare (now the Department of Health and Human Services) to estimate the costs and distributional consequences of virtually all the welfare reform proposals of the 1970s. Also, as the first highly visible large-scale social experiment, the New

Jersey Experiment had an enormous influence on the development and widespread use of experimental methods for the evaluation of social policies.

Estimating the Effects of Discrete Program Components in Ongoing Programs

The designs discussed previously are useful when policymakers want to compare alternative policy options, whether they be alternative program strategies or alternative combinations of program components. In these designs, a common pool of potential participants are randomly assigned to one or more policy options and a control group. This creates well-matched treatment and control groups and allows estimation of the effects of different policies on the same population (i.e., differential impact estimates). In certain circumstances, however, it is useful to know the effects of different policies on different populations.

This will be the case when evaluating an ongoing program that has several distinct components that are applied to different participants, either at the discretion of program staff or by choice of the participants. For example, job training programs typically provide a range of different services, such as job search assistance, occupational skills training, and on-the-job training. The specific services to be received by each participant are determined through an ongoing interaction between the participant and program staff once the participant is enrolled in the program. Some participants receive multiple services, either simultaneously or sequentially, and service plans may change over time, depending on the results of initial services.

In this case, direct random assignment of potential participants to different program services would run counter to the fundamental objective of the evaluation, which is to measure the impacts of the program as it normally operates. Part of the normal operation of the program is the application of staff judgment or participant preferences in deciding which participants are to receive specific services. Overriding these judgments or preferences with random assignment to services would certainly change the way the program operates and would arguably reduce its effectiveness by providing inappropriate services to some participants.

Ideally, one would like to conduct random assignment after program staff have assigned potential participants to services, as shown in Figure 3.7. This design provides a well-matched control group for the participants assigned to each service. Thus, the impact of each service on those assigned to it can

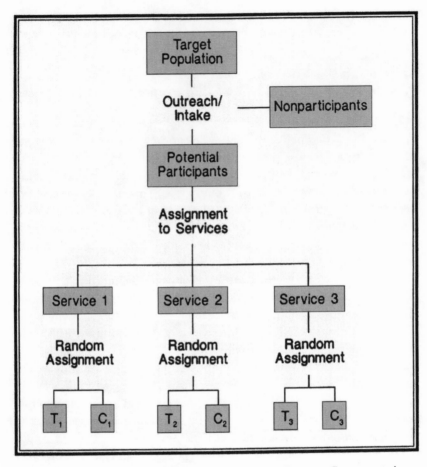

Figure 3.7. Design for Estimating Impacts of Discrete Program Components in an Ongoing Program

be estimated. In effect, this design provides a separate experiment for each program component. In addition, an estimate of the overall impact of the program on the entire participant population can be obtained by comparing the entire treatment group, across all components, with the entire control group.

It is important to recognize, however, that because assignment to service was judgmental, the groups assigned to different services are potentially different. Therefore, the estimated impacts of different services are not directly comparable. Suppose, for example, that Service A is found to have a larger positive impact on those assigned to it than Service B has on those assigned to it. We cannot therefore conclude that Service A is "better" in the sense that if those assigned to Service B had instead been assigned to Service A they would have experienced larger impacts. It may be that those assigned to Service A were more motivated or talented than those assigned to Service B. It may also be that even though Service A works well for those assigned to it, it would not be a good match to the abilities and aptitudes of those assigned to Service B. All that can be determined from this result is that Service A works better for those assigned to it than Service B does for those assigned to it.

Such a result is nevertheless of substantial value to policymakers. It allows them to identify the components of the program that are working well for those they serve and those components that are not. This in turn allows policymakers to focus their attention on those components in need of improvement or elimination rather than continuing to spend resources on ineffective services. It does not, however, indicate to policymakers how to improve these components; to do this would require testing alternatives to the ineffective components for the populations that they serve.

Therefore, improving existing programs must be a two-stage process. First, one must determine which parts of the program are achieving their objectives and which are not. For this purpose, experimental designs of the type described in this section, with assignment to program components prior to random assignment, are appropriate. Then, one must test alternatives to those program components found to be ineffective in the first stage using designs such as those described previously, which randomly assign potential participants to different program components, thereby yielding differential impact estimates.

Illustrative Example: The National JTPA Study

Since 1962, the federal government has provided job training for economically disadvantaged workers. During this period, attempts have been made to estimate the impact of such training on participants' earnings. One of the most ambitious attempts to evaluate these programs was a series of comparison group evaluations of the Comprehensive Employment and Training Act (CETA) program in the late 1970s and early 1980s (see Chapter 1). These evaluations revealed that, even when the same database was employed, different nonexperimental methods gave substantially different impact estimates (Barnow, 1987). This result was confirmed in methodological studies that applied various different nonexperimental estimation techniques to data from an employment and training demonstration for which unbiased experimental estimates of impact were available (LaLonde, 1996; Maynard & Fraker, 1987).

Because of the uncertainties involved in nonexperimental evaluation methods, a panel of experts convened by the Department of Labor to advise it on the evaluation of the program that replaced CETA, the Job Training Partnership Act (JTPA), unanimously recommended that the evaluation employ experimental methods (Stromsdorfer et al., 1985). The resulting evaluation was conducted in 16 local JTPA service delivery areas from 1987 to 1992.

Because the evaluation was designed to estimate the effects of JTPA on those who normally participate in the program at these sites, program staff conducted program outreach, eligibility determination, and applicant screening in the usual manner. The final step in the regular JTPA intake process is an assessment of applicant needs and interests. On the basis of this assessment, the intake worker recommended one of three service strategies for each potential participant: a strategy based on on-the-job training (OJT), one based on classroom training in occupational skills, or one based on other less intensive services.[23] The potential participants were randomly assigned after the assessment was conducted and the intake workers' service recommendations were recorded. Thus, the experimental design was essentially that shown in Figure 3.7, with the exception that the intake workers' service recommendations were not strictly binding.

Because service recommendations were made before random assignment, they were not affected by experimental assignment. Thus, the treatment group within each service strategy subgroup was well matched to its control group and constituted a subexperiment that yielded unbiased estimates of impact on those for whom that service strategy was recommended. In addition, the combined treatment and control groups across all three subgroups yielded an experimental estimate of the overall impact of the program on the entire treatment group.

In interpreting the results of such a design, it is important to bear two caveats in mind. First, as noted earlier, the service strategy subgroup estimates are not differential impact estimates; because potential participants were assigned to the three subgroups judgmentally, rather than randomly, they represent different participant populations. It is clear, for example, both

from discussions with program staff and from data on participant characteristics and outcomes, that staff tended to assign the more job-ready applicants to the OJT subgroup.[24] Therefore, the impact estimates derived for one
subgroup cannot be applied to another. For example, among adult trainees it
was found that the OJT subgroup had larger earnings gains than the classroom training subgroup, but this does not necessarily mean that if those in
the classroom training subgroup had been assigned to the OJT subgroup
instead they would have had larger earnings gains. It may simply mean that
the more job-ready applicants assigned to the OJT subgroup were better able
to benefit from the program.

The second caveat that must be borne in mind is that the treatment-control
differences for each subgroup represent the impact of recommending a
certain set of services for that subgroup and not the actual receipt of these
services. Because the process of matching participants to services is an
ongoing one in JTPA, not all treatment group members received the services
that were recommended for them, and some received services that were not
recommended for them. This was the unavoidable outcome of two constraints
on the research design: the need to define service subgroups prior to random
assignment and the need to avoid disturbing the normal operation of
the program. This caveat notwithstanding, however, the three subgroups
experienced very different patterns of service receipt that were highly correlated with the service recommendations. Thus, the impacts estimated for the
three groups can be viewed as the result of meaningfully different service
strategies.

More than 20,000 potential participants were randomly assigned in the
National JTPA Study sites. Baseline data were collected as part of the
program intake process, and 30 months of follow-up data on employment
and earnings, non-JTPA education and training, welfare benefits, and other
economic and social outcomes were collected through a combination of
personal interviews and administrative records.

Separate analyses were conducted for adult men, adult women, female
youths, and male youths.[25] The overall effect of the program on earnings (i.e.,
the average effect across all three service strategies) was statistically significantly positive for the two adult groups but not significantly different from
zero for either of the two youth groups. Indeed, none of the estimated effects
for any of the six youth service strategy subgroups were statistically significantly different from zero. When estimated program benefits in the form of
increased earnings were compared with program costs, JTPA had positive

net social benefits for five of the six adult service strategy groups but not for any of the six youth service strategy subgroups.

These findings had a dramatic and immediate effect on the policy deliberations regarding JTPA. As noted previously, as a direct result of these findings, annual funding for the youth component of JTPA was reduced by more than $500 million, whereas funding for the adult component remained essentially unchanged. This represented a savings to taxpayers at no loss to the intended beneficiaries of the program because the training was totally ineffective. A portion of the resources that would have been wasted on ineffective services was devoted instead to experimental demonstrations designed to test alternative training strategies for youths in the hope of identifying more effective service approaches. These experiments are currently under way.

Notes

1. It would also be possible to derive estimates of the impacts on applicants, eligible applicants, or potential participants using variants of the no-show adjustment.

2. In subsequent chapters, I discuss the uses of baseline data and procedures for its collection.

3. Alternatively, all eligibles could be randomly assigned and the invitation to participate extended only to the treatment group. Those who refuse the invitation could then be treated as no-shows and the impact on participants derived from the estimated impact on all eligibles using the no-show correction. Because only the treatment group is invited to participate, this approach reduces the number of individuals to whom the program must be explained, avoids the necessity of explaining random assignment to potential participants, and eliminates the necessity of informing controls that they will not be allowed to participate. For any given sample size, however, impacts on participants are estimated less precisely if all eligibles are randomly assigned than if only those who agree to participate are randomly assigned. (The effect of the position of random assignment on the precision of the estimates is discussed in a subsequent chapter.)

4. This statement and similar statements that follow apply to the eligible population within the experimental sites—that is, the eligible population identified in the first step of the intake process. Whether this population is representative of the broader eligible population in other localities and the implications if it is not are issues that are addressed in a subsequent chapter.

5. This assumes that the program being tested would not affect the composition of the eligible population if it were implemented on an ongoing basis. This may not be the case. A mandatory work program for welfare recipients, for example, might deter some individuals from applying for welfare. Because this effect cannot be captured experimentally, the experimental sample would not perfectly represent the population that would be eligible for an ongoing program.

6. As will be shown in a subsequent chapter, the experimental impact estimates provide information that is necessary, but not sufficient, to address this question. In addition, one must take into account the costs of the program.

7. If the participation rate were the same in both treatments, the no-show correction would be the same for the two so that the impacts of the two experimental programs on participants would be proportional to their impacts on the overall treatment group. One cannot know in advance, however, the participation rates in the two programs.

8. Additional families may be added in several sites if, as anticipated, additional vouchers are made available to the demonstration by the local public housing authorities.

9. To do so formally will require application of nonexperimental statistical adjustments of the impact estimates. Thus, the research question cannot be fully addressed with experimental methods. Nevertheless, random assignment is extremely valuable in this case because it avoids the potentially severe selection bias that would be involved in comparing families that were successful in moving to low-poverty areas with a comparison group composed entirely of families that were unsuccessful or, worse, that were not interested in moving.

10. See Friedman and Weinberg (1983). The Housing Allowance Demand Experiment also tested other, more complex, subsidy formulae.

11. For a detailed description of the Health Insurance Experiment, see Newhouse (1993).

12. A subsidiary issue that played an important role in the initiation of the experiment was related to the work disincentive posed by the Medicaid "notch"—the abrupt cessation of all benefits when covered families' earnings rose above the Medicaid eligibility level. Some policy analysts proposed smoothly phasing out health insurance coverage of the poor through the use of income-related cost sharing under which the share paid by the beneficiary would rise with income. Feldstein (1971) proposed this approach as a way to ensure that cost sharing did not deter the poor from receiving needed care under a universal plan with cost sharing.

13. The experiment included 15 treatments. Ten comprised all the possible combinations of the 25%, 50%, and 95% coinsurance rates with three different levels of the annual expenditure limit (5, 10, and 15% of family income, up to $1,000), plus the free (0% coinsurance) plan, to which the annual limit did not apply because the plan paid all the family's medical expenses. Four of the remaining experimental treatments incorporated different cost-sharing provisions for different types of care (inpatient vs. outpatient and mental health and dental care vs. all other services). The final treatment was enrollment in a Health Maintenance Organization (HMO). In addition, data were collected on a representative sample of regular enrollees in the same HMO for comparison with the randomly assigned HMO sample.

14. The aged were excluded on the grounds that, because they were already covered by Medicare, they were unlikely to be strongly affected by any new national health insurance plan, and because their behavior was likely to be sufficiently different from that of the nonaged population that they would have required a separate experiment.

15. The difference in duration of coverage was one of several "subexperiments" conducted within the larger experiment. A randomly selected 25% of the sample in each insurance plan (50% in the first site) was assigned to receive coverage for 5 years. This allowed better estimation of steady-state impacts on demand for care and health status and provided a test for any bias that might have arisen from the limited duration of the experiment. Other subexperiments measured the effect of cash participation incentive payments, mail questionnaires, and initial physical examinations on the utilization of care.

16. Of these, approximately 4,000 were enrolled in fee-for-service plans, and about 1,800 were enrolled in a HMO.

17. The experiment measured impacts on a wide range of indicators of health status within five major categories: general health, including physical, mental, and social health; physiologic health (the presence and effect of various chronic diseases); health habits; prevalence of symptoms and disability days; and risk of dying from any cause related to various risk factors. These indicators were based on data from self-administered medical history questionnaires administered at enrollment and exit (3 or 5 years after random assignment), a screening examination administered to a random 60% of all participants at enrollment and all participants

at exit, and biweekly self-administered health reports that provided data on disability days. See Newhouse (1993) for a full description of the analysis of impacts on health status.

18. The experimental results for the HMO plan (not discussed here) are also highly relevant to the recent policy interest in managed care plans.

19. Doing so requires a multivariate regression analysis, in which the effects of both components are estimated simultaneously, rather than a simple comparison of mean outcomes. I discuss this analytic approach in a subsequent chapter.

20. An eighth plan, incorporating a fourth guarantee level (125% of the poverty level) and a 50% tax rate, was subsequently adopted when New Jersey adopted a welfare program for two-parent families headed by unemployed workers that provided more generous benefits than several of the experimental plans. See Kershaw and Fair (1976) and Watts and Rees (1977) for a detailed discussion of the design of the New Jersey Experiment.

21. A companion project begun a year later, the Rural Income Maintenance Experiment, tested similar treatments in rural areas.

22. When the experiment began, the principal welfare program in New Jersey and Pennsylvania, AFDC, excluded families with two able-bodied parents. Thus, virtually all the control families were ineligible for welfare at the outset. In January 1969, however, New Jersey instituted an AFDC program for two-parent families (AFDC-UP) with benefits that were among the highest in the country.

23. In some cases, multiple services were recommended. These sample members were still categorized on the basis of whether OJT or classroom training in occupational skills (as distinct from basic education) was recommended, regardless of the other services that were recommended, on the grounds that these are the most intensive services that JTPA offers. See Orr et al. (1996) for a detailed description of the National JTPA Study.

24. The clearest way in which this selection process can be gauged is by comparing the post-random assignment earnings of controls in the three service strategy subgroups. Among adult women, for example, those in the OJT subgroup averaged approximately $15,000 in earnings during the 30-month follow-up period, whereas those in the classroom training and less intensive services subgroups averaged only about $11,500 and $10,250, respectively (see Orr et al., 1996).

25. In JTPA, participants ages 16 to 21 are classified as youths. The experimental sample included only out-of-school youths.

References

Barnow, B. S. (1987, Spring). The impact of CETA programs on earnings: A review of the literature. *Journal of Human Resources, 22,* 157-193.

Campbell, D. T., & Stanley, J. C. (1963). *Experimental and quasi-experimental designs for research.* Chicago: Rand McNally.

Fein, R. (1971, February 22 and 23). *Testimony on Health Care Crisis in America: Hearings Before the Subcommittee on Health of the Committee on Labor and Public Welfare,* U.S. Senate, p. 146.

Feldstein, M. S. (1971). A new approach to national health insurance. *Public Interest, 23,* 93-105.

Friedman, J., & Weinberg, D. H. (Eds.). (1983). *Urban affairs annual review, Vol. 24: The great housing experiment.* Beverly Hills, CA: Sage.

Kershaw, D., & Fair, J. (Eds.). (1976). *The New Jersey Income-Maintenance Experiment. Volume I: Operations, surveys, and administration.* New York: Academic Press.

LaLonde, R. J. (1986, September). Evaluating the econometric evaluations of training programs with experimental data. *American Economic Review, 76,* 604-620.

Maynard, R., & Fraker, T. (1987, Spring). The adequacy of comparison group designs for evaluations of employment-related programs. *Journal of Human Resources, 22,* 194-227.

Newhouse, J. P. (1993). *Free for all? Lessons from the RAND Health Insurance Experiment.* Cambridge, MA: Harvard University Press.

Orr, L. L., Bloom, H. S., Bell, S. H., Doolittle, F., Lin, W., & Cave, G. (1996). *Does job training for the disadvantaged work? Evidence from the National JTPA Study.* Washington, DC: Urban Institute Press.

Rosenbaum, J. E. (1991). Black pioneers—Do their moves to the suburbs increase economic opportunity for mothers and children? *Housing Policy Debate, 2,* 4.

Stromsdorfer, E., Bloom, H., Boruch, R., Borus, M., Gueron, J., Gustman, A., Rossi, P., Scheuren, F., Smith, M., & Stafford, F. (1985). *Recommendations of the Job Training Longitudinal Survey Research Advisory Panel.* Washington, DC: U.S. Department of Labor, Employment and Training Administration.

Watts, H. W., & Rees, A. (Eds.). (1977). *The New Jersey Income-Maintenance Experiment. Volume II: Labor-supply responses.* New York: Academic Press.

Chapter ❹

Sample Design

"Estimates of program effects are just that—estimates. They are facts, not truth, and once we have them we are still left with the problem of deciding what, if anything, they tell us about truth and whether what they tell us is enough to guide our actions. Conversely, in setting out to collect facts, we want to design evaluations so that their results will be a useful guide to action once we get them."

—*Stephen D. Kennedy (1996, p. 1)*

In this chapter, I discuss the issues involved in designing the experimental sample to achieve the most valid and precise estimates of the experimental impact. Specifically, I address the following issues:

- Site selection and the external validity of the experimental impact estimates
- Sample size and the statistical power of the design
- The point in the sample intake process at which random assignment is conducted and the power of the design
- Allocation of the sample among multiple treatments
- The optimal number of experimental sites
- Random assignment of groups of individuals.

Site Selection and the
External Validity of the Estimates

As noted in Chapter 1, experimental estimates are *internally valid*—that is, they provide unbiased estimates of the impact of the experimental treatment on the population to which it was applied. For the experimental estimates to be **externally valid**, the experimental sample must accurately represent the population of interest for policy. External validity is sometimes characterized as **generalizability**. To provide the most reliable guidance for policymakers, experiments should be both internally and externally valid. In designing experiments, then, it is important to pay careful attention to a number of threats to the external validity of the estimates.

Ideally, the experimental sample would be a random sample of the population of interest for policy.[1] Just as random assignment creates two groups that do not differ systematically in any way, random selection of the experimental sample from the broader population of interest would produce a sample that does not differ systematically from that population. Thus, if the experimental sample is a random sample of the population of interest, the impact estimates are unbiased estimates of what the impact of the program would be in the larger population.

In most applications, however, simple random sampling from the population of interest is not feasible. It would probably not be possible, for example, to conduct an experiment with a simple random sample of all Aid to Families with Dependent Children (AFDC) recipients in the United States or even in a single state. Such a sample would be spread so thinly over a large number of program offices and geographic areas that the costs of experimental administration and data collection would be prohibitive. Instead, experimental samples are generally clustered in a small number of sites.

It is still possible to obtain a random sample of the overall population (e.g., all AFDC recipients in the United States or in a given state) if the experimental sites are randomly selected from all sites in that population, and experimental participants are randomly selected from the population of interest within each site. Such a sample design is known as a **multistage random sample**. This type of sampling procedure was used in the national evaluation of the Food Stamp Employment and Training Program (FSETP) (Puma, Burstein, Merrell, & Silverstein, 1990). In this experimental study, a sample of 60 local food stamp agencies (FSAs) was randomly selected from among 410 FSAs containing 85% of the national population of program participants.[2] An intensive site recruiting effort resulted in the agreement of 55 FSAs to participate in the evaluation.[3] A sample of 12,000 potential FSETP participants were then randomly selected within these experimental sites and randomly assigned to the program or a control group.

As this example illustrates, one of the potential barriers to obtaining a representative sample of the population of interest is the need to obtain the cooperation of local program staff. Program staff typically resist participating in social experiments for a variety of reasons, including the added burden of experimental sample intake and random assignment procedures, fear of disruption of ongoing program activities, and ethical concerns about denial of service to controls (ways to address these concerns are discussed in a subsequent chapter). If the refusal rate is high among selected sites, selection bias can creep into the impact estimates via self-selection of sites. For example, if only the most effective schools agree to participate in an experimental test of a remedial education program, the experimental estimates are likely to overstate the impacts of the program.

Because of the expected cost and difficulty of recruiting a randomly selected sample of sites that are representative of the population of interest, many social experiments have opted instead for *convenience samples* of sites that, for one reason or another, are easy to recruit. Often, these are programs that have expressed interest in participating in the experiment or that have established relationships with the researchers or funding agency for other reasons. In other cases, in which the visibility and added resources associated with participation in a demonstration project are viewed as a benefit to the local program, sites have been selected by sponsoring agencies on political grounds. Often, such selections are a *fait accompli* before the research team has been selected.

At best, convenience samples of sites leave the experimenter with no knowledge of the relationship between the estimated program impacts at the experimental sites and what these impacts would be in the broader population of interest for policy. At worst, by concentrating the experimental sample within a self-selected set of sites, they inject the very selection bias that social experiments are intended to avoid. Of course, in most cases it is possible to compare the characteristics of the experimental sites and participant sample with those of the broader population from which they were drawn. Such comparisons can identify ways in which the experimental sample differs from the population of interest. They can never demonstrate conclusively, however, that it is truly representative of that population because it is possible that the two differ in unmeasured characteristics that affect the outcomes of interest.

An alternative to both random selection of sites and convenience samples is *purposive selection* of sites that are well matched to the population of interest in observable characteristics. For example, sites for the Washington State Self-Employment and Enterprise Development Demonstration were selected by choosing the combination of sites that minimized a weighted index of differences between the sites and the state overall on a number of characteristics (Orr, Johnson, Montgomery, & Hojnacki, 1989).

This approach is an improvement over convenience samples of sites in that it ensures that the experimental sites are well matched to the overall population on at least the most salient observable characteristics. Indeed, it can be argued that purposive selection is preferable to random selection of sites when the number of sites is small because in small samples sampling error can create large differences between the sample and the population from which it was drawn.[4] Purposive selection directly controls such differences in observable characteristics. Also, if sites are selected solely on the basis of observable characteristics, there is no reason to expect systematic differences in unobservable characteristics between the study sites and the overall population once they are matched on observable characteristics (as there is when the sites are self-selected or selected on political grounds). The principal disadvantage of purposive selection is that, unlike random selection, there is no way to quantify the sampling error involved. Also, as with random sampling, the experimenter must still convince local program staff in the purposively selected sites to participate in the experiment, and any refusals to participate can inject selection bias into the sample.

A final site-selection strategy that is sometimes used is purposive selection of sites that represent different social, economic, or programmatic environments in dimensions believed to affect the impact of the program rather than to match the distribution of these characteristics in the overall population. For example, in testing a training program for welfare recipients, one might try to pick some sites with high welfare benefit levels and some with low benefits, some sites in areas with high unemployment rates and some in areas with low unemployment rates, and so on. Such an approach can help researchers to understand how the impact of the experimental program varies with these conditions. If these conditions do influence program impacts and their distribution among the sample sites differs from their distribution in the population of interest for policy, however, then the experimental estimate of the average program impact in the sample will not be an unbiased estimate of the average impact that could be expected in the broader population. To obtain an unbiased estimate of what the impact would be in the broader population, one would have to "reweight" the sample to reflect the composition of that population in these dimensions. Doing so will reduce the precision of the impact estimates relative to the estimates that would have been obtained from a more representative sample. This approach also suffers from the other shortcomings of purposive sampling discussed previously.

Achieving externally valid impact estimates requires not only that the experimental sites be representative of all sites in the broader population of interest but also that the sample of individuals within these sites be representative of this population. As discussed in Chapter 3, this means that the intake and random assignment process must be designed to yield a sample of the relevant population—whether this is the overall target population, eligible applicants, or potential participants. Also, the intake process must be designed to be as similar as possible to that which would be employed in an ongoing program or, in the case of an evaluation of an ongoing program, the implementation of the experiment must disturb the existing intake process as little as possible.

In practice, it is often extremely difficult to achieve an externally valid experimental sample. Experimenters often lack the resources needed to recruit a truly representative sample of sites and to compel or induce local program administrators at all the selected sites to participate in the experiment. The results of their efforts in this regard must be judged not only in comparison to the ideal of a perfectly representative sample but also in comparison to the strengths and weaknesses of the alternative available evidence. If the only alternative source of information for policymakers is the anecdotes and success stories of local program operators, experimental evidence from even a badly nonrepresentative convenience sample may be an enormous contribution. The choice would be more difficult if the alternative were a nonexperimental study based on nationally representative data on the population of interest. In this case, one would have to weigh the risks of using a potentially internally invalid method (the nonexperimental estimator) against the risks of using a potentially externally invalid method (the experiment). There is little that can be said in general about this trade-off; each case must be examined on its own merits.

Finally, it must be recognized that the exact policy context within which the experimental results will be used is often not known when the experiment is designed. It is therefore critical that the experimental treatment and sample selection procedures be carefully documented so that future policymakers will know how closely these correspond to the program or policy with which they are concerned and its intended target population.

Sample Size and the Statistical Power of the Design

As explained in Chapter 2, even the best designed study—either experimental or nonexperimental—cannot measure the exact impact of a program, or even determine with certainty whether the program had an impact at all. What a well-designed experiment can do is provide an unbiased estimate of the impact, indicate whether we can be confident that the impact is nonzero, and specify a confidence interval around the estimate within which we can be reasonably certain the true impact lies. In designing an experiment, one of the central objectives is to ensure that the confidence with which we can state whether the program had a nonzero impact is great enough, and the interval within which we can bracket the true impact is narrow enough, for policy purposes. These objectives are captured by the statistical concept of the *power of the design*.

Measuring the Power of the Design

The power of the design is the probability that, for a specified value of the true impact, we will reject the null hypothesis of zero impact. Suppose, for example, that we want to estimate the impact of a training program on its participants' earnings. If the true impact of the program is positive, we would like the test of statistical significance of the experimental estimate to reject the null hypothesis of zero effect. The greater the probability that it will do so, the greater is the power of the design.

Figure 4.1 shows how the power of the design can be calculated for one specific value of the true impact, a $100 increase in earnings. That is, it shows how to calculate the probability that, if the true effect of the experimental program is to increase earnings by $100, the experimental impact estimate will be significantly greater than zero. The normal curve to the left in Figure 4.1 is the sampling distribution of the impact estimator under the null hypothesis that the true impact is zero. The darkly shaded area under the right-hand tail of the distribution is the critical region for the test of the null hypothesis at the 5% significance level.[5] (Note that one must specify the significance level of the test to calculate the power of the design.) As explained in Chapter 2, if the experimental estimate lies within the critical region, we reject the null hypothesis of zero impact. To calculate the power of the design, then, we must determine the probability that the experimental estimate will lie within the critical region when the true impact is $100.

This can be determined by the sampling distribution of the experimental estimate when the true impact is $100; this is the distribution on the right in Figure 4.1. It is centered on $100, and its shape is determined by the standard error of the experimental estimator. The probability that the experimental estimate will fall in the critical region if the true impact is $100 is given by the area under this curve to the right of the critical value I_c. This probability is the power of the design for a true impact of \$100—in this example, 70%. That is, there is a 70% chance that we would reject the null hypothesis of zero effect when the true effect is \$100. (Later, I explain how the numerical value of this probability is calculated; here, our interest is in its conceptual derivation.)

Power and Sample Size

As the previous example demonstrates, the power of the design depends on the shape of the two sampling distributions in Figure 4.1. Also, as noted in Chapter 2, the shape of the sampling distribution of the experimental estimate depends on the size of the experimental sample. In particular, the larger the experimental sample, the more tightly the sampling distribution will be clustered around its mean. Figure 4.2 shows what happens to the power of the design if we use a larger experimental sample than the sample used in Figure 4.1. As shown in Figure 4.2, the tighter sampling distribution around a true impact of \$100 increases the probability of the experimental estimate exceeding any value to the left of \$100, including the critical value for the test of significance. Moreover, the tighter sampling distribution around the null hypothesis of zero impact lowers the critical value for the significance test; this also has the effect of increasing the proportion of the area under the sampling distribution around \$100 that lies above the critical value (compare the shaded area under the right-hand curve in Figure 4.2 with the corresponding shaded area in Figure 4.1). For both reasons, increasing the size of the experimental sample increases the power of the design.[6]

Power and the Significance Level of the Test

A second way in which we could increase the power of the design would be to raise the significance level for the test of the null hypothesis of no effect. Suppose, for example, that instead of testing at the 5% significance level, we were to test at the 10% significance level. This would lower the critical value, I_c, thereby increasing the proportion of the area under the right-hand sampling distribution that falls in the critical region—that is, it would increase the probability of rejecting the null hypothesis of zero effect when the true effect is \$100.

Note, however, that raising the significance level of the test also increases the probability of rejecting the null hypothesis when it is in fact true from

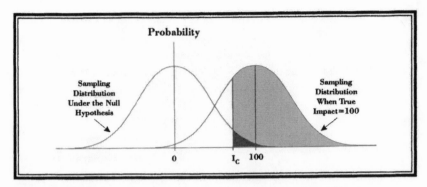

Figure 4.1. Derivation of the Power of the Design (for True Impact = 100)

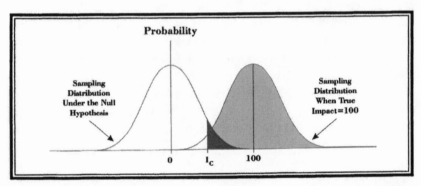

Figure 4.2. Power of the Design (for True Impact = 100) With Larger Sample Size

5% to 10%. Thus, in specifying the significance level of the test, there is a trade-off between two risks: the risk of falsely concluding that there is a positive effect (i.e., rejecting the null hypothesis) when in fact there is no effect and the risk of failing to reject the null hypothesis of zero effect when in fact the true effect is positive. The probability of the former error is given by the significance level of the test of the null hypothesis. The probability of the latter error is 1 minus the power of the design.[7] Thus, in the design depicted in Figure 4.1, there is a 5% risk of falsely concluding that the program effect was positive when in fact it was zero and a 30% risk of falsely concluding that the program effect was zero when it was in fact $100.

In making the trade-off between these two risks, researchers typically accept a higher risk of mistakenly concluding that the effect is zero than of falsely concluding that it is positive, on the grounds that the costs of the latter error are greater than the costs of the former error. Suppose, for example, we are testing a new program that, if found to be effective, will be implemented on an ongoing basis at a cost of $100 million per year. If we mistakenly conclude that the program is effective when in fact it has zero effect, over time billions of dollars will be wasted on it. If we make the converse error—concluding that the program has zero impact when its true effects are positive—we miss an opportunity to implement an effective program, but we do not waste large sums of money.[8]

However one views these risks, it is essential that the trade-off be made explicitly. Far too often, researchers unthinkingly apply the "conventional" significance levels of 5% or 10% without examining the implications for the power of the design. The result can be an extremely weak test of the null hypothesis—that is, only a low probability of detecting a positive impact if it exists. In such cases, one should consider increasing the sample size to strengthen the design, lowering the significance level to achieve a better balance between the two types of risk, or—if it is not possible to obtain a sufficiently large sample to yield adequate power—not conducting the experiment at all.

Power Functions

The discussion so far has been cast in terms of the power of the design at a single positive value of true impact. Obviously, the power of the design can be calculated similarly for any value of true impact. If power is calculated for all possible levels of true impact, the resulting probabilities trace out the *power function* for the design. Figure 4.3 shows an illustrative power function. The height of the curve measures the power of the design for each value of true impact (the horizontal axis). The curve has the characteristic shape of power functions, with a minimum when true impact is zero (where the null hypothesis is true) and power rising asymptotically toward 1.0 at values of true impact further away from zero.[9]

The power function is conditional on the significance level of the test and the sample size. For a given significance level, the power function corresponding to a larger sample size will lie above the power function for a smaller sample size—that is, the larger sample size will have greater power for all true impact values (except zero). For a given sample size, the power function for a higher significance level (e.g., 10%) will lie entirely above the power function for a lower significance level (e.g., 5%); this illustrates the trade-off between the two types of risk discussed previously.

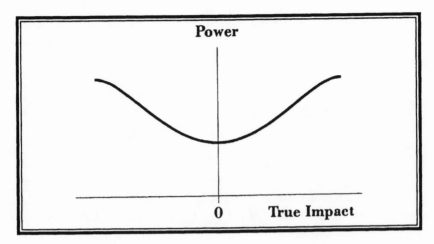

Figure 4.3. Power Function

Minimum Detectable Effects
and the Design of Experiments

Choosing the sample size and significance level for an experiment is equivalent to choosing the power function for the experiment. In practice, however, rather than attempting to calculate all the possible power functions corresponding to different sample sizes and significance levels, experimenters typically specify the desired power for a specified value of true effect and significance level of the test and then solve for the sample size that will yield that level of power.[10] To do so, they use the concept of *minimum detectable effect*—the smallest true impact that would be found to be statistically significantly different from zero at a specified level of significance with specified power.

Suppose that, in the case of the training program discussed previously, we want to have an 80% probability of detecting a true impact of $100 if it occurs, and that we are willing to take a 10% risk of rejecting the null hypothesis of zero when it is in fact true. We therefore want to know the sample size that will yield a minimum detectable effect of $100 with 80% power at the 10% significance level. Figure 4.4 shows how we can calculate this sample size.[11]

The left-hand curve in Figure 4.4 is the sampling distribution of the experimental estimate under the null hypothesis of zero effect; the shaded region in its right tail is the critical region for rejection of the null hypothesis

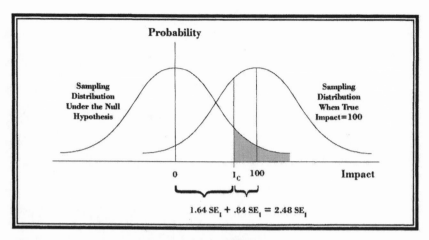

Figure 4.4. Calculation of Minimum Detectable Effects

at the 10% significance level. In large samples, the critical value that defines this region (I_c) will be 1.64 times the standard error of the impact estimate (SE_I). The right-hand curve in Figure 4.4 is the sampling distribution of the experimental estimate when the true impact is $100. For an 80% probability of rejecting the null hypothesis of zero effect when the true impact is $100, 80% of the area under this sampling distribution must lie to the right of the critical value 1.64 SE_I. This will be the case when the mean of the distribution ($100) lies 0.84 standard errors above the critical value.[12] As shown in Figure 4.4, to make this condition hold exactly we need only choose the sample for which $100 equals 2.48 (= 1.64 + 0.84) times the standard error of the impact estimate. That is, we choose n_t and n_c, the numbers assigned to the treatment and control groups, so that

$$100 = 2.48 \ SE_I = 2.48 \sqrt{\frac{V_Y}{n_t} + \frac{V_Y}{n_c}}$$ [4.1]

where V_Y is the variance of Y, the outcome of interest.

Alternatively, for any specified combination of treatment and control group samples we can calculate the minimum detectable effect (MDE) achievable with 80% power at the 10% significance level:

$$MDE = 2.48 \sqrt{\frac{V_Y}{n_t} + \frac{V_Y}{n_c}} \qquad [4.2]$$

Choice of a different level of power or significance simply changes the multiplicative constant in Equations 4.1 and 4.2. For example, for 80% power at the 5% significance level, the constant would be 2.80. Thus, more generally

$$MDE = k \sqrt{\frac{V_Y}{n_t} + \frac{V_Y}{n_c}} \qquad [4.3]$$

where k is a constant that reflects the chosen levels of power and significance.

As is clear from Equation 4.3, all that is required to compute the minimum detectable effect for any given value of k and combination of treatment and control sample sizes is knowledge of the variance of the outcome. This is usually available from existing data. For example, the variance of the earnings of low-income workers can be computed on the basis of data from nonexperimental evaluations of training programs or from national surveys such as the Current Population Survey.[13] In using existing data sources for this purpose, it is important to ensure that the population represented in the data is very similar to the planned experimental population.

An important property of experimental designs is readily derived from Equation 4.3: For any given division of the sample between treatment and control groups, minimum detectable effects are inversely proportional to the square root of the overall sample size (later, I discuss the optimal allocation of the sample between the treatment and control groups). For example, let s_t be the share of the total sample N allocated to the treatment group and s_c be the share of the total sample allocated to the control group. Then Equation 4.3 can be written as

$$MDE = k \sqrt{\frac{V_Y}{s_t N} + \frac{V_Y}{s_c N}} = k \sqrt{\frac{1}{N}} \sqrt{\frac{V_Y}{s_t} + \frac{V_Y}{s_c}} \qquad [4.4]$$

Thus, for example, doubling the sample reduces the minimum detectable effect by a factor of $1/1.41 = 0.71$. To halve the minimum detectable effect, one would have to quadruple the sample.

The minimum detectable effect is an extremely useful indicator of the power of any particular design. Small minimum detectable effects indicate that policymakers can be quite confident that if the program has even a small effect on the outcome, the experiment will have a good chance of detecting it (i.e., of rejecting the null hypothesis of no effect). Large minimum detectable effects indicate that the effect of the program would have to be large for the experiment to have a good chance of detecting them. Prior analysis of the power of the design is the best protection against ending up in the situation described previously—obtaining experimental estimates with confidence intervals so broad that they are consistent with both large effects and no effect at all.

Of course, "small" and "large" are relative terms, and there is no obvious way to decide what size effects we want to be reasonably sure of detecting. One rule that is sometimes suggested is to set the minimum detectable effect at the level that would make the program cost-effective—that is, design the experiment so that if the program is cost-effective we can be reasonably certain that the experiment will have a nonzero effect.[14] Although this rule has a certain intuitive appeal, it ignores the relationship between minimum detectable effects and the cost of the experiment. Achieving smaller minimum detectable effects requires larger samples, which increases the cost of the experiment. Thus, a truly general rule for deciding on sample sizes and the power of the design would have to specify the trade-off between experimental costs and the social value of more powerful estimates of program impact.[15] In the absence of such a general rule, the best advice that can be given is that the experimenters and policymakers compute and review a "menu" of alternative designs, with different costs and minimum detectable effects on the outcomes of central interest, to make a judgmental trade-off between power and cost.

The Point of Random Assignment and the Power of the Design

In some cases, the power of the design will be influenced by the design of the random assignment process as well as by sample size. This will be the case when interest focuses on estimating program impacts on participants and not on all those randomly assigned to participate in the program. In this section, I discuss this case.

As shown in Chapter 2, under the assumption that the program had no effect on nonparticipants, an unbiased estimate of program impact on participants (I_P) can be obtained by dividing the estimated impact on the overall treatment group (I_T) by the participation rate among those randomly assigned (r):

$$I_P = \frac{I_T}{r} \qquad\qquad [4.5]$$

The standard error of the estimated impact on participants (S_{I_P}) can be derived from the standard error of the estimated impact on the overall treatment group (SE_T) by the same procedure:[16]

$$S_{I_p} = \frac{SE_T}{r} \qquad\qquad [4.6]$$

Our measure of the power of the design, the minimum detectable effect on participants (MDE$_{Ip}$), is

$$MDE_{IP} = k\, SE_{IP} = k\, \frac{SE_T}{r}, \qquad\qquad [4.7]$$

Thus, the minimum detectable effect on participants depends not only on sample size and the variance of the outcome (which determine SE_T) but also on the participation rate among those randomly assigned. The lower the participation rate, the larger will be the minimum detectable effect on participants—that is, low participation rates result in low statistical power.

The principal way in which the experimenter can influence the participation rate, and thereby improve the power of the design, is through the design of the random assignment process. Figure 4.5 (which is adapted from Figure 3.1) shows the intake process for a voluntary program. As can be seen, individuals drop out of the intake process at various points between the initial response to outreach and participation in the program. Because the participation rate in Equations 4.5, 4.6, and 4.7 is defined as the proportion of those randomly

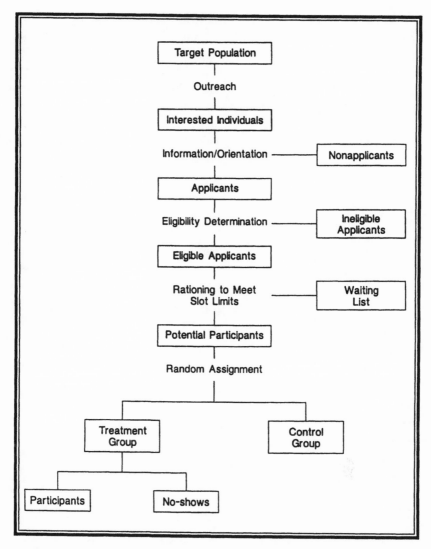

Figure 4.5. Design for Estimating Impacts on Participants in a Voluntary Program

assigned who participate in the program, the later in the intake process that random assignment is administered, the higher the participation rate. Thus, the principal way the experimenter can increase the participation rate and reduce minimum detectable effects is by conducting random assignment as late in the intake process as possible.[17]

Consider, for example, the choice between randomly assigning all applicants and randomly assigning only eligible applicants. Suppose that the ineligibility rate is 20% so that for every 100 applicants there are only 80 eligible applicants, and that of these 80, 60 would ultimately participate in the program in the absence of random assignment. The participation rate for applicants, then, is .60 (= 60/100), whereas the participation rate for eligible applicants is .75 (= 60/80). As shown in Equation 4.7, the minimum detectable effect on participants for a sample composed of applicants is

$$MDE_{IP,A} = k \frac{SE_{T,A}}{r_A} \qquad [4.8]$$

and the minimum detectable effect on participants for a sample composed of eligible applicants is

$$MDE_{IP,E} = k \frac{SE_{T,E}}{r_E} \qquad [4.9]$$

where r_A and r_E are the participation rates of applicants and eligible applicants, respectively.

The relative power of the two designs is indicated by the ratio of these two minimum detectable effects:

$$\frac{MDE_{IP,A}}{MDE_{IP,E}} = \frac{\left(k \dfrac{SE_{T,A}}{r_A}\right)}{\left(\dfrac{k\, SE_{T,E}}{r_E}\right)}. \qquad [4.10]$$

By equation 4.4:

$$[4.11]$$

$$\frac{SE_{T,A}}{SE_{T,E}} = \sqrt{\frac{N_E}{N_A}} = \sqrt{\frac{80}{100}} = \sqrt{.8}.$$

Substituting this expression into equation 4.10 yields:

$$\frac{MDE_{IP,A}}{MDE_{IP,E}} = \frac{\sqrt{.8}}{.8} = \frac{1}{\sqrt{.8}} = 1.12. \qquad [4.12]$$

Thus, random assignment of all applicants results in minimum detectable effects on participants that are 12% larger than if only eligible applicants are randomly assigned. Note that this is true even though by construction the number of program participants is the same in both designs. Note also that even though the applicant sample provides less precise estimates, it is 25% larger than the eligible applicant sample; thus, data collection costs will be approximately 25% greater if all applicants are randomly assigned.

For these two designs to have the same power, one would have to set their relative sample sizes so that

$$MDE_{IP,A} = \frac{k \, SE_{T,A}}{r_A} = MDE_{IP,E} = \frac{k \, SE_{T,E}}{r_E} \qquad [4.13]$$

which implies

$$\frac{SE_{T,A}}{SE_{T,E}} = \frac{r_A}{r_E} = .8. \qquad [4.14]$$

By equation 4.4:

$$\frac{SE_{T,A}}{SE_{T,E}} = \sqrt{\frac{N_E}{N_A}}. \qquad [4.15]$$

Substituting this expression into equation 4.14:

$$\sqrt{\frac{N_E}{N_A}} = .8 \qquad\qquad [4.16]$$

or

$$N_A = \frac{N_E}{(.8)^2} = 1.56 \; N_E. \qquad\qquad [4.17]$$

Thus, the applicant sample would have to be 56% larger than the eligible applicant sample to achieve the same power.

Although the numbers used in this illustrative example are purely hypothetical, they are typical of the orders of magnitude involved in the choice of placement of random assignment in the intake process. As these numbers suggest, this choice can have a substantial effect on the power of the design and/or the cost of the experiment. In the example, assigning eligible applicants rather than all applicants would entail either a 12% increase in minimum detectable effects and a 25% increase in sample size or a 56% increase in sample to maintain the same power. In most cases, an increase in sample size would increase the costs of implementing the experiment and collecting data by nearly the same factor. In any specific experiment in which impacts on participants are to be estimated, it is important to predict the likely participation rate so that realistic estimates of minimum detectable effects can be derived and to consider how participation rates and minimum detectable effects will vary with the placement of the point of random assignment.

Unfortunately, program staff typically resist placing random assignment late in the intake process. Late random assignment increases the burden on staff members because they must continue to process those who will ultimately be assigned to the control group in addition to those who will be allowed to participate in the program. Moreover, staff often feel that it is unfair to applicants to require them to invest additional time and effort, and to raise their expectations, only to be assigned to the control group. Finally, intake staff find it much more difficult to inform controls that they are excluded from the program after they have had extensive contact with the controls. For these reasons, it may ultimately be necessary to conduct random assignment at a point in the intake process that is not absolutely the latest point at which it could occur. Experimenters, however, must be cognizant of the analytic losses, monetary costs, or both involved in such a compromise decision.

Allocation of the Sample Among Multiple Treatments

The essence of social experimentation is comparison of outcomes among randomly assigned groups of individuals. In this section, I discuss how the relative number of individuals to be randomly assigned to each experimental group is determined. I begin with the simple case of a single treatment group and a single control group and then generalize the analysis to multiple treatment groups. Next, I consider the allocation of the sample when experimental costs vary from one experimental group to another. Finally, I discuss the issues that arise when multiple treatments are implemented at multiple sites.

Allocating the Sample Among Experimental Groups

The objective of sample allocation is to maximize the power of the design. Thus, in a simple experiment with one treatment group and one control group, we want to choose n_t and n_c to yield the smallest possible minimum detectable effect. Previously, it was shown that, for any given allocation of the sample between the treatment and control groups, the minimum detectable effect is inversely proportional to total sample size. Here, we keep total sample size constant and focus on the allocation of the sample among experimental groups; that is, we pose the problem in terms of choosing the ratio n_t/n_c for any given total sample. Thus, we choose n_t/n_c to minimize

$$MDE = k \sqrt{\frac{V_Y}{n_t} + \frac{V_Y}{n_c}} \,, \qquad [4.18]$$

subject to the constraint

$$n_t + n_c \leq N.$$

It can be shown that this expression is minimized when $n_t/n_c = 1$—that is, when equal numbers of individuals are assigned to the treatment and control groups.

Of course, we allocate the sample among experimental groups through random assignment. The desired sample allocation determines the **random assignment ratio**—the ratio of the probability that a given individual will be assigned to one group to the probability that he or she will be assigned to another. In the simple two-group case just described, the optimal treatment-control random assignment ratio is 50:50—that is, there is a 50% chance of being assigned to each group. Random assignment ratios need not be equal across experimental groups. As will be shown, in some cases the optimal sample allocation assigns very different numbers of individuals to different experimental groups; in these cases, random assignment probabilities would vary commensurately.

When there are multiple treatment groups, we face a trade-off among experimental objectives. Within a fixed total sample, allocating more of the sample to one treatment group will increase the power of the design for estimating the impact of that treatment at the expense of the power of the design for other treatments. To determine the optimum allocation in this situation, we must specify the importance we attach to each of the impact estimates to be derived. We do this by specifying an objective function W that is a weighted sum of the minimum detectable effects for the k treatments:

$$W = w_1 MDE_1 + w_2 MDE_2 + \ldots + w_k MDE_k, \qquad [4.19]$$

where w_i is the "policy weight" attached to the impact estimate for the ith treatment. Because smaller minimum detectable effects are preferred to larger ones, we wish to allocate the sample to minimize W, subject to the constraint

$$n_1 + n_2 + \ldots + n_{k+1} \leq N$$

where

n_i = the number of individuals assigned to the ith of $k + 1$ experimental groups (k treatment groups, plus a control group)
N = the total sample size

Consider, for example, an experiment with two treatment groups and a control group. Such an experiment can produce two different types of impact estimate: the impact of Treatment 1 and the impact of Treatment 2. If we put equal weight on these two different estimates (i.e., if $w_1 = w_2 = 1$), then we wish to minimize

$$W = MDE_1 + MDE_2 = \sqrt{\frac{V_Y}{n_{tl}} + \frac{V_Y}{n_c}} + \sqrt{\frac{V_Y}{n_{t2}} + \frac{V_Y}{n_c}} \qquad [4.20]$$

subject to the constraint

$$n_{t1} + n_{t2} + n_c \leq N$$

It can be shown that W is minimized (i.e., the power of the design is maximized) when $n_{t1}/n_{t2} = 1$ and $n_c/n_{t1} = n_c/n_{t2} = 2$. That is, in the optimal allocation, the samples assigned to the two treatment groups are of equal size and the sample assigned to the control group is twice as large as each of the treatment groups. This means that half the sample should be assigned to the control group and one quarter to each treatment group.

To understand why we obtain this asymmetric result, consider the effect of adding one individual to each of the three experimental groups. Adding one individual to treatment group 1 reduces the minimum detectable effect for this treatment (the first term in Equation 4.20) but has no effect on the minimum detectable effect for Treatment 2 (the second term in Equation 4.20); the converse holds for adding an individual to the sample assigned to the second treatment. In contrast, adding an individual to the control group reduces the minimum detectable effect for both treatments because the control group is involved in both experimental comparisons. Of course, the more sample members already assigned to a particular group, the less difference will the addition of one more individual make. If one considers starting with an equal allocation among the three groups and then shifting sample from the two treatment groups to the control group, the reduction in minimum detectable effect resulting from each additional control group member exceeds the increase in minimum detectable effect resulting from the loss of a treatment group member until the control group is exactly twice the size of each of the treatment groups.

This result for the three-group case can be generalized to a simple rule that applies to any number of groups as long as equal weights are placed on each experimental comparison: Allocate the sample in proportion to the number of experimental comparisons in which each group is involved. If, for example, the impact of seven different experimental programs is to be derived on the basis of seven treatment groups and one control group, each treatment group will be involved in one experimental comparison, and the control group will be involved in seven comparisons. Thus, if there is equal policy interest in each of these comparisons, the optimal allocation would place 1/14 of the sample in each treatment group and one half (7/14) of the sample in the control group.

If there is unequal policy interest in the different experimental comparisons, the sample allocation must be derived by minimizing the expression for W in Equation 4.19, subject to the constraint that the sum of the samples assigned to the various experimental groups cannot exceed the fixed total sample.

Sample Allocation Subject to a Fixed Budget

So far, we have used a fixed total sample as the constraint on sample allocation. This will sometimes be the case, as in an experimental evaluation of an ongoing program in which all eligible applicants who apply within a given time period are to be randomly assigned. More commonly, however, the binding constraint is not a fixed total sample size but rather a fixed budget that can be devoted to the experimental treatments and data collection. In this case, minimum detectable effects should be minimized subject to the constraint of a fixed budget rather than a fixed total sample size.

If the cost of assigning an individual to one experimental group is the same as that of assigning him or her to any other, then having a fixed budget is the same as having a fixed sample size; the total sample size is simply the budget divided by the (uniform) cost of assigning an individual to an experimental group. A common situation in which this is the case is that in which the experimental treatments are not funded through the budget of the agency sponsoring the experiment. This would be the case, for example, for evaluations of ongoing programs, in which the treatment is provided out of the regular program budget and the evaluation is funded through a separate research budget. In this case, the cost to the evaluation budget of assigning an individual to an experimental group is simply the cost of collecting data on the individual; because the same data are collected for all experimental groups, this cost does not vary from one group to another.

If the cost of treatment is included in the experimental budget, then the cost per sample member will generally vary from one experimental group to another. When multiple treatments are tested, some are likely to cost more than others; in any case, costs per sample member are likely to be higher in the treatment group than in the control group because controls receive no experimental services. Within a fixed budget, unequal costs per sample member indicate that a larger sample can be supported by assigning more individuals to the cheaper experimental groups.

The general solution for the optimal sample allocation when costs vary among experimental groups is to minimize W (as defined in Equation 4.19) subject to the constraint

$$n_1 c_1 + n_2 c_2 + \ldots + n_{k+1} c_{k+1} \leq C, \qquad [4.21]$$

where

n_i = the number of individuals assigned to the ith group
c_i = the cost per sample member in the ith group
C = the total budget for experimental treatment and data collection

Although the solution to this problem is mathematically straightforward, when there are multiple treatment groups the solution is somewhat complicated. In the simple case of a single treatment group and a single control group, the optimal allocation is

$$\frac{n_t}{n_c} = \sqrt{\frac{c_c}{c_t}} . \qquad [4.22]$$

That is, the sample should be allocated between the treatment and control groups in inverse proportion to the square root of the relative costs per sample member in the two groups.

A simple example will illustrate the importance of taking variations in the cost per sample member into account in sample allocation. Suppose we have a budget of $500,000 to evaluate a social service program for low-income families. For each family assigned to the treatment group, we will incur a cost of $4,000 for experimental services. Data collection will cost $500 per family regardless of experimental assignment. Thus, the total cost per treatment group family will be $4,500, and the total cost per control family will be $500. If we allocate equal numbers of families to the treatment and control groups, our budget will support 100 families in each group. Taking the relative costs of the two groups into account, however, the optimal allocation is to put three times as many families in the control group as in the treatment group. With this allocation, our budget will support 83 families in the treatment group and 250 families in the control group. Minimum detectable effects under this allocation will be 10% smaller than they would have been with equal-sized groups.[18] To achieve this reduction in minimum detectable effects with equal-sized groups would have required a 24% increase in total sample size.[19] Thus, switching from an equal allocation to the optimal allocation is equivalent to increasing the budget for the experiment by 24%, or $120,000.

"Unbalanced" Designs

The sample allocation procedures discussed in the preceding section take into account differences in average cost per sample member among experimental groups. In some cases, experimental costs may vary systematically not only with the experimental group to which an individual is assigned but also with the individual's characteristics. For example, negative income tax plans provide larger payments to low-income families than to higher-income families.

Therefore, assigning a high-income family to the treatment group is less costly to the experiment than assigning a low-income family to the treatment group. Income level does not affect the cost of families assigned to the control group, however, because controls receive no income-conditioned payments.

If one extends the logic of the preceding section, one would assign relatively more high-income families to the treatment groups, for which they cost less than low-income families, than to the control group, for which they cost the same as low-income families. This is in fact what was done in the early income maintenance experiments.

Although taking the variation of experimental cost with family type into account in the sample allocation arguably improves the power of the design that can be supported with a fixed budget, it is important to recognize that it fundamentally changes the nature of the experimental sample. In all the allocations considered to this point, although sample size might vary across experimental groups, the composition of the groups did not vary systematically; except for sampling error, each group was well matched to every other group. When we allow assignment to experimental group to be affected by individual characteristics, this is no longer true—the composition of the experimental groups differs systematically by design. Such designs are called *unbalanced designs* and are somewhat controversial in the literature on social experimentation.[20] In part for this reason, and in part because the cost of experimental treatments seldom varies so systematically with family characteristics, the only major social experiments to employ unbalanced designs were the early income maintenance experiments. The issues involved in the analysis of data from unbalanced designs are beyond the scope of this book. Therefore, although I note their existence, I continue to focus on designs in which all experimental groups are well matched.

Allocation to Multiple Treatments at Multiple Sites

Because program impacts may vary across sites, when multiple treatments are to be tested at multiple sites it is essential to avoid confounding site effects with program effects. As an extreme case, suppose we were to randomly assign unemployed workers in City A to classroom training or a control group and unemployed workers in City B to on-the-job training or a control group. Comparison of the treatment and control groups in City A will provide unbiased estimates of the impact of classroom training in City A; likewise, comparison of the treatment and control groups in City B will yield unbiased estimates of the impacts of on-the-job training in City B. If we find that, for example, classroom training in City A was more effective in raising workers' earnings than on-the-job training in City B, however, we will not know whether to conclude that classroom training is a more effective training strategy than on-the-job training or that, because of the nature of the workers or the local economy in the two cities, it is simply easier to raise the earnings of unemployed workers in City A. Because classroom training in City B or on-the-job training in City A were not attempted, we cannot distinguish between these two potential explanations. In this example, treatment and site are completely confounded.

To avoid confounding treatment and site, we want the distribution of each experimental group across sites to be the same as that of every other experimental group. This can be achieved by randomly assigning individuals to all experimental groups, in the same proportions, at every site. If this is done, the overall samples assigned to the different treatments, and to the control group, will be well matched, and fully comparable differential impact estimates can be derived.

Perhaps the most common reason for confounding of treatment and site is that tests of different treatments are conceived and executed as independent studies—often by the same funding agency. In this situation, it is almost

TABLE 4.1 Sample Design for Multiple Treatments in Multiple Sites When Not All Treatments Can Be Implemented at Each Site

Site	Treatment					
	1	2	3	4	5	6
A	X				X	X
B	X	X				X
C	X	X	X			
D		X	X	X		
E			X	X	X	
F				X	X	X

unavoidable that the experiments will be conducted at different sites, resulting in complete confounding of treatment and site. Unfortunately, in the policy process the results of these independent tests are nearly always treated as if they reflected only the differential impacts of the different treatments. In these cases, much more reliable guidance for policy could have been obtained at the same cost by combining the tests at a common set of sites.

In some cases, however, confounding of treatment and site is unavoidable for practical reasons. This is especially likely to be the case when a large number of treatments are being tested and the experiment is to be run through existing program agencies. Suppose, for example, that we wish to test six different approaches to increasing the employment of AFDC recipients. If all six approaches were to be implemented in the same welfare office, the staff of that office would not only have to become knowledgeable about all six treatments but also have to consistently apply the rules of each approach to those recipients, and only those recipients, assigned to that treatment. The burden on staff and the potential for contamination of the treatment in this situation are probably untenable.

Even in this situation, however, one can avoid complete confounding of treatment and site if program staff are willing to administer more than one treatment in the same office. Table 4.1 shows how the experimental sample can be allocated across sites to allow differential impacts to be estimated with no more than three of the six treatments implemented at any one site. For example, the impacts of Treatments 1 and 2 could be compared for well-matched samples at Sites B and C. Similarly, Treatments 2 and 3 could be compared at Sites C and D. As can be seen from the table, each treatment can be compared with all but one of the other five treatments at least at one site. Each comparison is based on only one third or two thirds of the sample assigned to the treatments being compared, however, depending on the number of sites involved. This is therefore a less powerful design than one in which individuals are assigned to all treatments at all sites.

Moreover, because different pairs of treatments are compared in different combinations of sites, the experimental comparisons cannot, by themselves, establish the relative magnitudes of impacts across all six treatments or even rank order the six treatments by impact, holding site effects constant. To do so requires some assumption about the interaction of treatment and site—for example, that although treatment effects may vary across sites, site effects do not vary across treatment. Data from this design are most conveniently analyzed by multivariate methods, which will be discussed in a subsequent chapter.

The Number of Experimental Sites

In designing an experiment, one generally has a choice between concentrating the sample at a small number of sites or spreading it over a larger number of sites. If cost were not an issue, it is clear that a larger number of sites is preferable. Just as increasing the number of individuals in the sample reduces the standard error of the impact estimate by "averaging out" sampling error, including a large number of sites should average out site-specific variations in the impact of the experimental program.

There are usually substantial costs associated with adding experimental sites, however. If the treatment is to be administered by existing program agencies, there are costs of recruiting these agencies and training agency members in the experimental procedures. If it is to be administered by the researchers themselves, it may be necessary to set up an office at each site. Similarly, if data are to be collected from sample members in person, it will be necessary to hire and train a data collection staff at each site, and it may be necessary to establish a field office at each site. Even if data are to be collected from administrative systems, such as welfare records, additional sites may increase the number of systems that must be accessed.

The choice of the number of experimental sites is a trade-off between the increased power that additional sites provide and the increased costs they entail. Within a fixed budget, this is a trade-off between sample size and number of sites because the costs of recruiting and administering additional sites must be deducted directly from the funds available for the experimental treatment or data collection or both.

A relatively simple technique is available for estimating the optimal number of sites in any particular experiment.[21] Unfortunately, it requires data that may not be available in all cases. This approach poses the problem as one of choosing the number of experimental sites (q) that minimizes the standard error of the impact estimate subject to a budget constraint that takes fixed site costs into account. If the sample is evenly distributed across sites, with n sample members at each site, the standard error of the overall impact estimate can be expressed as

$$SE_I = \left(\frac{1}{q}\right)\sqrt{\frac{4V_Y}{n} + V_{IS}} \qquad [4.23]$$

where

V_Y = the variance of the outcome of interest in the population
$4V_Y/n$ = the variance of the impact estimate within a single site[22]

V_{IS} is the variance of the experimental impact across sites (which is independent of the within-site sample size). Thus, the standard error of the estimate can be partitioned into a within-site component and a between-site component. We want to choose q so as to minimize SE_I subject to the following budget constraint:

$$C = q(C_s + cn) \qquad [4.24]$$

where

C = the total budget for the experimental treatment and data collection
C_s = the fixed cost of each additional site
c = the marginal cost per sample member

This formulation demonstrates the trade-off between sample size and number of sites within a fixed budget. Other things being equal, increases in the number of sites (q) reduce the standard error of the impact estimate, as shown in Equation 4.23. As shown in Equation 4.24, however, increasing q also increases the fixed site costs of the experiment (qC_s) so that to stay within a fixed budget, total sample size (qn) must be reduced.[23] This increases the within-site variance component of the standard error of the impact estimate (see Equation 4.23). The optimal value of q is that which just balances the gains from additional sites against the loss in sample size that results from additional fixed site costs.

To solve this problem, we must specify the values of the parameters in Equations 4.23 and 4.24. In most cases, the overall budget (C) will be known, and the cost parameters (C_s and c) can be estimated with reasonable accuracy. Moreover, the within-site variance of the experimental estimator can usually be estimated from existing data on the outcome of interest.[24] The between-site variance of the experimental impact, however, is generally unknown.

In some cases, however, it is possible to derive at least a proxy for the between-site variance of the impact from nonexperimental data. In the Health Insurance Experiment, for example, the experimenters used the variance of the difference in medical expenditures between insured individuals and uninsured individuals across regions of the country as a proxy for the between-site variance of the impact of cost sharing on medical expenditures. More generally, there may be prior multisite nonexperimental impact studies of the same, or a similar, intervention from which an estimate of the cross-site variance (i.e., the variance of site-specific impacts) can be derived.

If all else fails, the cross-site variance can be "guesstimated" as follows: Posit the range that you would expect to include 95% of all site-specific impacts. (In most cases, the lower bound of this range will be zero.) If site-specific impacts are normally distributed, this range will correspond to 1.96 standard deviations of the distribution of site-specific impacts. An estimate of the between-site variance of impacts, then, is approximately the square of one-half this range.

Whatever the source, if estimates of the parameters involved in Equations 4.23 and 4.24 can be obtained, an estimate of the optimal number of sites can be obtained. Archibald and Newhouse (1988) provided an analytic solution for the minimization of Equation 4.23 subject to the constraint in Equation 4.24, developed by Carl Morris (1974). In the case of the Health Insurance Experiment, Morris found that the optimal number of sites was in the range of four to six for reasonable values of the parameters. A more direct method is simply to compute the value of SE_I from Equation 4.23 for every integer value of q between 1 and the maximum number of sites that could be supported by the experimental budget ($= C/C_s$) and then choose the value that minimizes SE_I directly.[25] This approach has the advantage of also showing the loss in power associated with a nonoptimal number of sites.

As in all design decisions, the quality of the result obtained from this procedure—that is, the likelihood that the choice truly maximizes the power of the design—depends on the quality of the information that was used when making the decision. As the forgoing discussion makes clear, in many cases only relatively low-quality information about some of the critical parameters may be available. Some information is almost certainly preferable to none, however, because a decision must be made. Even fairly unreliable information about the critical parameters may be sufficient to establish the right order of magnitude.

Random Assignment of Groups of Individuals

To this point, we have assumed that the focus of policy interest is on program effects on individuals, and that experimental subjects are randomly assigned one at a time. This will be the case in most social experiments. There are two situations, however, in which it may be necessary to randomly assign groups of individuals.

The first occurs when policy interest focuses on impacts at the aggregate level, and random assignment of individuals is inconsistent with unbiased estimation of aggregate effects. Consider, for example, an experiment designed to test the effects of a worker training program on productivity at the plant level. In such an experiment, one cannot randomly assign individual workers to the training program; only if all the workers in the plant are subject to the same policy regime will we obtain unbiased effects at the plant level.[26] Instead, one would have to randomly assign plants to treatment or control status. In the treatment group, the program would be implemented plantwide; in the control group, it would not be implemented at all. All the principles of sample design discussed in this chapter would apply if one simply defines the plant, rather than the individual worker, to be the unit of analysis.

Of course, it may be difficult to obtain a sufficient number of plants to generate the sample size needed for reliable estimates. Whereas experimental samples of thousands of individuals are quite common, it may be difficult to recruit more than, for example, 10 or 20 plants to participate in an experiment. Whether such sample sizes would be sufficient depends on the minimum detectable effects attainable with the feasible sample size, which in turn depends on the variance of the outcome of interest across plants. Fortunately, aggregate outcomes are frequently much less variable than outcomes at the individual level. In any case, minimum detectable effects can be computed for this case just as for samples of individuals using the number of plants as the sample size and the variance of the outcome of interest at the plant level.

Although experiments of this type are much less common than those in which individuals are randomly assigned, several have been conducted in recent years. For example, the National Home Health Agency Prospective Payment Demonstration randomly assigned 142 home health agencies to alternative Medicare reimbursement formulae to test their effects on the use of care (Goldberg, 1997). Similarly, the San Diego Nursing Home Incentive Reimbursement Experiment randomly assigned 36 nursing homes to an incentive payment system designed to reward facilities for achieving various admission, treatment, and discharge objectives or to a control group that received only the regular Medicare reimbursements (Jones & Meiners, 1986).

A second case in which random assignment of groups arises occurs when policy interest focuses on program effects on individuals, but it is infeasible to randomly assign individuals. This might be the case, for example, if one were interested in the effects of alternative teaching methods on students' achievement, but for institutional reasons it was not possible to randomly assign students to different classes. In this situation, one might be forced to randomly assign whole classes to different experimental groups. Similarly, when the experimental treatment applies to the family as a whole, the entire family must be randomly assigned as a group. This was the case in the income maintenance experiments and the Health Insurance Experiment, in which all members of the family were assigned to the same negative income tax or health insurance plan, respectively.

Calculation of minimum detectable effects at the individual level is more complex in this case because the standard error of the impact estimate depends on the correlation among the outcomes within the "clusters" of individuals who were assigned together. Specifically, if SE_{I^*} is the standard error of the impact estimate for random assignment of N sample members individually, the standard error of estimate for a sample of the same size randomly assigned in m clusters of n individuals is

$$SE_{Ic} = SE_I \sqrt{1 + d(n-1)}, \qquad [4.25]$$

where d is the ***intraclass correlation*** of the outcome.[27] The intraclass correlation is a measure of the homogeneity of sample members, in terms of the outcome Y, within the clusters randomly assigned. Its values range from $-1/(n-1)$ to $+1$, with positive values indicating similarity among individuals within clusters and negative values denoting dissimilarity within clusters relative to the makeup of the overall sample.[28] When $d = 0$, the clusters are just as heterogeneous with respect to Y as the overall sample.

As can be seen from Equation 4.25, when $d = 0$, the "cluster effect" (the second term under the square root sign) is zero, and the standard error of the estimates based on random assignment of clusters is the same as the standard error of estimate based on random assignment of single individuals. When d is positive, the standard error of estimate is higher under random assignment of clusters, and when d is negative, the standard error of estimate is lower. Thus, minimum detectable effects will be larger under random assignment of clusters than under random assignment of individuals if d is positive and smaller if d is negative. If $d = 0$, minimum detectable effects will be the same under the two approaches.

Suppose, for example, that we randomly assign classrooms of 25 students each to alternative teaching methods. Further suppose that students have been assigned to classrooms in part on the basis of ability, leading to a positive intraclass correlation of grade point average (the outcome of interest) of 0.20. According to Equation 4.25, the cluster effect will increase the standard error of estimate, and therefore minimum detectable effects, by a factor of 2.4. That is, when classrooms are randomly assigned rather than individual students, the experimental effect on grade point averages would have to be 2.4 times as large to be detectable at a given level of statistical significance. In contrast, if students were randomly assigned to classrooms, then the intraclass correlation would be zero and random assignment of clusters would have no effect on minimum detectable effects.

As this illustrative example suggests, random assignment of groups can result in a substantial loss of power, relative to random assignment of individuals. The size of the loss will depend on the intraclass correlation of the specific outcome of interest and the size of the groups randomly assigned. In cases in which random assignment of groups is the only feasible approach, it is therefore critical to estimate the minimum detectable effects attainable with the proposed sample size and design, taking cluster effects into account, to ensure that the design will yield estimates of sufficient power to be worthwhile.

Notes

1. Random sampling should not be confused with random assignment. In random sampling, a group of individuals is randomly selected from a larger population to obtain a sample for analysis that is representative of the population from which it was drawn. In random assignment, the analysis sample is randomly divided into two or more groups to be subjected to different policy regimes.

2. FSAs serving less than 50 participants per year were excluded from the sampling frame.

3. Among the original 60 randomly selected sites, 13 refused to participate in the study and 6 of these were in three states that refused at the outset to participate. Seven of the selected sites were found not to be implementing the program in the study year and were dropped from the sample. Backup sites were randomly selected for sites that refused. Time constraints, however, limited the site selection and recruiting process, and it was ultimately decided to implement the study for a sample of 55 sites. Subsequent problems with random assignment procedures at 2 sites reduced the final sample to 53 sites. See Puma et al. (1990) for further details.

4. The eminent sampling statistician Leslie Kish (1965, p. 29) summarized the matter as follows: "If a research project must be confined to a single city in the United States, I would rather use my judgment to choose a 'typical' city than select one at random. Even for a sample of 10 cities, I would rather trust my knowledge of U.S. cities than a random selection. But I would raise the question of enlarging the sample to 30 or 100 cities. For a sample of that size, a probability selection should be designed and controlled with stratification."

5. The exhibit develops the power of the design for a one-tailed test. Similar reasoning applies to two-tailed tests, although this case is more difficult to show graphically.

6. When the critical value is initially higher than the mean of the right-hand distribution in Figure 4.1, these two effects are offsetting. It can be shown, however, that their net effect is to increase the power of the design. Thus, an increase in sample size always increases the power of the design.

7. Rejecting the null hypothesis when it is true (i.e., falsely concluding that there is a positive effect) is known as a Type I error. Failing to reject the null hypothesis when it is false (i.e., failing to detect a true positive effect) is known as a Type II error.

8. Similar reasoning applies to the evaluation of an ongoing program. A false positive results in the continuation of a waste of resources, whereas a false negative results in unnecessarily terminating the program. The social cost of the latter will depend on the alternative use of the resources formerly devoted to the program.

9. The minimum value of the power function is equal to the significance level and occurs at zero. This follows from the definition of power as the probability of rejecting the null hypothesis when the true effect is I_0. When I_0 is zero, this probability is the same as the probability of rejecting the null hypothesis of zero effect when it is true—that is, the significance level.

10. This is equivalent to specifying the family of power functions defined by a given significance level and then choosing among them on the basis of their levels at a single value of true impact.

11. This method of illustrating the derivation of minimum detectable effects is adapted from Bloom (1995).

12. The numerical values in this example are obtained from a standard table of values of the t statistic. Recall that the t statistic is defined as the impact estimate divided by its standard error.

13. For one important class of outcomes, the variance can be computed from the mean of the outcome. For dichotomous outcomes (i.e., outcomes that can take on only two values, 0 or 1),

the variance of the outcome is $m(1 - m)$, where m is the sample mean. (Because m is also the proportion of the sample taking on the value 1, it can also be thought of as the proportion of the sample with positive outcomes.) The expression $m(1 - m)$ is maximized when $m = 0.5$. Therefore, even if the mean is unknown, one can compute the worst-case minimum detectable effect for such an outcome. Outcomes such as "completed high school," "employed at follow-up," and "left welfare" belong in this class.

14. This assumes that program costs can be predicted, which is often the case, at least approximately.

15. A framework within which this could be done is presented by Burtless and Orr (1986).

16. This assumes that the participation rate would be constant across replications of the experiment. This is almost certainly not strictly true, but if each individual has a constant probability of participating, in large samples the variation of the overall participation rate will be so small as to be negligible.

17. It might appear that the participation rate could also be increased by taking administrative measures to reduce the number of individuals dropping out of the intake process (e.g., by following up with individuals who fail to apply for the program and encouraging them to do so or by tracking down no-shows and encouraging them to participate). If such steps would not be taken in an ongoing program, however, taking them in the experiment would result in a different composition of the participant population from that which would occur in an ongoing program, thereby undermining the external validity of the experiment.

18. This result is obtained by calculating the ratio of the minimum detectable effects under the two allocations using Equation 4.18.

19. This result is derived from the fact that, for any given sample allocation, minimum detectable effects are inversely proportional to the square root of total sample size.

20. For an excellent discussion of the advantages and disadvantages of unbalanced designs, see Hausman and Wise (1985).

21. This technique was developed by Morris (1974). It is described by Archibald and Newhouse (1988).

22. This follows directly from the following expression for the variance of the within-site impact estimate (V_{IW}), setting $n_t = n_c = n/2$: $V_{IW} = V_Y/n_t + V_Y/n_c = 2V_Y/n + 2V_Y/n = 4V_Y/n$.

23. Note that, if there are no fixed-site costs (i.e., if $C_s = 0$), then qn is a constant ($= C/c$), and the within-site variance component of Equation 4.23 is a constant. In this case, increases in q would reduce the variance of the impact estimate without limit, and the optimal number of sites would be the maximum attainable (C/c) with a single sample member at each site.

24. Under the null hypothesis, the within-site variance of the experimental impact estimate is $V_I = V_Y/n_t + V_Y/n_c$, where V_Y is the variance of the outcome, and n_t and n_c are the numbers of treatment and control group members, respectively, at a single site. Existing data are usually available to estimate V_Y.

25. For each value of q, Equation 4.24 must be solved for n to calculate SE_I.

26. This is not to say that all workers in the plant must participate in the training for the estimates to be valid, only that none who would participate in an ongoing training program be artificially excluded through random assignment.

27. See Hansen, Hurwitz, and Madow (1965), or any standard text on sampling statistics, for a formal definition of the intraclass correlation.

28. Note that the lower bound of the intraclass correlation approaches zero as the cluster size n becomes large.

References

Archibald, R. W., & Newhouse, J. P. (1988). Social experimentation: Some why's and how's. In H. J. Miser & E. J. Quade (Eds.), *Handbook of systems analysis: Craft issues and procedural choices* (pp. 173-214). New York: North Holland.

Burtless, G., & Orr, L. L. (1986, Fall). Are classical experiments needed for manpower policy? *Journal of Human Resources, 21,* 606-639.

Bloom, H. S. (1995). Minimum detectable effects: A simple way to report the statistical power of experimental designs. *Evaluation Review, 19*(5), 547-556.

Goldberg, H. B. (1997, February). Prospective payment in action: The National Home Health Agency demonstration. *CARING Magazine, 17*(2), 14-27.

Hansen, M. H., Hurwitz, W. N., & Madow, W. G. (1965). *Sample survey methods and theory. Volume 1: Methods and applications.* New York: John Wiley.

Hausman, J. A., & Wise, D. A. (1985). *Social experimentation.* Chicago: University of Chicago Press.

Jones, B. J., & Meiners, M. R. (1986, August). Nursing home discharges: The results of an incentive reimbursement experiment. In *Long-term care studies program research report* (DHHS Publication No. PHS 86-3399). Rockville, MD: U.S. Department of Health and Human Services, Public Health Service, National Center for Health Services Research and Health Care Technology Assessment.

Kennedy, S. (1996). *Notes on statistical power.* Unpublished handout for a class on evaluation at the John F. Kennedy School of Government, Harvard University, Cambridge, MA.

Kish, L. (1965). *Survey sampling.* New York: John Wiley.

Morris, C. (1974). *An estimate of the optimal number of sites.* Unpublished Health Insurance Study memorandum No. SM-1093. Santa Monica, CA: RAND.

Orr, L. L., Johnson, T., Montgomery, M., & Hojnacki, M. (1989). *Design of the Washington Self-Employment and Enterprise Development (SEED) Demonstration.* Bethesda, MD: Abt/Battelle Memorial Institute.

Puma, M. J., Burstein, N. R., Merrell, K., & Silverstein, G. (1990). *Evaluation of the Food Stamp Employment and Training Program.* Bethesda, MD: Abt.

Chapter ⑤

Implementation
and Data Collection

“The government are very keen on amassing statistics. They collect them, add them, raise them to the nth power, take the cube root, and prepare wonderful diagrams. But you must never forget that every one of these figures comes in the first instance from the village watchman, who just puts down what he damn pleases.”

—Sir Josiah Stamp, Inland Revenue
Department (England), 1896-1919

To this point, I have focused on the rationale and design of experiments. In this chapter, I discuss the more operational issues involved in implementing the experiment in the field and collecting data on the experimental subjects.

In the first part of the chapter, I address the following aspects of implementing the experiment:

- ◆ Administration of the experimental treatment
- ◆ Gaining the cooperation of program staff
- ◆ Implementing random assignment
- ◆ Maintaining the integrity of random assignment

In the second part of the chapter, I discuss the collection of the following types of data that will be required for the experimental analysis:

- Individual identifiers and indicators of treatment status
- Baseline data
- Outcome data
- Program participation data
- Cost data

Implementation of the Experiment

The early social experiments (e.g., the income maintenance experiments and the Health Insurance Experiment) were administered by the researchers conducting the study. The researchers set up offices at the experimental sites, recruited participants, and issued income maintenance or health insurance benefits according to rules designed especially for the experiment.

These administrative functions required that the experimenters engage in activities far afield from the usual scope of academic research. They were required, for example, to specify in detail the rules of the experimental program—in the case of the income maintenance experiments, what amounted to a model negative income tax statute, and in the case of the Health Insurance Experiment, a set of detailed health insurance policies. These basic ground rules had to be supplemented with detailed operational forms and procedures to be followed by administrative staff. The researchers then had to set up field organizations to recruit participants—in the case of these two studies, literally by knocking on doors[1]—and administer the experimental benefits. This meant, in effect, that the researchers had to run a welfare office or a small health insurance company.[2]

There were certain advantages to administering the experimental treatment directly. It allowed the researchers to specify the experimental program in detail, to ensure that it was implemented as intended, and to document exactly how it operated.[3]

There were also distinct disadvantages, however. It was very costly and time-consuming for researchers unschooled in program administration to develop the requisite expertise for such an undertaking and to create *de novo* the administrative forms and procedures required. Moreover, having done so, it was not clear that the treatment was administered in the same way it would have been by regular staff in an ongoing program. In the case of the income maintenance and health insurance experiments, in which the experimental benefits were relatively clearly defined in monetary terms, this may not have been a serious problem.[4] In an experiment in which the content of the treatment is less well-defined—for example, a counseling program or a drug treatment program—the replicability of the experimental treatment in a regular program could be highly questionable if it is delivered by research staff.

For these reasons, recent experiments have been administered by the staff of existing programs. For example, tests of employment and training services for welfare recipients have been administered by regular welfare caseworkers, experimental housing vouchers have been administered by the staff of local public housing authorities, and experiments testing home care services for the elderly have been administered by local social service agencies, such as Administrations on Aging. In each case, of course, the experimental treatment was specified, at least in general terms, by the researchers who oversaw and documented its provision. In all cases, however, the researchers were able to take advantage of existing organizational structures, procedures, and staff expertise to deliver an experimental treatment that closely replicated how an ongoing program would be administered.

There are undoubtedly cases in which the experimental treatment is so novel that no existing program structure is appropriate for its administration. (This was, in fact, probably true of the income maintenance experiments.) In most cases, however, the policy to be tested in the experiment arises in the context of some existing program, and the most sensible way to administer it in the experiment is through that program. Of course, evaluation of ongoing programs involves administration by regular program staff by definition. In the following sections, we assume that the experimental treatment will be administered by regular program staff under the supervision of the researchers. Therefore, one of the first tasks in implementing the experiment will be to gain the cooperation of program staff.

Gaining the Cooperation of Program Staff

As noted in Chapter 4, program staff tend to resist random assignment for a variety of reasons. Many program operators have a basic distrust of research and evaluation. At best, they view it as an irrelevant distraction from their main mission, the day-to-day delivery of services to their clientele. At worst, they view it as a threat to the program. Many view researchers as naive intellectuals who do not understand the reality of program operations but who nevertheless have the power to adversely affect the funding of their program through an erroneous finding that the program is not working as intended.

This basic distrust is compounded in experimental evaluations by concerns about random assignment. Program staff often view random assignment as an unethical denial of service to deserving individuals. Moreover, they expect program applicants who are assigned to the control group to share the same view; as a result, they anticipate having to deal with complaints and objections from the control group, up to and including physical attacks or lawsuits or both. Similarly, they may foresee objections from community groups sympathetic to the program clientele, unfavorable publicity in the local media once it becomes generally known that eligible, deserving applicants are being randomly excluded from the program, or both.

Program operators are usually concerned about the administrative burden and disruption that a research project, especially one involving random assignment, is likely to entail. The requirement that additional applicants be processed to provide for a control group is seen (quite correctly) as creating additional work for a staff that may already be stretched thin or raising the costs of a program that is (in the staff's view) already underfunded or both. In addition, staff must spend time explaining random assignment to applicants and dealing with their questions and complaints as well as responding to queries and requests from the research staff or collecting data for the experiment or both. Program operators are concerned that this diversion of staff effort will adversely affect the quality of service the program can provide to its regular clientele.

A closely related concern is that, by diverting some applicants into a control group, random assignment will reduce the flow of program participants. For programs that have difficulty recruiting enough participants to fill all their program slots (or as many of a particular subgroup as they would like), this can be a serious concern.

These concerns arise with varying force depending on the experimental setting. They tend to be most strongly felt when the experiment is intended to evaluate an ongoing program. They are less salient in the case of special demonstrations in part because the experiment is viewed as less of a threat to the program's central mission and in part because the funding for special demonstrations normally takes into account the added costs attributable to the experimental design. Researchers, however, are almost certain to encounter these objections, in one form or another, in virtually any experiment that involves regular program staff.

The following general strategies can be used by the experimenter to counter these concerns:

♦ Establishing the legitimacy and ethical acceptability of the study
♦ Minimizing staff burden and cost
♦ Ensuring an adequate flow of program participants
♦ Providing positive inducements for program staff to cooperate.

Establishing the Legitimacy and Ethical Acceptability of the Study

The researchers' first task in dealing with local program staff is to convince them that the study should be taken seriously (i.e., that it is important and legitimate). In part, this involves convincing them that the researchers themselves should be taken seriously—that they know and understand the program they are evaluating (or within whose context they are proposing to experiment). This means that the members of the research team must do their homework so that they do in fact understand the program. It will be helpful if the research team includes some individuals who have worked in the program or other peers whom program staff respect, such as members of local or national professional associations related to the program.[5] For example, in the National Job Training Partnership Act (JTPA) Study, the site recruiting team included several former directors of local training programs as well as representatives of the National Association of Counties, the National Alliance of Business, and the National Governors' Association. It is also extremely helpful for the state or federal agency that funds the program to play a prominent role in the initial discussions with local program staff to underscore the importance the agency attaches to the study.

A necessary part of establishing the legitimacy of an experiment is convincing program staff that it is ethically sound.[6] Doing so requires that staff concerns about denial of service to the control group be taken seriously and addressed directly through frank and thorough discussion. As discussed in Chapter 1, there are strong arguments for the ethical acceptability of random assignment in most cases (and, presumably, experiments are only undertaken where such arguments can be made): Most social programs and demonstrations can serve only a fraction of those who are nominally eligible; in such cases, random assignment is arguably the fairest way to ration scarce program benefits or services. Moreover, it can be argued that it is unethical not to evaluate ongoing programs with the strongest possible methodology. It is important to know whether the program is achieving its intended objectives; continuing an ineffective program is a disservice to its intended beneficiaries as well as to the taxpayers who fund it. If, however, the program is achieving its intended effects—as virtually all program operators believe—the evaluation will provide the information needed to justify its continuation.

Generally, this dialogue must occur twice at two different levels: with program management staff, who will decide whether the local program is willing to participate, and with the line staff, who must implement the experiment.[7] It is important to recognize that, even after program management has agreed to participate, it is essential that the program staff's ethical concerns about random assignment be thoroughly discussed before advancing to any other aspect of experimental design or implementation. If these concerns are not discussed, they will continue to arise, disrupting the dialogue with the site and making it impossible to focus on implementation of the study. Even if staff are not entirely convinced by the experimenters' arguments, it is important that they have an opportunity to express their views. If given that opportunity, line staff will generally accept whatever decision their superiors have made, even if they do not fully agree with it. The objective here is as much to allow the staff to work through their feelings about denial of service to controls, which can be quite strong and emotional, as to convince them intellectually of the ethical acceptability of the study. In some cases, this takes several meetings with staff; these sessions can become quite heated.

In cases in which staff resistance to random assignment threatens to undermine the integrity of the experiment or the site's willingness to participate, it may be necessary to make some modifications to the design to secure site cooperation. For example, staff members at the site can be given a limited number of discretionary exemptions from random assignment to be used in cases in which, in the staff's view, the applicant is in such dire need of program services that it would be unethical to deny him or her in any circumstances. The effect of such exemptions, from an evaluation standpoint, is to limit the applicability of the impact estimates to the nonexempt participant population—that is, the experimental results will not apply to those exempted from random assignment. If the number of exemptions is small, however (e.g., on the order of 1% or 2% of all participants), this will have only a negligible effect on the overall impact estimates.[8]

Exemptions from random assignment can also be used to deal with legal barriers to excluding certain individuals from the program. For example, if the program receives court-mandated referrals that it is required to serve, these can be exempted from random assignment. Again, however, it must be recognized that the experimental estimates will not apply to this segment of the participant population.

A second type of design modification that has sometimes been used in evaluations of ongoing programs to overcome staff objections to random assignment is shortening the "embargo" period during which controls are excluded from the program. Ideally, controls should be excluded from the program throughout the follow-up period during which outcome data are collected. In some cases, however, realistically there is little risk that controls will reapply after an embargo period of a year or more so that little is lost by shortening the exclusion period. In the National JTPA Study, for example, controls were excluded from JTPA for only 18 months, even though data collection extended for 30 months after random assignment. Less than 1% of all controls enrolled in JTPA after the embargo period ended; the effect of such a low incidence of "crossovers" on the impact estimates was probably negligible.[9] Caution must be exercised in adopting this type of design modification, however; the threat posed by reapplication of controls before the end of the follow-up period depends on the institutional context so that each case must be judged on its own merits. Moreover, it must be recognized that if virtually none of the controls reapply after the end of the embargo period, this "concession" is of little value to them.

A third design compromise that has sometimes been used to address staff concerns about the effects of random assignment on controls is to allow intake staff to provide controls with lists of local providers of services similar to those offered by the experimental program. This not only assuages staff concerns that needy applicants may go without assistance because of the study but also allows them to avoid being placed in the uncomfortable position of having to face disappointed controls empty-handed. It may even serve to prevent more active intervention by program staff on behalf of controls, such as individual referrals to specific providers. To the extent that providing lists of alternative providers leads controls to receive services that they would not have obtained in the absence of the experimental program, however, it biases the impact estimates relative to that standard. Because the effects of such information are unknowable in advance and may be large, I do not recommend this approach. Rather, I recommend that the experiment be designed so that controls are informed of their status by letter, and program staff have no personal contact with controls after random assignment. This removes both the opportunity and the need for program staff to respond to requests for assistance from controls.

It might be argued that providing no information to controls biases the impact estimates upward by artificially reducing the amount of service controls receive below what they would have received if the experimental program did not exist. According to this argument, the fact that the controls volunteered for the experimental program is evidence that in the absence of the program they would have sought assistance from some other program. Assignment to the control group may discourage some applicants to the point that they give up on seeking assistance. Thus, a hands-off policy toward controls does not faithfully replicate the desired counterfactual, in which they would all seek assistance.

Although conceding that this argument has some validity, I argue that the preferred solution is not to give controls extensive lists of local service providers. Rather, in cases in which this argument is persuasive, it is probably better to refer controls to the single source of assistance that they were most likely to contact in the absence of the experimental program. In the case of the JTPA evaluation, for example, it seems most likely that controls would have gone to the Employment Service had JTPA not existed. Thus, referring controls to the Employment Service may provide the conceptually correct counterfactual.

A closely related strategy for assuaging staff concerns about denial of services to controls is to provide some minimum level of service to the control group rather than attempting to exclude controls from the experimental program altogether. If policy interest focuses on the effects of the experimental treatment relative to no additional service, however, rather than relative to this minimum level of service, this design will underestimate the impact of the experimental program by an unknown amount. Only if the services provided to the controls have no effect—in which case, they are a placebo and not a real treatment—will this design provide unbiased estimates of the incremental impact of the experimental program relative to no additional service. For this reason, if the ethical conditions for a no-service control group are met, I do not recommend adopting this approach simply to appease program staff.

Minimizing Staff Burden and Cost

Although less emotional than the issues surrounding denying service to controls, the added staff burden and cost imposed by an experimental study are very legitimate concerns for local program operators. Although some added burden and cost are unavoidable, there are several ways in which these can be minimized by experimenters.

Perhaps the most important way to minimize added burden is to integrate random assignment and baseline data collection into the regular program intake process with as little disruption of normal program activities as possible. Generally, implementation of random assignment involves adding four steps to the intake process: (a) informing applicants about random assignment and (if required) obtaining their informed consent, (b) collecting baseline information, (c) randomly assigning the applicants, and (d) informing applicants of the outcome of random assignment. Wherever possible, these steps should be "piggy-backed" onto existing program activities to avoid unnecessarily complicating and lengthening the intake process.

Consider, for example, an experiment designed to test a new training program for welfare recipients. Figure 5.1 shows the normal intake process for the welfare program: Individuals interested in applying for welfare receive an oral explanation of the program and its application procedures from program staff. Those still interested in applying for program benefits are given an application form. Applicants complete the form and submit it, along with any required documentation, to program staff.[10] Program staff review the applications and determine eligibility for the program. Those found eligible are notified and informed of any steps they must take to receive program benefits; ineligible applicants are informed that they will not receive benefits.

Figure 5.2 shows how random assignment might be integrated into this process. At the initial step, along with an explanation of the regular program, program staff would give individuals who express interest in the program a brief explanation of the experiment and the use of random assignment to select those to be invited (or required) to participate in the experimental training program.[11] The application package given to potential applicants would include a baseline survey form and (if required) an informed consent form to be completed and submitted along with the regular program application form. Staff would then determine the eligibility of those who apply in the usual manner, and ineligibles would be informed that they do not qualify for program benefits. Eligible applicants would be randomly assigned to treatment or control status. All eligible applicants would then be notified that they qualify for regular program benefits, and those assigned to the treatment group would be invited to participate in the experimental training program (or, if the program is mandatory, informed that they are required to participate).

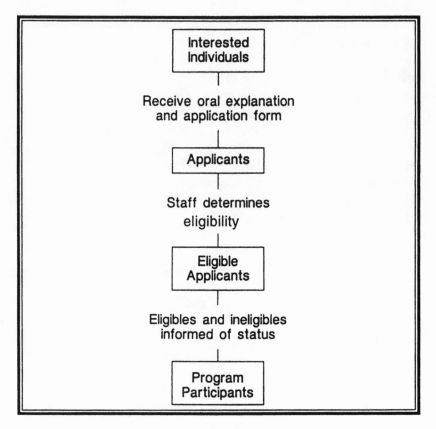

Figure 5.1. Normal Program Intake Process

This integration of random assignment into the intake process has the advantage that it does not change the order or content of any of the regular intake steps. Moreover, it does not increase the number of times that staff must meet with applicants to complete the process.

There are other steps that experimenters can take to minimize burden on intake staff. Because intake staff must respond to applicants' questions about the baseline survey form, it is important to keep the baseline form as short and simple as possible. Where more complex baseline data are required, it may be necessary for study staff to collect these data through personal interviews with the applicants rather than through a self-administered baseline form or by asking program staff to interview the applicants. Similarly, there are various options for conducting random as-

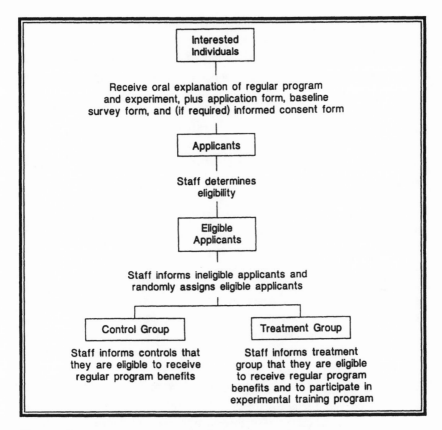

Figure 5.2. Program Intake Process With Random Assignment

signment, some of which entail less burden on program staff than others. The options for both baseline data collection and random assignment procedures are discussed later.

In evaluations of ongoing programs, the random assignment ratio will be an important determinant of the added cost and burden for program staff. Suppose, for example, that the program normally serves 1,000 participants per year. Random assignment of equal numbers of eligible applicants to the treatment and control groups means that for every 1,000 program participants (treatment group members), the program must process enough applications to produce 2,000 eligible applicants—that is, the need to provide for a control group doubles the number of applicants that must be processed. If, instead, an assignment ratio of two treatment group members to every control were adopted, only 500 controls would be needed for every 1,000 participants, and the required increase in intake would be only 50%.

Quite aside from considerations of intake costs, assigning more applicants to the program than to the control group may help to assuage staff concerns about denial of service to controls because it reduces the number of applicants excluded from the program. In the National JTPA Study, for example, a 2:1 assignment ratio was adopted primarily for this reason.

Such a change in the random assignment ratio is not costless, however. As noted in Chapter 4, equal-sized treatment and control groups yield the most precise impact estimates (when there are only two experimental groups). Thus, if a different ratio is adopted, the experimenter must either settle for less precise impact estimates or increase the sample size to maintain precision. In the previous example, if the assignment ratio is changed from 1:1 to 2:1 and the number assigned to the program held constant at 1,000 so that the number assigned to the control group declines to 500, minimum detectable effects will rise by 22.5%. If, instead, the overall sample size (treatment group plus controls) were held constant at 2,000, with 1,333 assigned to the program and 667 assigned to the control group, the increase in minimum detectable effects would be only approximately 6%.

To achieve the same minimum detectable effects with a 2:1 assignment ratio as with a 1:1 ratio, the overall sample size would have to be increased by 12.5% to 1,500 treatment group members and 750 controls. This increase in sample size would require extending the length of time for which random assignment is conducted by 50%, thereby offsetting somewhat the apparent benefit to the program of the higher assignment ratio.[12] More important, it would increase data collection costs in proportion to the increase in sample size. For large samples or extensive (or expensive) data collection strategies or both, this can be a substantial cost.[13]

Another important determinant of the added burden posed for intake staff is the point in the intake process at which random assignment is conducted. As noted in previous chapters, random assignment late in the process means that intake staff must take applicants who will ultimately become controls through more steps in the intake process. Program staff resist late random assignment for other reasons as well. Late random assignment makes exclusion of controls more difficult both for the applicants, whose expectations are raised by prolonged contact with the program, and for the staff, who have become more invested in helping the applicants.

As with changing the random assignment ratio, however, changing the point of random assignment has important analytic costs. Conducting random assignment earlier in the intake process is almost certain to increase the number of "no-shows"—individuals assigned to the treatment group who do not enter the program. Although a methodological adjustment is available to remove the effect of no-shows on the impact estimates (see Chapter 2), this adjustment increases the minimum detectable effects attainable with any given sample size. If the point of random assignment is changed to accommodate program staff, the experimenter must either accept less precise impact estimates or increase the experimental sample size to maintain the power of the design. This choice can be analyzed in terms very similar to those presented in connection with a change in the random assignment ratio.

Where the issue is primarily one of the added cost of processing additional applicants, it may be cheaper to reimburse the program for those costs than to increase the sample size sufficiently to maintain the precision of the estimates. In an evaluation of the California Conservation Corps, for example, the program agreed to conduct random assignment after eligibility had been determined only after the study sponsor agreed to reimburse the cost of the physical examinations administered as part of the program's normal intake process for applicants who were subsequently assigned to the control group.

Ensuring an Adequate Flow of Program Participants

Program staff may also resist random assignment because of the difficulty of recruiting a sufficient number of applicants to fill all program slots and to provide for a control group. One response to this problem is to change the random assignment ratio to reduce the number of applicants assigned to the control group. Another is to commit to temporarily reducing the random assignment ratio if the program experiences difficulty recruiting enough applicants to fill all its slots. In the National JTPA Study, for example, local programs were required by Department of Labor regulations to spend 40% of their training budgets on youth. Many sites had difficulty recruiting enough youth to meet this requirement when one third of all applicants were assigned to the control group. To address this problem, the evaluators temporarily changed the assignment ratio from 2:1 to 3:1 or even 6:1 at several sites.

Although this change may have kept these sites from dropping out of the study, it posed difficult problems for the analysis, as will be discussed in Chapter 6. These same analytical difficulties arise if the random assignment ratio varies across sites. Therefore, if a nonoptimal random assignment ratio is adopted, the experimenter should at least adopt the same ratio at all sites.

The experimenters can also provide technical assistance to improve program outreach or to reduce the number of applicants who drop out prior to program entry or both. Although the researchers conducting the experiment may not have the expertise to provide such technical assistance, they can usually hire consultants who do have expertise.

Providing Positive Inducements for Program Staff to Cooperate

In exchange for the added burden and cost that experiments entail, experimenters can offer some positive inducements to participating programs. Although many of these benefits to study sites are intangible, they are nevertheless real and should be emphasized in the initial dialogue with staff at prospective sites.

An important inducement for many local program operators is the opportunity to take part in an important national study. Local program staff often feel powerless to affect national policy; participation in a study that may influence national policymakers provides them a way to do so. In evaluations of ongoing programs, local program staff may view the study as a way to demonstrate the value of the program. In special demonstrations, they may be attracted by the chance to show the efficacy of new service approaches, hoping that they will be funded on a regular basis. As this implies, however, local staff willingness to participate in a demonstration will be strongly conditioned by their view of the desirability of the experimental program being tested.

Local program operators may also be attracted by the opportunity to obtain information and feedback on their own programs, even if they do not fully understand or accept the argument for a rigorous experimental evaluation. Most local programs have little systematic information about what happens to their participants after they leave the program. For these program operators, the experiment's follow-up data collection offers a rare opportunity to observe the long-term outcomes of their participants. A commitment to provide such data can therefore be an important incentive for local programs to participate.

Experimental studies can also provide an opportunity for members of participating programs to learn from each other. Many multisite experiments hold periodic conferences at which staff of participating sites can share their experiences and discuss issues and problems of common interest. In studies in which this type of forum has been provided, staff of local programs have almost uniformly found it very useful.

In many cases, the researchers can also provide valuable technical assistance to the participating programs. Much of this assistance is, of course, focused on the implementation of the experiment and collection of data for the study. Although this assistance would appear to benefit primarily the experiment, for many local programs the knowledge of research and evaluation methods gained by participating in an experiment is quite useful in program evaluation efforts. The researchers are also in a unique position to advise local program operators on how staff at other study sites have dealt with difficult operational problems or at least to put them in touch with knowledgeable staff at other study sites. The researchers may also be able to draw on their own expertise to assist local program staff in dealing with operational problems. For example, expertise in data collection and data processing can often be helpful in setting up program information systems and tracking program participants. Experience acquired in evaluating other programs can often be applied to problems such as recruiting program applicants or reducing attrition among applicants or participants.

Unfortunately, the value of some of these relatively intangible benefits may become apparent only once the study is under way. A more obvious, and sometimes more convincing, inducement to participate is monetary reimbursement. In the National JTPA Study, for example, the Department of Labor made payments averaging $170,000 to the local service delivery areas to compensate these programs for study-related costs (Doolittle & Traeger, 1990). Although it is appropriate to reimburse local programs for the added costs associated with the experiment, researchers should take care that such payments do not devolve into simple bribes, lest staff at prospective study sites adopt a strategy of withholding their agreement to participate to maximize the monetary payment.

Where the experiment is being conducted by the federal or state agency that administers the program, the agency can also provide some nonfinancial inducements to participate. For example, in programs with performance standards systems, staff at study sites might be held blameless with respect to any adverse effects that participation in the experiment might have on their performance indicators. Staff at study sites might also be given more flexibility in meeting other program regulations during the study period, in recognition of the special demands of the experiment.

Implementing Random Assignment

The actual assignment of potential participants to treatment and control groups is quite straightforward. In virtually all modern experiments, this is done by a computer algorithm that assigns each potential participant to an experimental group on the basis of a random number generated by the computer.[14] The more complex and difficult aspect of implementing random assignment in a real-world program is establishing procedures to be followed by the research and program staffs that allow the assignment to be made without delaying the program intake process or unduly inconveniencing applicants. Moreover, random assignment procedures must be designed to ensure that intake workers cannot manipulate the assignments to admit favored applicants to the program, and that program staff do not inadvertently subject sample members to the wrong treatment. Finally, the process must be designed to accurately capture certain information that will be critical to later data collection and analysis—principally, permanent identifiers for each individual (e.g., name and Social Security number), the date of random assignment, and the assignment itself.

Two principal approaches have been developed to achieve these objectives: centralized random assignment and on-site random assignment. I discuss each in turn, and in the final part of this section, I discuss the random assignment algorithm.

Centralized Random Assignment

In all the early social experiments, random assignment was conducted centrally by the research staff in charge of the study. In studies such as the income maintenance experiments, in which the sample was identified through household surveys at the study sites, sample members were randomly assigned as their completed baseline interviews were returned to the study office. Research staff then recontacted the families and invited them to participate in the experiment.

This approach had the advantage of maximizing the experimenters' control over the random assignment process. It provided tamper-proof assignments that were accurately implemented because all the steps in the process were under the control of research staff. Reliable identifying information for each sample member was obtained from the baseline interview, and the assignment and date of assignment were recorded in the study computer at the time the assignment was made.[15]

Because it relied on obtaining hard-copy interviews from the field, this assignment process could take days or weeks to complete. Such delays, however, were not an important consideration in these experiments because the potential participants had not applied for any program and were not expecting any further contact beyond the interview.

In later experiments, in which the experimental sample was drawn from applicants to special demonstrations or ongoing programs, the time required to conduct random assignment became a more critical issue. Program staff strongly resisted putting applicants "on hold" for days or weeks while the researchers conducted random assignment. In response to this concern, a number of later experiments adopted a procedure in which random assignment was conducted by telephone. When local program staff had completed their eligibility determinations for one or more applicants, they would call a specially designated random assignment clerk and submit their identifying information. The clerk would enter this information into the computer, obtain the assignment, and inform the intake worker of the individual's experimental assignment.

This process was substantially faster than communicating with the site by mail. It was also very error prone, however; oral transmission of names and Social Security numbers led to numerous errors in these critical identifiers. In nearly all cases, these errors could be corrected later by comparison with the hard-copy baseline interview forms, but the reconciliation process was time-consuming and expensive. Moreover, to maximize responsiveness, the researchers had to have full-time random assignment clerks to take calls; for smaller studies, this was inordinately expensive. A compromise arrangement, which was somewhat less responsive but much cheaper, involved allotting each study site specific hours within which to call for assignments.

To avoid the errors induced by oral transmission of information, in some recent studies program staff have transmitted sample identifiers and received the resulting experimental assignments by fax rather than by telephone. This approach is particularly suitable when applicants are recruited and assigned in batches. For example, many training programs recruit participants in "waves" to fill a specified number of slots in a training class starting on a specific day. In contrast, welfare programs accept and process applications continuously. Both telephone and fax transmission are somewhat cumbersome when applicants are to be randomly assigned individually.

On-Site Random Assignment

In cases in which quick turnaround is important, the fastest, most flexible approach is to allow program staff to conduct random assignment on-site. Until recently, however, on-site random assignment was quite error prone and potentially subject to manipulation by program staff.

In the earliest studies to use this approach, random assignment was based on the applicant's Social Security number. For example, all applicants with Social Security numbers ending in an even digit might be assigned to the treatment group and those with numbers ending in an odd digit assigned to the control group.[16] Faithfully implemented, this algorithm would indeed generate two well-matched groups because the last four digits of the Social Security number are, for all practical purposes, randomly assigned to individuals.

Such an algorithm is easily manipulated by local program staff, however, by the simple expedient of misreporting Social Security numbers. By changing the last digit of the reported Social Security number from odd to even, program staff can ensure that favored applicants—for example, those deemed most needy or simply most likely to complain if assigned to the control group—are admitted to the experimental program. Even if they do not deliberately falsify information in this way, the fact that each applicant's treatment status can easily be known from the beginning of the intake process may lead intake staff to treat those destined to be controls differently from those who will be allowed to enter the program. For example, they might discourage (or simply fail to encourage) those with odd numbers from filling out long application forms, or they might be less diligent about determining the eligibility of those whom they know will be controls.

Some protection from these threats to random assignment can be obtained by making the random assignment algorithm somewhat more complex and giving responsibility for its application to a single "random assignment coordinator" at each site—in effect, conducting centralized random assignment within the site. For example, each two-digit number between 00 and 99 could be randomly assigned to treatment or control status and a list of these assignments given to the random assignment coordinator. Individual intake workers would then submit applicants' Social Security numbers to the random assignment coordinator, who would use the last two digits of the numbers to obtain assignments from this list. As long as the random assignment coordinator can be trusted not to photocopy the list and hand it out to the intake workers, this approach provides reasonable protection against manipulation of the assignment or asymmetric treatment of the different experimental groups or both—at the cost of some loss of flexibility and rapid turnaround.

An alternative method of on-site random assignment that provides protection against staff manipulation can be employed in some experiments. When the existing participants in a program are to be randomly assigned, the assignments can be conducted, and the experimental status of each individual recorded, in the program's central computer system. This approach could be used, for example, when a new service or requirement for the existing welfare caseload is to be tested. Randomly assigning the entire caseload en masse, using a computerized algorithm, rules out manipulation by program staff to assign specific individuals to the treatment group.

This approach may have other drawbacks, however. To maintain well-matched treatment and control groups, all individuals who were randomly assigned must be included in the experimental analysis. If the experimental treatment is voluntary or if only a subset of participants are eligible to receive it, randomly assigning all participants rather than only those who volunteer or are eligible or both will result in a higher proportion of nonparticipants in the treatment group. Thus, the estimates of impact on participants will be less precise.

The advent of virtually universal availability of microcomputers has opened the way for more flexible but secure methods of on-site random assignment. Software that will run on virtually any microcomputer is available that allows individual intake workers to randomly assign individual program applicants in much the same way as the random assignment clerk in a centralized random assignment procedure.[17] The intake worker need only enter the identifiers needed for data collection and analysis purposes (usually the applicant's name, Social Security number, and date of birth). The software will check to see if this person has been assigned previously and immediately return the individual's assignment on the screen.[18] The software automatically records the identifiers, assignment, and date in an encrypted file that cannot be changed by site staff. This file is periodically submitted to the researchers, either electronically or on a diskette, to create the initial record for each person randomly assigned. On command, the software will also print lists of treatment and control group members for use by program staff. This approach allows random assignment to be quickly and easily conducted at the agreed on point in the intake process, with virtually no risk of manipulation or tampering by program staff and minimal risk of error in the sample identifiers or recorded treatment status.

It must be recognized that any method of random assignment—centralized or on-site—is subject to the risk that program staff will erroneously assign the wrong individuals or assign them at the wrong point in the intake process. I further discuss these risks later.

The Random Assignment Algorithm

As noted previously, in modern experiments random assignment is generally based on a computerized algorithm that uses random numbers to assign individuals to groups. The simplest approach would be to draw a random number for each person to be assigned, with the assignment depending on the range within which the number falls. For example, to assign treatment and control group members in a 1:1 ratio, one could draw a random number between 0 and 1.0 and assign all those with numbers > 0.5 to the treatment group and all those with numbers 0.5 or less to the control group. This is the computerized equivalent of flipping a coin for each person to be assigned.

This approach will produce two well-matched experimental groups, but it has a significant disadvantage. Just as flipping a coin repeatedly will sometimes generate long strings of consecutive heads or long strings of consecutive tails, randomly assigning each individual independently will sometimes produce—purely by chance—long strings of consecutive assignments to the same group. Although this is not a problem for the analysis, it can sometimes create operational problems. For example, program staff may lose faith in the fairness of random assignment if they see a large number of applicants assigned to the control group—especially if it occurs early in the experiment.

Assignment of unbalanced numbers of individuals to the two groups may also complicate program planning. Suppose, for example, that the experimental treatment is a training program, and that the program staff wants to start a class of 10 trainees. With a 1:1 assignment ratio, they would expect to just fill the class if they submitted 20 names for random assignment. With independent random assignment of each person, however, they would sometimes receive 15 assignments to the treatment group and sometimes receive only 5.

Relatively close balance in the numbers assigned to each experimental group can be ensured by a technique known as **blocked random assignment**. In blocked random assignment, short "blocks" of assignments are created in advance. Within each block, the numbers of individuals assigned to the various groups exactly equal the random assignment ratio, but the order in which they occur is random. Figure 5.3 shows a schematic diagram of a

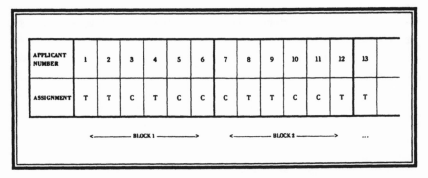

Figure 5.3. Blocked Random Assignment: Illustrative Assignments (Block Size = 6)

set of such blocks. In this example, each block contains six assignments, divided equally between the treatment and control groups.[19] These blocks of assignments are then stored in the computer (in order), and each person submitted for random assignment receives the next assignment in the block.[20]

Using this procedure, at the end of each block the ratio of assignments to the two groups exactly equals the intended random assignment ratio. Within each block, the relative number of assignments to the two groups cannot differ from the desired ratio by more than three persons (if the block size is six).[21] Also, because the assignments were randomly ordered within blocks, assignment to the two groups is entirely random.

Blocked random assignment does raise the theoretical danger of intake staff being able to manipulate random assignment. Program staff cannot, of course, see the upcoming assignments that are encoded within the computer. If, however, an intake worker knew that the assignments were in blocks of six, he or she would know that any time the numbers of treatment and control group members differed by three, the next assignment would be to the group with fewer members. Thus, by holding a favored applicant until there were three more controls than treatment group members, he or she could ensure that applicant of admission to the program. In my experience, program staff are neither this analytic nor this determined to subvert random assignment. In any case, if this type of strategic behavior is considered to be a realistic threat, it can be prevented by simply using blocks of different length in random order.

In implementing a system of blocked random assignment, it is important to consider the organizational level at which balanced assignments are desired. Blocked random assignment ensures only that the assignments made by a single computer are balanced. If these assignments are distributed across multiple sites or offices, there is no guarantee of balance at an individual site or office. Alternatively, if multiple computers are used to make assignments at a single site or office, there is no guarantee of balance at the overall site or office level. Generally, operational considerations argue for balanced assignments within each program office. This means that the optimal arrangement will generally be to use one computer in each office. If random assignment is centralized, separate assignment sequences can be reserved for each office.

Maintaining the Integrity of the Experimental Design

Careful design of random assignment procedures will go a long way toward ensuring that the experimental design is implemented as intended. As with any field undertaking, however, a number of problems can arise during the implementation of an experiment, and the researcher must anticipate the potential threats to the design so that implementation problems can be avoided or at least detected and dealt with promptly. The major potential threats to the design that arise in the field include

- ◆ Nonrandom assignments as a result of deliberate or inadvertent subversion of random assignment procedures by program staff or problems with the random assignment algorithm
- ◆ Random assignment of ineligible program applicants
- ◆ Failure to maintain adequate records of all individuals randomly assigned
- ◆ Controls receiving an amount or kind of service or benefit that they would not have received in the absence of the experiment ("control group contamination")
- ◆ Failure to serve treatment group members

All these threats involve some degree of lack of understanding of, or cooperation with, the experimental procedures by the local program staff. One general prescription for avoiding these kinds of problems, therefore, is a concerted up-front effort to gain the willing cooperation of the staff and to train them thoroughly in the experimental procedures. To work out any problems in the system, wherever possible it is prudent to implement the random assignment procedures on a test basis for approximately a week, with all applicants being assigned to the treatment group, before making any "real" assignments. As the experiment proceeds, the researchers must also closely monitor events in the field to ensure that the prescribed procedures are being followed and provide any necessary retraining. Provision of a written procedures manual for staff reference and availability of research staff to respond to program staff questions will also help ensure adherence to correct procedures.

Nonrandom Assignment

If the computerized random assignment techniques described in the previous section are employed—on either a centralized or decentralized basis—there is little chance that program staff can manipulate, or inadvertently distort, the actual random assignment process. In these circumstances, the only real threat of nonrandom assignments is a malfunction of the random assignment algorithm itself. Given the critical importance of random assignment to the success of the experiment, however, it is prudent to guard against even this unlikely event.

In experiments that rely on noncomputerized random assignment—especially where it is conducted on-site by program staff—the risk of nonrandom assignment is very real. For example, in a pilot test of an evaluation of the Women, Infants, and Children's Feeding Program, local staff recruited women in health clinic waiting rooms and randomly assigned them using an algorithm based on the women's Social Security numbers. Proper application of the algorithm would have produced equal-sized treatment and control groups. At one site, nearly two thirds of the women were assigned to the treatment group; it seems clear that recruiters falsified Social Security numbers to allow women who should have been controls to be assigned to the program (Puma et al., 1991).

Several steps can and should be taken to detect departures from random assignment. First, the numbers of treatment and control group members assigned should be closely monitored. As explained in the previous section, under blocked random assignment, the numbers in the two groups should never differ from the desired random assignment ratio by more than a specified number. For example, if the random assignment ratio is 1:1 and the block size is six, the numbers in the two groups should never differ by more than three (one half the block size). Any larger difference would be a clear indication of a breakdown in the random assignment algorithm. In experiments in which blocked random assignment is not used, the indications are not as clear-cut—virtually any difference in group sizes could be produced by pure chance. Large deviations from the intended ratio, however, are unlikely and should be treated as strong indications of a failure of random assignment.

Second, as baseline data on the sample become available, it is possible to compare the characteristics of the treatment and control groups to determine whether they are well matched. Again, any degree of mismatch between the two groups is possible due to chance alone. A finding of more statistically significant differences between the two groups than would have been predicted on the basis of chance alone (e.g., significant differences at the 10% level on more than 1 of 10 characteristics), however, should be treated as an indicator of potential problems.

If either of these checks sound a warning signal, the experimenters should review the entire random assignment process, including both site procedures and the random assignment algorithm, to determine whether there has been a breakdown. In any case, the researchers should periodically conduct on-site reviews of local program procedures to ensure compliance with the experimental design.

Random Assignment of Ineligible Individuals

One of the most frequent departures from the experimental design, especially early in the experiment, is random assignment of ineligible individuals.[22] This can happen for a variety of reasons. For example, staff may, either inadvertently or because they misunderstand the correct timing of random assignment, randomly assign individuals before an eligibility determination is made. Even when the individual has been determined to be eligible prior to random assignment, sometimes information subsequently comes to light that proves this determination to have been in error. Program staff may also randomly assign individuals previously determined to be ineligible—again, either inadvertently or because they misunderstand the random assignment procedures.

Ineligibles who have been randomly assigned by mistake are usually detected—if detected at all—by program staff in the course of their normal program activities. For example, a caseworker may make the discovery in the course of an initial counseling session with a client to determine his or her service needs. This discovery is generally followed by a frantic call to the research staff asking, "What do we do now?"

Several approaches are available to deal with random assignment of ineligible individuals. If the ineligibles assigned to both the treatment and control groups can be identified, they can be removed from the experimental sample—in effect, "unassigned." Removal of all ineligibles from both groups leaves two well-matched groups of eligibles, just as if the ineligibles had never been assigned in the first place.

It is critical, of course, that the ineligibles in both groups be identified if this approach is to be used. Frequently, the process that leads to detection of ineligibles applies only to the treatment group. For example, at one site of the Moving to Opportunity demonstration, counselors working with the experimental group assigned to receive housing vouchers that could be used only in low-poverty areas found that 20 of the first 148 families assigned to this group (14%) were ineligible. Because the experimental groups should be well matched on all characteristics, one can infer that a similar proportion of those assigned to the other experimental groups were ineligible. Among those assigned to unrestricted housing vouchers, who received no counseling, program staff identified only 7% as ineligible, and they found no ineligibles among those assigned to the control group, with whom program staff had no further contact. Clearly, the probability of detection of ineligibles varied with the amount of staff contact with the families.

As this example suggests, one can usually determine whether the ineligibles in all experimental groups have been identified by examining the relative numbers of known ineligibles in each group and the process by which they were discovered. If the proportion of sample members known to be ineligible differs substantially among groups, the process by which the sample members were detected seems more likely to identify ineligibles in one group than in another, or both, the ineligibles should not be removed from the sample.

Even when ineligibles cannot be removed from the sample, an analytic correction is available if the ineligibles in the treatment group can be identified and excluded from the program before they receive any services. In this case, they can usually be treated as no-shows, and the no-show correction described in Chapter 2 can be applied to remove their effect on the impact estimates. The only assumption required for this correction to yield unbiased estimates of program effects on eligible participants is that the program have no effect on the outcomes of the no-shows in the sample, including the ineligibles. Thus, even in those instances in which it is unlikely that ineligibles can be identified in the control group, it is important to attempt to identify any ineligible individuals in the treatment group as early as possible.

If the assumption required to apply the no-show correction is not satisfied, the experimenter has no choice but to include the ineligibles in the sample and to recognize that the resulting impact estimates apply to a somewhat different population than the intended eligible population.

Failure to Maintain Adequate Records

To conduct a valid experimental analysis, we must know the identity of all individuals assigned, when they were assigned, and the group to which they were assigned. If random assignment is conducted using a computerized algorithm designed by the researchers, as suggested in the previous section, a record containing these pieces of information is automatically created at the time of assignment.

When the sample is assigned by noncomputerized methods, however, errors and omissions can creep into these data, especially when local program staff are responsible for random assignment. Program staff have a natural tendency to focus on program participants; they may keep only minimal records of those assigned to the control group or of treatment group members who do not enter the program. Moreover, they may be very careless about retaining the records of these latter groups; unless the researchers collect this information soon after random assignment, it may be lost.

In an experiment to test the delivery of family support services by local nonprofit agencies, for example, random assignment was conducted by the local programs before the evaluation contractor was selected. Later, when the evaluation contractor attempted to collect random assignment information, staff at some of the sites could not produce accurate lists of assignments.[23] In these cases, evaluation staff had to search through hard-copy records in the local program office to reconstruct the assignments. At one site, the researchers were simply unable to identify the complete sample of families that were randomly assigned; this site had to be dropped from the experiment.

Similar experiences in other experiments in which the design and implementation of random assignment were entrusted to local program staff with little or no oversight by the research staff lead me to conclude that random assignment should always be designed and supervised by researchers. Although local staff may actually perform the assignments—as in the decentralized random assignment approaches described previously—they should do so only after thorough training, using systems and procedures designed by the research staff.

Control Group Contamination

Perhaps the most difficult problem to deal with after the fact is controls receiving an amount or type of service that they would not have received in the absence of the experimental program. It is important to recognize that the mere fact that controls receive some nonexperimental services does not necessarily mean that control group contamination has occurred. In cases in which services similar to those of the experimental treatment are available from nonexperimental sources, the desired counterfactual involves some receipt of services by the control group.[24] Because we do not know the amount or type of services the control group would have received in the absence of the experiment (after all, this is the purpose of the control group!), it is virtually impossible to measure control group contamination once it has occurred and therefore virtually impossible to correct for any resulting bias. Therefore, it is critically important to prevent control group contamination from occurring in the first place.

Control group contamination can arise from several sources. Program staff may refer controls to other sources of assistance, either out of a simple desire to be helpful or as a "consolation prize" for having been excluded from the experimental program. The mere fact of having been recruited for, then excluded from, the experimental program may change controls' behavior in seeking similar services from nonexperimental sources. On the one hand, outreach for the experimental program may prompt some individuals who would not have sought services at all to seek them. Once assigned to the control group, some of these individuals may go on to seek nonexperimental services. In these cases, the existence of the experiment encourages a higher rate of service receipt than controls would have experienced in its absence. On the other hand, assignment to the control group may discourage some individuals from seeking nonexperimental services, even though they would have done so in the absence of the experiment. Thus, we cannot even be certain of the direction of any bias.

Little can be done to prevent any contamination that occurs simply as a result of program outreach. A number of steps can be taken, however, to prevent program staff from taking actions that may contaminate the control group. Perhaps the most effective way to protect against program staff undermining the experimental design by helping controls obtain nonexperimental services is to make sure that the staff understand and accept the reason for this prohibition. In my experience, the greatest threat of control group contamination comes from staff who either do not understand what they can and cannot do, and therefore violate the prohibition unintentionally, or believe that random assignment is unfair and deliberately attempt to compensate for what they view as an injustice to controls. Therefore, in training local program staff in random assignment procedures, it is important to be clear about the prohibition on special efforts to help controls and to take enough time to work through staff concerns about random assignment so that they feel comfortable abiding by this prohibition.

An effective way to remove both the opportunity and the temptation for program staff to refer controls to nonexperimental services is to inform controls of their experimental status by letter rather than in person. This has the added advantage of ensuring that each control receives a full, clear explanation of the reason for exclusion from the program and their rights to receive services from other sources (without identifying those sources). It also creates a permanent record of what the controls were told.

The opportunity for control group contamination can also be reduced by minimizing contact between program applicants and service providers prior to random assignment, especially when experimental services are purchased from outside vendors. Service vendors often receive funding from multiple programs; in these cases, well-meaning staff may tell applicants that if they are assigned to the control group the provider will serve them under another program. It is therefore preferable for the central administrative organization of the experiment to conduct intake and random assignment rather than entrusting these functions to service providers.

Of course, it is also necessary to take steps to prevent controls from receiving the experimental treatment. Here again, the willing cooperation of program staff, and their thorough understanding of the prohibition on services to controls, is essential. Given these, perhaps the greatest risk of controls receiving experimental services arises from controls who reapply to the experimental program. The random assignment software can be programmed to detect those who reapply while random assignment is still ongoing.[25] If the program continues to accept applicants after the end of the random assignment period, the embargo on services to controls can be enforced by creating a record for each control in the program's central participant information system, with a flag or note indicating that these persons should not be accepted as participants until after the end of the embargo period.

In Chapter 6, I discuss an analytic correction that can be used to correct for any crossovers (controls who receive the experimental treatment) that do occur. Here, I note only that crossovers should not be dropped from the experimental sample because this will unbalance the treatment and control groups. Rather, they should simply be identified in the database and included in all regular data collection activities so that the analytic correction can be applied.

Failure to Serve Treatment Group Members

Just as it is important that controls not receive services that they would not have received in the absence of the experiment, it is important that the treatment group receive the experimental treatment. As noted earlier, the presence of individuals in the treatment group who do not receive the treatment degrades the precision of the estimates. A 30% nontreatment rate has the same effect on minimum detectable effects as a 50% reduction in sample size; a 50% nontreatment rate is equivalent to losing three fourths of the experimental sample.

Of course, there will be some no-shows in virtually any program. Some individuals will change their minds after being accepted into the program, or their situation will change so that they no longer need, or cannot take advantage of, program services. High rates of nontreatment, however, are probably a sign of problems in the administration of the program or of random assignment itself.

Perhaps the most common reason for nontreatment of those randomly assigned to enter the program is long lags between random assignment and entry into the program. This typically occurs because program applicants are assigned before the program is ready to enroll them. For example, early in the AFDC Homemaker-Home Health Aide Demonstration, several sites started recruiting potential trainees well in advance of the scheduled start of training and randomly assigned applicants as they were approved. This resulted in long lags between assignment and the start of training for the earliest applicants, and many of the applicants dropped out before entering training. In a few cases, inadequate numbers of applications caused classes to be postponed, again resulting in long lags and high no-show rates. These problems were resolved by better coordination of recruiting activities with the start of training and by adopting a practice of holding applications until just before the class was about to begin and then reconfirming the applicants' availability before randomly assigning them.

As this example suggests, high rates of nontreatment can often be reduced by improved management of the intake flow or by changing the timing of random assignment to reduce the lag between random assignment and program entry.

In some cases, high rates of nontreatment arise because the random assignment model is flawed or severely constrained by institutional factors. If, for instance, all program applicants are randomly assigned rather than only those who are eligible for the program, the resulting treatment group will contain a number of individuals who do not participate in the program because they are ineligible. Sometimes this is unavoidable. For example, some programs employ extensive testing or in-person screening as part of the eligibility determination process; in these programs, it would be extremely expensive or burdensome or both (for both staff and applicants) to carry all applicants through this process before randomly assigning a large fraction of them to the control group.[26] Although such circumstances will usually dictate placing random assignment before eligibility determination, the experimenter should be cognizant of the costs of doing so—in terms of reduced precision of the estimates or the need for a larger sample to maintain precision.

Data Collection

Several different types of data will be required in the experimental analysis. Perhaps the most fundamental data element is the ***treatment status indicator***, which shows the experimental group (treatment or control) to which each sample member was assigned. This information is needed to create the experimental contrast that measures program impacts. The ***date of random assignment*** is required to align outcome data in time across the sample. ***Personal identifiers*** will be needed to link data from various sources together. ***Baseline data*** on sample members' background and demographic characteristics are useful for describing the study population, improving the precision of the impact estimates, and defining subgroups of the study sample for separate analysis. Data on the ***outcomes*** of interest are needed to estimate the impacts of the experimental program. Data on ***program participation*** (including nonexperimental services received by both the treatment and the control groups) are required to determine the service differential that produced the estimated impacts. Finally, measures of the ***cost of services*** received by the treatment and control groups are necessary to allow comparison of program impacts with the net additional cost of the experimental services.

In the following sections, I discuss the collection of each of these types of data. I first consider the information generated by the random assignment process and then discuss the collection of baseline data, outcome data, program participation data, and cost data. The discussion is confined to those aspects of data collection that are directly related to the experimental nature of the study; I do not attempt to provide a comprehensive guide to the collection of these various types of data.

Two general rules apply to all data collection activities in an experiment. First, to the extent possible, all data elements should be collected for every individual randomly assigned. Experimental impact analysis involves comparison of the outcomes of the entire treatment group with those of the entire control group. If any sample members are eliminated from the sample, these two groups will no longer be well matched, and therefore the impact estimates will be biased. Thus, for example, treatment group members who fail to participate in the experimental program, or controls who do participate, should not be dropped from the sample.

Second, as a general rule, the same data collection procedures should be used for the treatment group and for the control group. If different methods are used for the two groups, differential errors in the data may be confounded with the impact of the experimental treatment.

I elaborate on the application of these two rules to specific types of data collection in the following sections.

The Random Assignment Record

As mentioned earlier, the random assignment process must be designed to record certain key pieces of information about each person randomly assigned: the treatment status indicator, the date of assignment, and at least one personal identifier. I refer to these data collectively as the *random assignment record*.

These data elements are perhaps the most critical pieces of information about the sample that will be collected or generated in the experiment. All the impact estimates rest squarely on knowledge of the group to which individuals were assigned, and all the follow-up data will be keyed to the date of random assignment. Personal identifiers are the key to linking data from different sources, including linking treatment status to outcome data; without this link, the other data collected by the experiment are useless. Sample members missing any of these three critical data elements usually must be dropped from the analysis.

The use of personal identifiers is illustrated by a typical random assignment and data collection process. One or more personal identifiers (e.g., name, Social Security number, or both) are entered into the random assignment record at the time of assignment. These same identifiers are entered on a separate baseline survey form, which contains background information on the sample member and contact information (e.g., address and telephone number) that can be used to conduct follow-up interviews. The same identifier may be used to access data from the experimental program's records for the person as well as from other administrative records (e.g., AFDC benefits). Each sample member's personal identifier(s) is then used to link all these data into a single record so that each person's background characteristics and treatment status can be related to his or her outcomes in estimating program impacts.

Fortunately, when random assignment is computerized, the treatment status indicator and date of random assignment are generated by the computer. As long as the assignment algorithm is working properly and the computer's internal clock is set correctly, these data will be error free.

Personal identifiers can be more problematic. Although it may seem a simple matter to obtain a sample member's name or Social Security number, these basic data can be remarkably error prone. Names change (as when women marry), and individuals may use different names at different times (e.g., nicknames or informal versions of their given name). Names may also be misspelled or incorrectly transcribed by program staff, especially if the sample member's handwriting is illegible. Moreover, more than one sample member may have the same name. For all these reasons, names do not serve well as primary identifiers, especially in large samples. They are, however, useful as a secondary identifier to resolve ambiguities that arise when using other identifiers. (Date of birth is also useful for this purpose.)

The ideal identifier would be permanent and unique to the individual. The identifier in common use that is closest to these characteristics is the Social Security number. The Social Security number has the added advantage that it is used as the primary identifier in many administrative record systems, such as AFDC and food stamp benefit records and unemployment insurance wage records. Thus, if the experiment needs to access outcome data from these systems, the Social Security number is the identifier of choice. Although in practice there can also be problems with this identifier (e.g., individuals with multiple Social Security numbers or none at all and transcription errors), it is widely used as an identifier in many research projects.

Baseline Data

As noted previously, baseline data on the sample serve several purposes. First, they are needed to describe the study population. In future policy applications of the experimental results, it will be important to know how closely the experimental sample resembled the population for whom the program is being considered. Second, baseline data can be used to improve the precision of the impact estimates. (I discuss the procedure for doing so in Chapter 6.) Third, baseline data can be used to define subgroups of the experimental sample for separate analysis. For example, it is often of interest to know whether program impacts differed between men and women, older and younger participants, and those with high school diplomas and those without. This information can be used to target the program on those for whom it is most effective or to identify those populations for which the program needs improvement or both. Finally, if follow-up surveys are to be conducted to collect outcome data, contact information must be collected at baseline. Contact information includes the address and telephone number of the sample member as well as those of friends or relatives who will know how to contact the sample member if he or she should move or change telephone numbers.

The kinds of baseline data required in any particular experiment can be derived from these analytic uses. They obviously include any personal characteristics or experience that would be useful in describing the sample for policy purposes or in defining subgroups of interest for policy. For example, in an experimental test of a job training program, one would want to collect data on the applicants' work experience and education level as well as standard demographic information, such as age, gender, and ethnicity. For purposes of improving the precision of the estimates, the most useful baseline variables are preprogram values of the outcomes of interest (e.g., employment and earnings) and any personal characteristics that can be expected to affect these outcomes.

In designing baseline data collection instruments, it is important to bear in mind the relatively limited role these data play in experimental analyses. A common error is to collect extensive retrospective data of the type one might use in a longitudinal study to "model" the development of the outcome variables over time. In an experiment, the control group provides a longitudinal picture of how the outcomes would develop in the absence of the experimental program, and the treatment-control difference in outcomes indicates to the researcher how the program changes this picture. Although there may be independent interest in how various background characteristics of the individual affect the outcomes, it is not necessary to estimate these effects to measure the impact of the program.

Generally, the best source of baseline data is the applicants themselves. Information can be collected directly from the applicants as part of the intake process in several different ways. Perhaps the simplest, most efficient way to collect baseline information is through the use of a self-administered form to be completed by the applicant along with the regular program application form. In some cases, however, in which the information required is too complex, the applicants' literacy level is too low to allow use of a self-administered form, or both, it may be necessary to collect baseline data through a personal interview. This can be done either by program intake workers or by interviewers employed by the experimenters. Generally, when personal interviews are required, it is highly preferable that they be conducted by interviewers employed and trained by the researchers, unless the program staff to whom this responsibility is assigned are thoroughly trained by the research staff and are fully committed to the study.

A middle ground between the self-administered form and the personal interview is the "staff-assisted" baseline form, which applicants are asked to complete in the presence of program staff, who are available to respond to questions and explain any parts of the form that may be confusing to the applicants. Because staff-assisted forms can be administered to groups of applicants, they require less staff time than personal interviews while providing more support to the applicant than the self-administered form.

Some types of baseline data can be obtained from administrative records. For example, in experiments involving welfare recipients, baseline values of welfare benefits are probably best collected from administrative records because these records constitute the official record of the amounts paid and are probably quite accurate. The records are also quite inexpensive to access because they are usually automated. For other background information, however, such as demographic characteristics or work history, administrative systems are notoriously inaccurate, especially if program benefits do not depend directly on the data in question. Moreover, the definitions used for such variables may vary considerably among local programs, making uniformity of data problematic in multisite experiments.

When baseline data are collected directly from the sample member, for several reasons it is essential that they be collected before random assignment. First, this requirement ensures that, by definition, baseline data are available for all individuals who are randomly assigned—that is, for the entire analysis sample. Attempts to collect baseline data after random assignment invariably result in missing data for a portion of the sample, either because the sample member cannot be located or because the sample member is unwilling to cooperate with the interview. Control group members tend to be more difficult to interview for both these reasons; thus, not only will data be missing but also the data are likely to be missing differentially for the treatment and control groups. Such disparities between the two groups can bias the impact estimates.

A second reason for collecting baseline data prior to random assignment is that it ensures that the sample member's responses will not be influenced by knowledge of his or her experimental assignment. This is particularly true of attitudinal data because attitudes can potentially be affected by exclusion from the experimental program. Other types of data may be influenced as well; individuals who have been excluded from the program may simply not give their responses as much time and thought as those who have been accepted into the program. Control group members, for example, may provide less complete work histories than treatment group members; this would result in the appearance of a mismatch between the two groups in terms of prior work experience. "Correcting" this mismatch in the analysis would produce biased impact estimates.

Outcome Data

Anything that the treatment group does after random assignment is potentially affected by the experimental program—even if only through the individual's knowledge that he or she is eligible to participate in the program. Therefore, the sole purpose of collecting data on the experimental sample after random assignment is to provide the outcome data needed to estimate program impacts.

A common error in designing follow-up data collection instruments is the collection of data on variables that are viewed as useful in "explaining" the postprogram outcomes. As noted previously in connection with baseline data, in an experiment it is not necessary to "explain" the outcomes; the control group provides all the information that is needed regarding what the outcomes would have been in the absence of the experimental program. In fact, because these "explanatory" variables may be affected by the experimental treatment, their inclusion in the model used to estimate impacts on other outcomes may bias the impact estimates by capturing part of the effect of the treatment. Thus, follow-up data collection should be focused on those variables that reflect the intended objectives of the program or any other potential consequences of program participation or both. (See the discussion of specification of outcomes in Chapter 2.)

Outcome data can be collected either through surveys of the experimental sample or from administrative records. Surveys are typically conducted by telephone or, for those who cannot be contacted by telephone, in person. Administrative data may come from any of a variety of program record systems—for example, the eligibility and benefit payment systems of social programs, health insurance records, or the employer-reported wage records maintained by state unemployment insurance (UI) agencies for all UI-covered workers.

Where available, administrative records have several distinct advantages compared to surveys.[27] First, for some variables, they are likely to be more accurate. For example, health insurance records of the amount and cost of medical care consumed by an individual are likely to be more accurate than the individual's recall of those items. Second, administrative records are not subject to nonresponse, as are surveys. Thus, one can often obtain data for virtually 100% of the population of interest rather than the 75% or 80% response rate that is typical in surveys. Third, it is often cheaper to collect computerized administrative data than to conduct surveys, especially for large samples, because the cost of accessing electronic files is largely independent of the number of records to be extracted. Finally, administrative data are often available for much longer retrospective periods than can be reliably collected in surveys because of respondent recall error.

Administrative records also have important limitations, however. For many outcomes of interest, they are simply not available. In some cases, they may cover only part of the population of interest. For example, state AFDC payment systems will provide accurate records of benefits paid to families within the state but no information on families that move to another state and receive benefits. Access to administrative records may also be restricted for reasons of confidentiality. Usually (although not always), this restriction can be removed by obtaining a signed release from the sample member; such releases are routinely collected as part of the baseline information form in many experiments.

Even where administrative records are available, they often contain some data elements that are highly inaccurate. In general, the most reliable administrative data are those that record program benefits in quantitative terms (e.g., welfare payments) or relatively objective personal characteristics that are central to eligibility for, or the amount of, program benefits (e.g., number and age of the children of welfare recipients). Descriptive data that are not essential for determining program eligibility or benefit amount (e.g., educational attainment) are often collected only sporadically or carelessly or both by program staff and may not be updated on a regular basis. Moreover, the content and definition of variables in administrative records may vary greatly from one local program to another, making it difficult to collect uniform data for all members of the sample.

Finally, for a variety of reasons, it is often difficult to obtain complete and accurate extracts of administrative records. Agency staff responsible for maintaining administrative data often give low priority to requests for such extracts because they view them as diversions from their programmatic mission. As a result, they may be careless in executing such requests or misunderstand what is wanted; for example, providing benefit records for current welfare recipients only rather than all sample members who ever received welfare during the follow-up period. Mistakes may also arise simply out of lack of experience in producing such extracts. For reasons such as these, the National JTPA Study was able to collect complete and accurate data on UI-covered earnings for only 12 of 16 study sites and on AFDC and food stamps benefits for only 4 and 2 sites, respectively.

The great advantage of surveys is their ability to collect detailed data tailored to the analysis at hand. Their greatest limitations are cost, nonresponse, and respondents' limited knowledge of, or ability to recall, certain outcomes. A typical follow-up survey costs $100 to $200 per completed interview, depending on its length and the difficulty of locating the respondent population. For a sample of 10,000 respondents, the total cost of such a survey can easily exceed $1,000,000. Follow-up survey response rates seldom exceed 80% to 85%, and respondents may have great difficulty answering certain questions. For example, most people cannot reconstruct their expenditures or amounts of program benefits received with much precision, and many cannot distinguish among the programs from which they or their families have received cash benefits (e.g., AFDC, General Assistance, Supplemental Security Income, and Social Security). These limitations notwithstanding, surveys are often the only available source of data on the experimental outcomes.

However the outcome data are collected, it is critically important to apply the same methods to the treatment and control groups to avoid treatment-control differences in measured outcomes that reflect differences in data collection methods rather than program impacts. Consider, for example, an experimental test of a health clinic in which utilization of medical care is an outcome of interest. One might be tempted to obtain medical utilization data for the treatment group from the clinic's administrative records and to use a survey to measure utilization among controls, who obtained their care from a wide range of providers in the community. Such a strategy would likely lead to differential underreporting between the two groups; this difference in reported utilization would then be mistakenly attributed to the impact of the program.[28]

A more subtle example of the confounding of experimental impacts with differences in data collection methods occurs when the records of the experimental program are used to update the contact information obtained at baseline. Because the program can provide updated information only for the treatment group, this results in more current information, and therefore higher survey response rates, for the treatment group than for controls. If survey respondents differ systematically from nonrespondents in ways that affect their outcomes, such differential nonresponse may lead to biased impact estimates. The only safe rule is to use only those sources of contact information that are available symmetrically for both treatment and control groups.

The timing of data collection must also be symmetric between the two groups. Figure 5.4 shows how differences in the timing of measurement can bias the impact estimates when there is a trend in the outcome of interest. In this hypothetical case, the proportion of the treatment group on welfare is measured at an earlier point relative to random assignment (t_0) than that of the control group (t_1). Because the rate of welfare receipt is declining in both groups, the treatment-control difference ($P_{T0} - P_{C1}$) measured this way understates the true impact of the program (the vertical distance between the two outcome lines) at either time t_0 (the distance from a to b) or time t_1 (the distance from c to d).

More generally, outcome data for all individuals in the experimental sample must be aligned according to time elapsed since random assignment to avoid confounding the experimental impact with trends in the outcome variables. This applies both to "snapshot" outcome measures, such as that depicted in Figure 5.4, and to outcomes measured continuously over time (e.g., monthly earnings).

Analysts sometimes attempt to key follow-up data collection to the point at which individuals leave the program—for example, conducting follow-up interviews 6 months after program exit. This approach is fundamentally flawed because program exit is not defined for controls, who were excluded from the program. Treatment group members who leave the program early (or never enter it) are likely to differ systematically from those who leave it later—for example, they may be less motivated or, conversely, they may be more successful. There is no way to identify the control counterparts of these different self-selected groups so that their follow-up interviews can be conducted at the same time.

Program Participation Data

In an experimental impact study, exclusion of the control group from the experimental program creates a service differential between the treatment

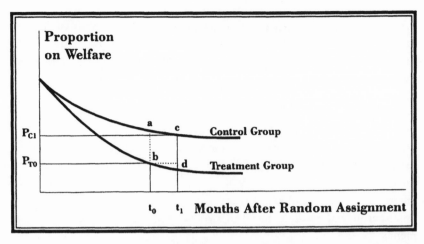

Figure 5.4. Effect of Asymmetric Timing of Data Collection on the Impact Estimate

group and the control group. Impacts are then estimated as the treatment-control differences in the outcomes of interest. Remarkably, no information on the actual treatment-control service differential is needed to estimate its impact. If the impact estimates are to be useful for policy, however, it is important to be able to describe the service differential that produced them so that the experimental program can be replicated on a larger scale. This information is also useful in interpreting the experimental results; for example, in some experiments these data have revealed that the reason the program had no impact was that the experimental program failed to create a significant service differential.[29]

For these purposes, it is useful to know the nature of the services or benefits provided and the duration of receipt of these services or benefits. For example, in a counseling program, we want to know the number of counseling sessions, their timing and content, the credentials and approach of the counselor, and any services to which the individual was referred by the counselor. In a training program, we want to know the dates of entry and exit, the type and number of hours of training received, the training curriculum, and whether the individual successfully completed the course.

In a program that does not displace services and benefits that would have been received from nonexperimental sources, the treatment-control service differential is simply the experimental services received by the treatment group. Thus, we need only collect information about these services to describe the treatment-control service differential. This information can usually be obtained from the administrative records of the organization providing the experimental services, although in some cases it will be necessary to set up special data collection systems to obtain this information during the course of the experiment. For example, a counseling program might not normally keep track of the number, length, or content of individual counseling sessions. In such a case, it will be necessary to design a form on which counselors are asked to record these data as each session is held.

Collection of program participation data is much more difficult in cases in which the experimental program can be expected to displace similar nonexperimental services. In such cases, to measure the net treatment-control service differential it is necessary to measure both experimental and nonexperimental services received by both treatment and control group members.

Several different approaches are available to measure these services. First, one can use the administrative data compiled by the experiment to measure the delivery of experimental services and attempt to access similar administrative data on nonexperimental services. For example, in an evaluation of a training program, one might search the records of other training providers in the community—for example, JTPA, the Employment Service, and the Job Opportunities and Basic Skills program—for services to the experimental sample.[30]

If successful, this approach can yield relatively accurate data on service receipt. There are several problems with this approach, however. As noted previously, programs may not routinely record detailed service information; in many programs, the administrative records may contain little more than the dates that the individual entered and left the program. Moreover, if there are a large number of potential alternative service providers—as is often the case, especially in multisite studies—it can be extremely expensive and time-consuming to identify all the relevant providers, negotiate access to their records, and extract the data for the sample. Finally, if there is a large number of providers, there is a substantial risk that some will be missed, resulting in an underestimate of the nonexperimental services received by the control group and an overstatement of the treatment-control service differential.

Because of these problems, service receipt is frequently measured through follow-up interviews with the sample members. The obvious problem with this method is that respondents may not know, or may not remember, detailed information about the services they received from various programs, especially if the recall period is more than a few months. Respondents may also have trouble identifying some of the services they have received. For example, in the National JTPA Study, sample members could not distinguish the subsidized employment they obtained through JTPA from regular jobs. Realistically, however, this may be the only feasible approach for measuring nonexperimental services when there is a large number of service providers at the study sites. In the National JTPA Study, for example, sample members reported receiving education and training services from more than 400 schools and training institutions.

In cases in which nonexperimental services must be measured through follow-up surveys, the experimenter must decide whether to measure all services through the survey or to rely on administrative data for experimental services and survey data for nonexperimental services. The latter approach uses the best available data for each type of service but probably measures experimental services more accurately than nonexperimental services, thereby confounding the treatment-control service differential with measurement error. The former approach avoids this problem at the cost of using less accurate data.

Which approach is preferred depends on the relative accuracy of the two types of data and the relative amounts of service received by the two groups. The trade-offs involved can be illustrated by a simple example. Suppose that the treatment group received an average of 100 hours of experimental service (only), whereas controls averaged 40 hours of nonexperimental service (only), resulting in a (true) service differential of 60 hours. Also suppose that administrative data from the experiment accurately represent all experimental services received, whereas survey respondents underreport services (both experimental and nonexperimental) by 20%. If services to the treatment group are measured with administrative data and services to controls with survey data, we will obtain estimates of 100 hours of service to the treatment group and 32 hours of service to the control group, resulting in a service differential of 68 hours. If services to both groups are measured with survey data, our estimates will be 80 hours of service to the treatment group and 32 hours to the control group, resulting in a service differential of 48 hours. The former overstates the service differential by 8 hours; the latter understates it by 12 hours.

In this example, the mixed-mode approach provides a more accurate measure of the true service differential. If the rate of underreporting on the survey were lower, or the treatment-control difference in service receipt smaller, however, using the survey to measure services to both groups might well yield the more accurate estimate.

A possible refinement to the mixed-mode approach is to compute an estimate of the underreporting rate in the survey based on the ratio of treatment group service receipt reported in the administrative data to that reported in the survey. This estimate can then be used to correct the controls' survey data for underreporting.

It should be noted that, in practice, it is often impossible for survey respondents to distinguish experimental services from nonexperimental services. In this situation, to use administrative data from the experiment to measure services one must assume that the treatment group received only experimental services and the control group received only nonexperimental services. The reasonableness of these assumptions will depend heavily on the nature of the services and the institutional setting of the experiment.

Cost Data

The great contribution of social experiments is to provide unbiased estimates of program impact. To be useful for policy, however, these estimates must be combined with information about the cost of the program. That is, policymakers must consider whether the program's impacts are sufficient to justify its costs. In Chapter 6, I describe how such benefit-cost analyses are conducted. Here, I focus on the issues involved in collecting data on program costs.

The cost that must be measured is the cost of the treatment-control difference in services or benefits that produced the estimated impacts of the program—that is, the net or incremental cost of the experimental program. If the experimental program does not displace any nonexperimental services or benefits, this cost is simply the cost of the experimental program. If the experimental program bears the full cost of the services or benefits it provides, this cost can usually be measured with data from the administrative records of the experiment.

As with the measurement of service receipt, if the experiment displaces nonexperimental services, measurement of the net cost of the experimental program is more complex. In this case, we wish to measure

$$C = c_t S_t - c_c S_c \qquad [5.1]$$

where

C = net cost of the experimental program per treatment group member

c_t = cost per unit of service received by the treatment group

S_t = average number of units of service received by treatment group members

c_c = cost per unit of service received by controls

S_c = average number of units of service received by controls

S_t and S_c are the treatment and control service levels whose measurement was discussed previously. The problem here is to measure c_t and c_c, the unit costs of services received by the typical treatment and control group members. The fact that treatment and control group members may, in general, receive different types and intensities of service means that service costs must be measured separately for the two groups.

If treatment group members receive only experimental services and the experiment bears the full cost of these services, then $c_t S_t$, the average cost per treatment group member, can be calculated simply by dividing the total cost of the experimental program by the total number of treatment group members. If either of these conditions is not satisfied, however, the cost of services received by treatment group members must be estimated with data from sources other than the experiment. In any case, cost data must be collected from sources other than the experiment to estimate c_c, the unit cost of services to controls. How this is done will depend heavily on the specific services involved. Rather than attempting to prescribe any general guidelines for this task, I illustrate some of the possible sources of cost data by describing the approach taken in one experimental evaluation, the National JTPA Study.

In the National JTPA Study, receipt of employment and training services (S_i in Equation 5.1) was measured through a combination of JTPA administrative data and a follow-up survey of the experimental sample.[31] JTPA administrative data were used to measure days of unpaid work experience and on-the-job training in subsidized jobs on the grounds that these services were provided only by JTPA and that JTPA bore their full cost.[32] For those services that were readily available in the community from sources other than JTPA, survey data were used to measure the number of days or hours of service received by both treatment and control group members. This included such services as classroom training in vocational skills, basic education, and job search assistance.

The unit costs of these various services (c_i in Equation 5.1) were estimated on the basis of data from several sources. The costs per day of providing job search assistance, unpaid work experience, and on-the-job training in subsidized jobs were obtained by dividing total JTPA expenditures on each of these services by the total number of days of each provided to JTPA enrollees, as measured in JTPA administrative data. The cost of job search assistance estimated in this way was applied to assistance received from both JTPA and non-JTPA sources, as measured in the follow-up survey.

JTPA administrative data were not used to estimate the cost of classroom training in vocational skills and basic education, primarily because JTPA frequently does not pay the full cost of these services. JTPA often obtains such services from public institutions, such as community colleges and high schools, that receive substantial tax subsidies. Therefore, in the follow-up survey, respondents were asked to identify the specific institution at which they received classroom training, and data on the costs of the institutions named were obtained from other sources.

Hourly costs of instruction for each of the public high schools or colleges named in the survey were computed on the basis of institution-specific data compiled by the U.S. Department of Education. The costs of training at private schools and training institutions were not included in the Department of Education data; therefore, a telephone survey was conducted to determine these costs. In the survey, each of the private institutions named by follow-up survey respondents was contacted to obtain their tuition rate. Because private schools receive no tax subsidy, their tuition can be treated as equal to the full social cost of the training they provide. The unit costs derived from these sources were then multiplied by the number of hours of classroom training reported on the follow-up survey to compute a total cost of training for each sample member.

Notes

1. In both cases, the experimental sample was recruited by conducting an in-person survey of households in randomly selected dwellings within randomly selected census tracts at the experimental sites to obtain a sample that was representative of the sites. Those households that were determined to be eligible for the experimental program on the basis of survey responses were then invited to participate.

2. The Health Insurance Experiment researchers contracted with a commercial claims processing company to handle the experimental insurance claims. Those in charge of the income maintenance experiments, however, directly hired and supervised the staffs administering the experimental payment plans.

3. See Kershaw and Fair (1976) for an example of the level of documentation of the income maintenance experiment treatments.

4. Even if the experimental benefits were delivered in exactly the same way they would have been in a regular program, it is possible that the experimental staff communicated the incentives embodied in the treatments more clearly—or less clearly—than would regular program staff; this could affect the response to the experimental treatment.

5. This type of program experience and expertise is, of course, valuable in its own right to ensure that the experiment is well designed as well as to reassure local program staff.

6. It may also be necessary or useful or both to demonstrate that random assignment is legal. In the National JTPA Study and the National Evaluation of the Food Stamp Employment and Training Program, the sponsoring agencies obtained opinions from the departments' chief legal officers that the agencies had legal authority to employ random assignment to evaluate their programs.

7. In some cases, several different organizations must agree to cooperate with the experiment. In the National JTPA Study, for example, it was necessary to obtain not only the agreement of the local Service Delivery Area, the organization that administers JTPA, but also the consent of the local Private Industry Council, which oversees the program, and usually that of one or more local elected officials, such as the mayor or county commissioners. Any one of these groups could effectively veto the study in the local area. This "multiple veto" problem made site recruiting for the study extremely difficult.

8. The expected value of the impact estimate in the absence of exclusions is the weighted average of the estimated impact on those excluded from random assignment and the estimated impact on those randomly assigned, where the weights are their relative proportions. Thus, the bias involved in excluding those who are exempted from random assignment is the difference in the impacts on the two groups multiplied by the proportion of participants exempted from random assignment. This bias will be small as long as the proportion exempted from random assignment is small. Suppose, for example, that 2% of all participants are exempted from random assignment, and that the estimated impact of the program is a 10% increase in the outcome of interest. In the extreme case in which the program has no effect on the outcome for those exempted, the estimated impact will overstate the true impact by 2%; that is, the estimated impact would have been 9.8% percent rather than 10% if the program's zero impact on the exempted individuals had been included in the estimate.

9. As with exclusions from random assignment, the bias due to crossovers will be small if their incidence is small. I discuss the analytic treatment and implications of crossovers later.

10. Program staff frequently gather application information in person, although the applicant is usually required to submit additional documentation, such as a birth certificate and proof of residence.

11. If participation in the experimental training program is voluntary, it may not be necessary to inform program applicants about this at this point. Those assigned to the treatment group could be informed, and invited to participate, at the same time that they are notified of their eligibility for regular program benefits. If the experimental program is mandatory, prospective applicants must be informed that, if randomly selected, they will be required to participate.

12. When staff at sites in the Minority Female Single Parent Program were given a choice between a 1:1 assignment ratio and a 2:1 ratio with a longer period of random assignment, staff at three of the four sites opted for the 1:1 ratio with a shorter random assignment period (Boruch, Dennis, & Carter-Greer, 1988).

13. More generally, the cost of adopting a nonoptimal assignment ratio can be measured by the savings (primarily in data collection costs) that would accrue if a smaller, optimally allocated sample with the same minimum detectable effects were adopted.

14. There are, however, a few exceptions to this rule. In one case, the first assignments were made by literally flipping a coin because the computer algorithm was not yet ready for use. In another study, assignment was made by drawing names from a hat, in the presence of the potential participants, to demonstrate the fairness of the process.

15. This approach had the further advantage that it ensured that baseline data were available for all sample members because they could not enter the study sample (i.e., be randomly assigned) until the baseline interview had been received. It also ensured that the baseline data were not collected after random assignment; as will be shown later, this is an important consideration in the experimental analysis.

16. Other random assignment ratios are readily implemented by using the last two digits of the Social Security number. For example, a 2:1 ratio can be achieved by assigning all those whose Social Security number ends in "67" or less to one group and those whose last two digits are "68" or greater to the other.

17. The software described here was developed by Abt Associates for use in the evaluation of the Head Start Family Service Centers, the National Community Service evaluation, and the Moving to Opportunity demonstration.

18. For individuals who have been previously assigned, the software simply returns the same assignment.

19. If the random assignment ratio were 2:1, rather than 1:1 as in the Figure 5.3, each block would contain four treatment group assignment and two control assignments, in random order.

20. Equivalently, the blocks can be created by the computer as needed. The essential point is that assignments are created in blocks containing a fixed ratio of assignments to the different groups rather than one at a time.

21. This would occur if the first three assignments in the block were all to the same group.

22. In this context, by "ineligible individuals" I mean individuals who are ineligible for random assignment. If random assignment is conducted after eligibility for the program is determined, these individuals are also ineligible for the experimental program. In experiments in which random assignment is conducted early in the intake process, however, individuals who are ineligible for the program could be eligible for random assignment.

23. In this experiment, bad recordkeeping was compounded by a complex design. At the sponsoring agency's suggestion, most of the sites had originally assigned families to three groups: a treatment group, a control group, and a "replacement group," which was intended to be a source of families to replace those that failed to enter the program or dropped out after entry. In some cases, families had been nonrandomly selected from this latter group to replace no-shows and dropouts; these families had to be identified and excluded from the analysis.

24. See the discussion of incremental impacts in Chapter 2.

25. If random assignment is conducted on a decentralized basis, however, this will detect only those who reapply to the same office. In these cases, separate procedures must be established to check each applicant against a master list of controls, as suggested for those who reapply after the end of the random assignment period. One way to eliminate the need to check for previous assignments while ensuring that individuals receive the same assignment when they reapply is to use a random assignment algorithm based on the applicant's Social Security number. Such an algorithm will always return the same assignment to those who reapply. Unfortunately, assignment on the basis of the applicant's Social Security number is incompatible with "blocked" random assignment (discussed previously).

26. Applicants to some youth corps, for example, are required to complete a tryout period that can last as long as 4 weeks before they are accepted as "appropriate" for the corps. Approximately one fourth of the applicants who begin this tryout period drop out before completing it.

27. For a discussion of the issues involved in using administrative data in one specific context—measuring the postprogram earnings of JTPA participants—see Baj and Trott (1991) or Office of Technology Assessment (1994). For a comparison of survey earnings data with administrative earnings records maintained by the UI system, see Kornfeld and Bloom (in press).

28. In this case, one could not even be sure of the direction of the bias. On the one hand, survey respondents are likely to underreport their utilization because of recall error, whereas the

clinic's administrative records will accurately record all care received at the clinic. On the other hand, the clinic's administrative records will miss any care received from other sources.

29. This can occur either because the program produces very little service or because the service it does produce simply displaces service from nonexperimental sources.

30. Note that in both cases, we would attempt to identify services to both the treatment group and the control group.

31. See Orr et al. (1996, Appendix B) for a detailed description of the procedures used to estimate costs in the National JTPA Study.

32. It would have been virtually impossible to measure these services through the follow-up survey because respondents could not reliably distinguish these types of employment from regular jobs.

References

Baj, J., & Trott, C. E. (1991). *A feasibility study of the use of unemployment insurance wage-record data as an evaluation tool for JTPA* (Research Report No. 90-02). Washington, DC: National Commission for Employment Policy.

Boruch, R. F., Dennis, M., & Carter-Greer, K. (1988). Lessons from the Rockefeller Foundation's experiments on the minority female single parent program. *Evaluation Review, 12*(4), 396-426.

Doolittle, F., & Traeger, L. (1990). *Implementing the National JTPA Study.* New York: Manpower Demonstration Research Corporation.

Kershaw, D., & Fair, F. (Eds.). (1976). *The New Jersey Income-Maintenance Experiment. Volume I: Operations, surveys, and administration.* New York: Academic Press.

Kornfeld, R., & Bloom, H. (in press). Measuring program impacts on earnings and employment: Do UI wage reports from employers agree with surveys of individuals? *Journal of Labor Economics.*

Office of Technology Assessment. (1994). *Wage record information systems, OTA-BP-EHR-127.* Washington, DC: U.S. Congress.

Orr, L. L., Bloom, H. S., Bell, S. H., Doolittle, F., Lin, W., & Cave, G. (1996). *Does job training for the disadvantaged work? Evidence from the National JTPA Study.* Washington, DC: Urban Institute Press.

Puma, M. J., DiPietro, J., Rosenthal, J., Connell, D., Judkins, D., & Fox, M. K. (1991). *Study of the impact of WIC on the growth and development of children. Field test: Feasibility assessment* (Final Report: Vol. I). Cambridge, MA: Abt.

Chapter ⑥

Analysis

"If the data were perfect, collected from well-designed randomized experiments, there would be hardly room for a separate field of econometrics."
—*Zvi Griliches, President, American Economic Association, 1993-1994*

One of the strengths of social experiments is the simplicity with which their results can be analyzed. In properly designed and implemented experiments, simple comparisons of the mean outcomes of the treatment and control groups provide unbiased estimates of the effects of the experimental intervention. Complex econometrics is not required to ensure the internal validity of the estimates.

This is not to say, however, that social experiments cannot provide a wide array of useful analyses. In this chapter, I discuss the rich variety of ways in which experimental data can be analyzed to inform the policy process. Specifically, I discuss

◆ The basic impact model
◆ Estimating the time path of impacts
◆ Estimating impacts on subgroups
◆ Estimating and explaining variations in impact across sites
◆ Dealing with potential biases
◆ Analyzing the social benefits and costs of the program.

The Basic Impact Model

As noted previously, the difference in mean outcomes between the treatment and control groups is an unbiased estimate of the impact of the experimental treatment. This estimate, however, is subject to sampling variability that arises from the random assignment of sample members to the two experimental groups. Outcomes depend not only on the experimental treatment but also on the characteristics of individual sample members. In a test of a remedial education program, for example, students' grade point averages in the follow-up period will depend not only on whether they were assigned to the experimental program but also on such individual factors as native ability, the quality of the student's previous education, and his or her home environment.

Random assignment guarantees that the treatment and control groups do not differ systematically in these characteristics, but it does not guarantee that they are identical in these dimensions. Therefore, random differences in the characteristics of the treatment and control groups, depending on the specific individuals assigned to each, contribute to the sampling variability of the impact estimate. Taking account of these differences will reduce this sampling variability and improve the power of the design—that is, it will allow us to detect somewhat smaller program effects than are detectable in a simple difference-in-means analysis.

The simplest way to "control for" or "hold constant" differences in the characteristics of the treatment and control groups is to use multivariate regression analysis to estimate a model of the form

$$Y_i = a + \Sigma b_j X_{ji} + cT_i + e_i \qquad [6.1]$$

where

Y_i = the outcome measure of interest (e.g., grade point average) for the ith individual

X_{ji} = a set of j individual background characteristics (e.g., age, gender, and past educational performance)

T_i = treatment status indicator (a dummy variable equal to 1 if the ith individual is a member of the treatment group and 0 if he or she is a control)

e_i = a random error term

In this model, the coefficient c estimates the impact of the program on this outcome, holding constant the *covariates* included in the set of personal characteristics X_{ji}. This estimate is called the *regression-adjusted impact estimate*. The set of coefficients b_j measures the effects of the various background characteristics on the outcome measure.[1]

The random error term, e_i, reflects the effects of all the individual characteristics and environmental factors not explicitly included in the model. The variance of the error term, $V(e_i)$, is related to the variance of the outcome Y_i according to the relationship

$$V(e_i) = V(Y_i)(1 - R^2) \qquad [6.2]$$

where R^2 is the proportion of the variance of the outcome Y explained by the regression equation.

The variance of the impact estimate c is proportional to $V(e_i)$:

$$V(c) = V(e_i)\left(\frac{n}{n_t n_c}\right) = V(Y_i)\left(1 - R^2\right)\left(\frac{n}{n_t n_c}\right), \qquad [6.3]$$

where n, n_t, and n_c are the total sample size and the number of treatment and control observations, respectively. Controlling for more individual characteristics increases the R^2 of the regression, thereby reducing the variances of e_i and the impact estimate. This, in turn, reduces the minimum effect size that can be detected with a given sample.[2]

Suppose, for example, that in the example of the compensatory education program we are able to explain 20% of the variance of students' grade point averages in the follow-up period on the basis of student attributes not related to program participation. The variance of the regression-adjusted impact estimate will then be 20% smaller than the variance of the simple difference-in-means estimator.[3] This translates into an 11% reduction in the standard error of the estimate and, therefore, an 11% reduction in the minimum detectable effect. This is fairly typical of the gains in precision attainable by controlling for the baseline characteristics of the sample.

Although an 11% reduction in minimum detectable effects may seem relatively small, it is equivalent to the gain in power associated with a 25% increase in sample size. Therefore, if it would be less costly to collect baseline data on characteristics of the sample than to increase the sample by

25% (as is nearly always the case), collecting baseline data on covariates would be a cost-effective investment of research funds.

In most applications, the single baseline characteristic that provides the greatest explanatory power, and therefore the greatest reduction in minimum detectable effects, is the preprogram value of the outcome variable itself. In the case of a compensatory education program, for instance, we would expect grade point average in the year prior to program entry to explain much of the variation across students in postprogram grade point average. This is because the preprogram value incorporates the effects of all the individual characteristics that influence grade point average; to the extent that these characteristics do not vary over time, differences in preprogram values of the outcome across the sample will be good predictors of postprogram differences across the sample. In the National Job Training Partnership Act (JTPA) Study, for example, the earnings of adult sample members in the five calendar quarters prior to random assignment explained approximately 10% of the variance in their postprogram earnings; the addition of a wide variety of other demographic and socioeconomic characteristics increased the explanatory power of the model only by an additional 10 percentage points (Abt Associates, unpublished data).

It is important to bear in mind that only characteristics measured prior to random assignment may be used as covariates in the impact model. Characteristics measured after random assignment could, in principle, be affected by the experimental treatment. If so, controlling for them in the impact regression would capture part of the effect of the program in the coefficients of the covariates, thereby biasing the impact estimate c.

It is also important to note that this basic model estimates the average impact of the program on the entire treatment group. If program impacts are expected to vary within the treatment group, there may be interest in estimating the impacts on subgroups of the sample. Later, I discuss variants on the basic model that can be used to estimate impacts on subgroups in such cases.

Estimating the Time Path of Impacts

In some cases, we expect the impact of a program to vary systematically over time. Many programs involve a short-term investment of time and resources to achieve a longer term goal; for example, training programs divert workers from the labor market while they are in training to increase their longer term earnings. In such cases, we might not expect the program's effects to become evident until the participant has left the program. In other programs, we might expect the strongest effects to occur while the participant is in the program—for example, tutoring programs intended to raise students' school performance. In either type of program, we would be interested to determine whether, and for how long, program effects persist after the participant leaves the program.

Basic Estimation Approach

In the absence of other complications (which will be discussed later), tracing out the time path of program impacts is quite straightforward. One simply uses the basic model presented in the previous section to estimate impacts for each time period (e.g., month, semester, and year) after random assignment.[4] In evaluating a training program, for instance, one might use the participant's earnings in each month after random assignment, seriatim, as the dependent variable in the impact model.[5] This will generate a sequence of monthly impact estimates—one for each month of the follow-up period.

An important point to note is that the data are aligned in terms of number of months after random assignment, not in terms of calendar time. In the training program example, the dependent variable in the first impact regression will be the earnings of each sample member 1 month after random assignment; in the second regression, it will be earnings in the second month after random assignment, and so on. Because sample members will have been randomly assigned at different points in calendar time, each regression may contain observations from a number of different calendar months.

Figure 6.1 shows the results of such an analysis for one of the Aid to Families with Dependent Children (AFDC) Homemaker-Home Health Aide Demonstrations. The two lines in the figure represent the earnings of the treatment and control groups in each month after random assignment. The vertical distance between the two lines in any given month equals the difference in earnings between the two groups in that month, or the estimated impact of the program.[6]

In the homemaker demonstrations, AFDC recipients received 4 to 6 weeks of training as homemaker-home health aides and were then guaranteed employment as aides for up to a year. As can be seen in Figure 6.1, there was little or no impact on earnings in the first several months after random assignment as the trainees participated in the training and awaited placement in their subsidized jobs. Once in subsidized employment, trainees' earnings quickly increased, showing large gains relative to the control group through-

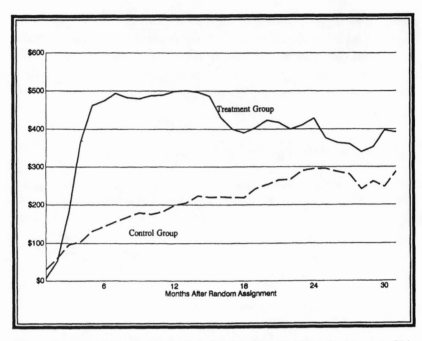

Figure 6.1. Total Monthly Earnings by Month After Random Assignment, Ohio AFDC Homemaker-Home Health Aide Demonstration

out much of the follow-up period. Toward the end of the follow-up period, however, the impact of the program declined slightly for two reasons. First, as trainees left their subsidized jobs, some of them had trouble finding unsubsidized employment, and their earnings declined slightly. Second, throughout the postrandom assignment period, the earnings of the control group steadily rose as many of them found employment even without the help of the demonstration program.

Figure 6.1 reveals that the effect of the experimental program was still relatively large at the end of the follow-up period. Therefore, some of the impact on earnings almost certainly extended beyond the follow-up period so that the evaluation did not capture the full effect of the program. This is important to know in comparing program benefits with program costs. In a program such as the homemaker demonstrations, program costs are incurred at the outset and therefore are fully captured by the evaluation. If some program benefits accrue after the end of the evaluation follow-up period, the evaluation will understate the net benefit of the program if it does not attempt to estimate these benefits. Later, I discuss ways to project program benefits beyond the evaluation follow-up period. For now, I simply note that it is important to determine whether there are likely to be benefits beyond the end of the evaluation follow-up period; estimation of the time path of impacts helps to make this determination.

Estimation Approach When There Are Start-Up Effects

For many new programs, there is an initial period during which staff are learning their roles and responsibilities, and operational problems are being worked out. During this period, the program may not be as effective as it will be once these start-up problems have been resolved. If so, impact estimates that include this initial period will understate the steady-state impact of the program. Moreover, because the length of time the program has been in operation will be positively correlated with time since random assignment, this bias will be strongest for the estimated impacts in the early months after random assignment. This will create the appearance of a more pronounced change in impacts over time than would be the case in a mature program. In evaluations of experimental programs that have been set up especially for purposes of evaluation, it is important to control for start-up effects.

This can be done relatively easily by including in the impact regression an interaction between the treatment status indicator and the length of time the program has been in operation. The following is one such regression specification:

$$Y_i = a + \Sigma b_j X_{ji} + cT_i + d\left(\frac{T_i}{t}\right) + e_i, \qquad [6.4]$$

where t is the length of time the program has been in operation at the point in the follow-up period for which impacts are being estimated. Note that t will vary across individuals because different individuals came into the program at different times relative to the start-up of the program.

In this model, the quantity d/t measures the effect of start-up on the impact of the program; therefore, $(c + d/t)$ measures the actual effect of the program, including start-up effects, when it has been in operation for t periods. The variable t enters the regression in reciprocal form to reflect the fact that start-up effects, by definition, disappear over time. In this specification, as t increases, d/t asymptotically approaches zero.[7] Thus, c is an estimate of the impact of the program in steady state.

In addition to allowing estimation of the time path of impacts of net start-up effects, this formulation provides a direct test for start-up effects. A coefficient d that is significantly different from zero is evidence of start-up effects.

Impacts on Subgroups

Program impacts may vary across individuals, as well as over time, for a variety of reasons. The program may be better suited to some participants; for example, a training program that presumes a minimum level of knowledge of mathematics may not work well for poorly educated trainees. Alternatively, some trainees may not apply themselves as diligently as others and may therefore not gain as much from the program. Also, the variation in impacts may be the result of environmental factors that are completely independent of the characteristics of the program or its participants. A training program may have large impacts on earnings in a locality with a booming economy, where there is ample demand for its graduates, but little effect in a locality where unemployment is high and demand for labor slack.

Knowledge of such variations in impact across individuals or localities can help policymakers in two ways. First, it can help them target the program to those individuals or areas where its impact will be greatest. Second, it can pinpoint weaknesses in the program that need to be addressed by identifying those participants for whom the program is ineffective.

As noted in Chapter 1, experiments cannot measure program impacts on specific individuals; they can estimate average impacts only on groups of individuals. Experiments, however, can be used quite flexibly to estimate impacts on subgroups of the overall sample that are of interest for policy. In the following sections, I consider the opportunities presented by subgroup analysis as well as the limitations of this analytic approach.

Basic Estimation Approach

We can estimate impacts on any subgroup that can be defined on the basis of baseline characteristics—that is, on the basis of data collected prior to random assignment—simply by applying the basic model in Equation 6.1 to this subgroup of treatment and control group members. If, for example, we wish to know whether the program was more effective for men than for women, we can simply divide the sample into the two gender subgroups and run separate regressions on each.

As noted previously, characteristics measured after random assignment may be affected by the experimental treatment; if so, they will define noncomparable subgroups of the treatment and control groups. Suppose, for instance, that we wish to know the impact of a training program on participants who moved out of the area after they left the program. We could divide the treatment and control groups into movers and stayers and estimate the regression-adjusted treatment-control differences in outcomes within each of these two subgroups. Suppose, however, that participation in the program encouraged the more highly motivated treatment group members to move out of the area to seek a better job. Among movers, members of the treatment group, on average, will be more highly motivated than the control group members, and their outcomes will be better because of this selection factor, regardless of the effects of the program. Thus, the treatment-control difference in outcomes among movers will provide an upward-biased measure of the impact of the program. Among stayers, the opposite will be true: The treatment group members will be less motivated than controls, on average, and the difference in outcomes between the two groups will understate the effects of the program.[8]

Fortunately, for the first purpose of subgroup analysis noted previously (targeting of program services), only subgroups defined on the basis of baseline characteristics are relevant. This follows from the fact that program managers can obviously target the program only on subgroups that can be identified prior to program entry. Even for the second purpose noted previously (weaknesses in the program), subgroups defined on the basis of baseline characteristics provide a wide array of participant types for analysis.

Separate estimation of impacts for different subgroups provides unbiased estimates of those impacts and a test of statistical significance for each. That is, for each subgroup taken by itself, we can test whether the estimated impact differs from zero by more than could be expected by chance alone. Such tests do not, however, indicate directly whether the difference in impacts among subgroups is greater than could be expected on the basis of random sampling variability.

Consider, for example, the estimated impacts of JTPA on the earnings of subgroups of women on welfare, shown in Table 6.1. The fact that the estimated impact on the earnings of women who had received welfare for 2 years or more is significantly different from zero means that we can be confident that the program had a positive effect for this subgroup. We cannot

Table 6.1   Impacts on Earnings of Adult Women, by AFDC Experience

Subgroup	Estimated Impact ($)
Never on AFDC	883
On AFDC < 2 years	1,582
On AFDC > 2 years	3,519*

SOURCE: Orr et al. (1996).
*Estimated impact statistically significantly different from zero at the 10% level.

have equal confidence that the program was effective for those who had been on welfare less than 2 years; the fact that this estimate is not statistically significantly different from zero at our chosen level of significance indicates that we cannot be confident that the program had a positive effect on their earnings, the positive estimate notwithstanding.

This does not mean, however, that we can be confident that the program had a greater impact on the earnings of longer term welfare recipients than on those of shorter term recipients, even though the latter estimate is much smaller and is not significantly different from zero. To compare two impact estimates, we must test whether the difference between them is significantly different from zero. This test depends on the sampling error of the difference between the two estimates, which in turn is a function of the sampling errors of the two estimates. We can compute the standard error of estimate of the difference between impact estimates for two independent subgroups as:[9]

$$SE(I_a - I_b) = \sqrt{SE_a^2 + SE_b^2} \qquad [6.5]$$

where SE_a and SE_b are the standard errors of the two impact estimates, and $SE(I_a - I_b)$ is the standard error of the difference between them. A t statistic to determine the statistical significance of the difference can be computed as follows:

$$t = \frac{I_a - I_b}{SE(I_a - I_b)} \qquad [6.6]$$

That is, the difference between the two impact estimates divided by the standard error of that difference.

When this test is applied to the estimated impacts in Table 6.2, it can be seen that the earnings gains of longer term recipients were not significantly larger than those of shorter term recipients. This type of finding is fairly common in subgroup analysis. One frequently finds that, although one can be confident of a positive impact for one subgroup and cannot be sure the program had any effect for another, one cannot determine that the program had a larger effect on the former group than on the latter.

This reflects the fact that a more powerful design is required to distinguish between two estimates, both of which are measured with some sampling error, than to distinguish between a single estimate and a fixed point (zero). If comparisons between subgroups are likely to be important in the analysis, this should be taken into account in the design of the experiment, and a sufficiently large sample should be randomly assigned to provide adequate power to detect subgroup differences that are of practical importance.

Estimating Subgroup Impacts Jointly

An alternative to estimating separate impact regressions for each subgroup is to estimate the impacts for the various subgroups jointly in a single regression equation of the following form:

$$Y_i = a + \Sigma b_j X_{ji} + \Sigma g_k Z_{ik} T_i + e_i \qquad [6.7]$$

where Z_{ik} equals 1 if the ith sample member belongs to the kth subgroup and is zero otherwise. This is the basic impact model introduced previously, with the single treatment status indicator T_i replaced by a set of subgroup dummies interacted with the treatment status indicator. In this model, the impact of the program on Y for the kth subgroup is given by g_k.

This approach has two advantages over estimation of separate equations for each subgroup. First, it usually provides more power because it uses the full sample to estimate the a and b coefficients.[10] Second, it allows one to test whether there are statistically significant differences in impact among the subgroups taken as a set (rather than between pairs of subgroups).

To test for significant differences among subgroups, one performs an *F test* on the g_k coefficients. The F statistic can be used to test the null hypothesis that the g_k coefficients are all equal. Detailed explanation of the F test is beyond the scope of this book; in essence, however, it tests whether adding the Z_{ik} variables to the impact model significantly improves its explanatory power. If the F test rejects the null hypothesis, we can be confident that program impacts vary across the subgroups, although we cannot be sure which subgroups' impacts differ without conducting pairwise tests of significance.[11] An efficient analysis strategy is to conduct F tests on each of the sets of subgroups of interest (e.g., subgroups defined by gender and those defined by ethnicity) and then, if desired, conduct pairwise significance tests within the sets in which the F test rejects equality of impacts.

Interpreting the Results of Multiple Tests

There may be policy interest in a large number of participant subgroups and, in fact, many studies estimate impacts for large numbers of subgroups. Although this is perfectly legitimate, in doing so one must be cognizant of the implications of performing large numbers of significance tests for the interpretation of the individual estimates.

Suppose, for example, that one estimates impacts for 20 subgroups and performs a t test on each at the 10% significance level. At this significance level, each test has a 10% chance of rejecting the null hypothesis of no effect when it is in fact true—that is, of producing a false-positive result. Therefore, even if there were no true program impacts in any of the subgroups, in 20 tests one would expect, on average, 2 positive test results due to sampling error alone. This has several implications for the interpretation of the test results.

First, if the proportion of impact estimates that are significantly different from zero is close to the significance level (in this case, 10%, or 2 of 20 estimates), there is a strong possibility that they represent false-positive tests. One cannot be sure, of course, that this is the case because there is no assurance that the actual number of false-positive tests will equal the expected number in any specific sample.

Second, even if the number of estimates that are significantly different from zero is larger than the number that would be expected by chance alone, one must bear in mind that some of these are likely to be false-positive results. Suppose, for example, that the null hypothesis is rejected in 6 of 20 tests at the 10% significance level. On average, we would expect approximately 2 of these 6, or one third of the statistically significant estimates, to be false positives.[12] Again, one cannot know the actual number of false positives in any given set of tests; we do know that, on average, some will be present.

Third, and perhaps most important, we cannot know which of the test results are likely to be erroneous. We know only that, among those subgroups with impact estimates that are significantly different from zero, the probability that the null hypothesis has been rejected incorrectly is higher than would be indicated by the significance level of the individual test.

The risk of false-positive test results when large numbers of tests are conducted suggests that experimenters should exercise restraint in the number of subgroups for which they estimate impacts and caution in the interpretation of the test results. In particular, I caution against "fishing" for subgroup impacts. Frequently, when the estimated impacts for the sample as a whole are not significantly different from zero, researchers begin estimating impacts for subgroups in search of positive impacts. If enough subgroup impacts are estimated, some estimates that are significantly different from zero will almost certainly be found; as the foregoing discussion indicates, however, these may simply reflect false-positive test results.

One way to reduce the danger of false-positive test results for a given number of subgroup estimates is to reduce the significance level of the test—that is, to impose a more stringent test. Suppose, for instance, that the significance tests in the previous example were conducted at the 5% level rather than the 10% level. At this significance level, we would expect only one false positive if there were no true nonzero impacts in any of the 20 subgroups.

Unfortunately, there is no simple rule for deciding on the reduction in significance level required to offset the performance of multiple tests. This is a complex issue that depends on, among other things, the number of tests, the number of true nonzero impacts among the subgroups analyzed, and the power of the design.

Multiple Tests: An Illustrative Example

To illustrate the principles discussed previously, Tables 6.2 and 6.3 present the results of a set of subgroup analyses performed in the National JTPA Study. Table 6.2 shows the estimated impacts of JTPA on the earnings of a number of subgroups of adult men, along with two types of significance test: t tests of the difference of the estimated impact from zero in each subgroup and F tests of the difference in impacts within each set of subgroups defined by a single baseline characteristic (e.g., three different ethnic groups).

Table 6.2 shows that the estimated impact of JTPA on the overall sample was a $978 increase in earnings. This estimate was significantly different

---

TABLE 6.2 Estimated JTPA Impacts on Earnings: Subgroups of Adult Men

Subgroup Defined by	Estimated Impact ($)
Full sample	978*
Ethnicity	
White, non-Hispanic	707
Black, non-Hispanic	931
Hispanic	1,784
F test, difference among subgroups	ns[a]
Welfare status	
Receiving cash welfare	305
No cash welfare	1,529*
F test, difference among subgroups	ns
Education	
High school diploma or GED certificate	931
No high school diploma or GED certificate	1,353
F test, difference among subgroups	ns
Recent work experience	
Worked < 13 weeks in past 12 months	735
Worked 13 weeks or more in past 12 months	1,140
F test, difference among subgroups	ns
Work history	
Never employed	−2,104
Earned < $4/hour in last job	245
Earned $4/hour or more in last job	1,647*
F test, difference among subgroups	ns
Household composition	
No spouse present	248
Spouse present	2,759*
F test, difference among subgroups	*
Family income in past 12 months	
$6,000 or less	733
More than $6,000	1,556*
F test, difference among subgroups	ns
Age at random assignment	
22-29	1,221
30-54	1,151
F test, difference among subgroups	ns

Source: Orr et al. (1996). Used with permission.
a. ns, estimate not significantly different at the 10% level.
*Estimate significantly different from zero at the 10% significance level.

from zero at the 10% significance level (as indicated by the asterisk). Next, the table shows estimated impacts for three ethnic subgroups. Although the estimated impacts for two of these subgroups are larger than the estimated

TABLE 6.3 Estimated JTPA Impacts on Earnings: Subgroups of Adult Women

Subgroup Defined by	Estimated Impact ($)
Full sample	1,837*
Ethnicity	
White, non-Hispanic	1,973*
Black, non-Hispanic	1,927*
Hispanic	467
F test, difference among subgroups	ns
Welfare status	
Receiving cash welfare[a]	2,359*
No cash welfare	1,634*
F test, difference among subgroups	ns
Education	
No high school diploma or GED certificate	1,499
High school diploma or GED certificate	1,753*
F test, difference among subgroups	ns
Recent work experience	
Worked < 13 weeks in past 12 months	2,100*
Worked 13 weeks or more in past 12 months	1,029
F test, difference among subgroups	ns
Work history	
Never employed	1,270
Earned < $4 hourly in last job	1,437
Earned $4 or more hourly in last job	2,540*
F test, difference among subgroups	ns
AFDC history	
Never AFDC case head	883
AFDC case head < 2 years	1,582
AFDC case head 2 years or more	3,519*
F test, difference among subgroups	ns
JTPA required for welfare, food stamps, or WIN program	
Yes	2,190
No	1,560*
F test, difference among subgroups	ns
Household composition	
No spouse or own child present	920
Own child under age 4, no spouse present	2,519*
Own child age 4 or older, no spouse present	598
Spouse present, with or without own children	2,617*
F test, difference among subgroups	ns
Family income in past 12 months	
$6,000 or less	1,199*
More than $6,000	2,448*
F test, difference among subgroups	ns
Age at random assignment	
22-29	1,746*
30-54	2,020*
> 54	833
F test, difference among subgroups	ns

SOURCE: Orr et al. (1996). Used with permission.
NOTE: WIN, Work Incentive program; ns, estimate not significantly different at the 10% significance level.
a. AFDC, General Assistance, or other welfare except food stamps.
*Estimate significantly different from zero at the 10% significance level.

impact on the overall sample (one of them substantially so), none of the subgroup estimates are significantly different from zero. This reflects the smaller sample sizes, and therefore reduced power, available at the subgroup level. Also, although the estimates vary substantially across subgroups, the F test shows that they do not differ significantly at the 10% level.

Interpretation of these results is as follows. We can be reasonably confident that JTPA had a positive effect on the earnings of adult men; the best estimate of this effect is an earnings gain of $978. When we consider any individual ethnic group (e.g., white men), however, we cannot be sure that the program had a positive effect. Our best estimate of the program's impact on the earnings of white men is a $707 gain, but the chance that there was no true effect in this subgroup is >10%. Also, although our best estimate of the program's impact on the earnings of Hispanic men is more than twice as large as the estimated impact on white men's earnings, we cannot confidently rule out the possibility that the program had the same impact on all three ethnic groups.

When we break the sample down by welfare status (Table 6.2), a similar pattern emerges. Setting aside the issue of multiple tests (to which I return momentarily), the test results here indicate that the program increased the earnings of men who were not receiving welfare at baseline; our best estimate of this gain is $1,529. We cannot be sure that men who were receiving welfare at baseline were helped by the program, although our best estimate for this subgroup is an earnings gain of $305. Also, despite the substantial difference between these two estimates, we cannot be confident that the former group gained more than the latter (as indicated by the F test); the difference in estimates could simply reflect sampling error.

The other data in Table 6.2 display similar patterns. The only breakdown for which a significant difference in impacts among subgroups emerges is that based on household composition. Here, the F test indicates that men with spouses present experienced significantly greater earnings gains than those with no spouses. This conclusion cannot be drawn with certainty, however. This is the only one of eight breakdowns tested to show a significant difference among subgroups; at the 10% level of significance, we would expect about one of eight F tests to reject the null hypothesis of no effect by chance alone. Thus, there is a good chance that this is a false-positive test result.

We can have somewhat more confidence in the conclusion that several of the individual subgroups of men experienced positive program impacts. Overall, Table 6.2 shows estimates for 18 different subgroups. If there were no true impacts at the subgroup level, we would expect approximately 2 of the estimates to be significantly different from zero at the 10% level by chance alone; in fact, 4 are different. Thus, it seems likely that at least 1 or 2 of the impact estimates that are significantly different from zero represent real effects. Among these estimates, however, we have no way to distinguish those that represent real effects from those that are false-positive test results.

Therefore, we must conclude that, although we can be confident that JTPA had a positive overall effect on the earnings of adult men, this experiment was not sufficiently powerful to identify the specific subgroups of adult men who benefited most from the program—or even to identify which ones benefited at all. This example illustrates the limits of subgroup analysis. The National JTPA Study sample included more than 5,000 adult men. Even this large sample, however, was not sufficient to allow precise estimation of impacts within subgroups. This is in part the result of the high variance of the outcome being analyzed (earnings) and in part a reflection of the relatively small impacts of the program in this demographic group.

A much clearer set of subgroup results was obtained for adult women in the National JTPA Study.[13] As shown in Table 6.3, in 15 of the 26 subgroups for which impacts on earnings were analyzed, the estimated impacts were significantly different from zero. Thus, we can be reasonably confident that the program had positive effects for these subgroups. Our ability to detect these effects is partly due to the slightly larger sample size for adult women (approximately 6,000) and partly the result of somewhat larger program effects among adult women than among adult men (an estimated overall effect of $1,837 for women compared with $978 for men). Even for adult women, however, the experiment was not powerful enough to detect differences among subgroup impacts of the size that actually occurred, as indicated by lack of significance of the F tests of differences among subgroups in Table 6.3.

Explaining Variation in Impacts Across Sites

One set of subgroups in which there is often great interest is the samples of program participants at different sites. In multisite experiments, the impact of the program may vary across sites for a variety of reasons. The most obvious is that the program may be implemented differently—either deliberately or inadvertently—at the different sites. Impacts may also vary, however, because of differences in the participant population that allow those at some sites to benefit more from the program or because the local environment (e.g., the labor market or the educational system) is more conducive to positive impacts at some sites. Distinguishing among these causes of variation—indeed, even determining whether there is meaningful variation across sites—is not a simple task.

Determining Whether There Is Meaningful Cross-Site Variation

Even in a perfectly designed and implemented experiment, the impact estimate for any given set of sample members will differ from the true impact of the program because of random sampling error. Thus, even if all sites were identical in terms of the experimental program, the program participants, and the local environment, we would expect them to yield different impact estimates due to sampling error alone. The first question that must be addressed with respect to site-specific impacts is whether the estimates differ by more than could be expected on the basis of chance alone.

The treatment group members at each site can be viewed as a subgroup of the overall treatment group. Thus, the subgroup estimation techniques and significance tests discussed previously can be applied directly to the analysis of site-specific impacts. That is, one can estimate site-specific impacts with an equation of the form given by Equation 6.7 and use an F test to determine whether these estimates differ significantly. Only if the F test rejects the null hypothesis that the true impact is the same at all sites does the experiment provide evidence of variation in impact across sites.

Table 6.4 shows an illustrative set of site-specific estimates taken from the National JTPA Study. The table shows estimated impacts for four major demographic groups for each of the 16 sites in the study.[14] As can be seen, even though the estimates vary widely across sites within each demographic group, in no case are they significantly different from one another (see F test results). As is always the case when a test of significance fails to reject the null hypothesis, this does not mean that the impact of the program does not vary across sites; it simply means that the experimental design was not powerful enough to detect any variation that did occur.

This example illustrates the difficulty of confidently estimating differences in impact across sites. Site-specific estimates are much less precise than estimates based on the overall sample because of the much smaller samples

TABLE 6.4 Site-Specific Impacts on Earnings, by Target Group—National JTPA Study

		Earnings ($)		
Site	Adult Women	Adult Men	Female Youth	Male Youth
1	2,628	5,310*	3,372*	9,473*
2	2,308*	4,338	2,320	5,464
3	2,095	3,908	1,404	1,918
4	1,786*	2,533	1,222	1,414
5	1,190	2,335	649	1,192
6	1,181	2,197	556	1,090
7	1,109	1,655	244	973
8	1,069	1,540	117	119
9	884	1,212	–432	–204
10	787	721	–1,064	–1,298
11	309	710	–1,298	–2,206
12	–438	630	–1,471	–2,876
13	–1,108	–484	–2,179	–3,029
14	–1,369	–1,083	–2,355	–4,147
15	–1,410	–2,412	–3,821*	–5,836
16	–2,033	–2,637	—	—
F test, difference among sites	ns	ns	ns	ns

SOURCE: Orr et al. (1996). Used with permission.
NOTE: Sites were ranked separately for each target group in order of size of estimated impact. Therefore, listings for different target groups in the same row do not necessarily refer to the same site. No youth were assigned at one site.
ns, Differences among sites not statistically different from zero at the 10% level.
*Significantly different from zero at the 10% level.

available at the site level. In this case, even with overall sample sizes as large as 6,000, the samples available at individual sites are too small (relative to the variance of the outcome of interest) to provide sufficient power to confidently identify whatever differences in impact exist across sites.

Explaining Cross-Site Differences in Impacts

Even when it is determined from the experiment that impacts differ significantly across sites, this finding is not, by itself, very helpful to policymakers. To be useful for policy, the analysis must explain why program effects were different at different sites. If the differences are due to differences in the local environment or participant population—factors that are outside the policymakers' control—analysis of site-specific impacts may be helpful in predicting the impact of implementing the program in other localities, but it will not help design a more effective program.[15] Only if the differences are due to differences in the implementation of the program across sites will knowledge of cross-site differences be useful for program design. In this case, policymakers can adopt those program features that maximize program impact.

Analysis of site-level impacts may well be the weakest area of the current practice of program evaluation, both experimental and nonexperimental. All too often, the analysis of variations in impact across sites proceeds as follows. The investigators perform significance tests on estimates of site-specific impacts to identify those that are significantly different from zero. These sites are then assumed to have larger impacts than those with estimated impacts that are not significantly different from zero—without benefit of the appropriate significance test. Finally, the researchers attribute this "difference" in impacts to whatever difference in site characteristics seems most salient to them—usually some feature of the program being evaluated—without testing for other potential causes of variation in impact.

This approach is subject to two potential errors. First, as noted previously, there may be no real difference in impacts across sites, even if some site-specific estimates are significantly different from zero and others are not. Second, even if there are real differences, they may be the result of any number of differences in the local site environment or participant characteristics rather than differences in the program being evaluated. Only through careful statistical analysis can we be confident that (a) there are real differences in impacts and (b) we know why they occurred.

A more rigorous approach to analysis of site-level impacts attempts to test formally whether impacts vary with program characteristics, holding constant characteristics of the local environment and program participants. We perform this analysis by estimating an impact model of the form

$$Y_i = a + \Sigma\, b_j\, X_{ji} + c T_i + \Sigma\, d_j\, X_{ji}\, T_i \qquad [6.8]$$
$$+ \Sigma\, f_k\, S_{ki} + \Sigma\, h_k\, S_{ki}\, T_i + \Sigma\, p_m\, P_{mi} + \Sigma\, q_m\, P_{mi}\, T_i + e_i\,,$$

where

S_{ki} = a set of k characteristics of the site in which sample member i lives (e.g., the local unemployment rate and average wages)

P_{mi} = a set of m characteristics of the experimental program in the site in which sample member i lives (e.g., type or duration of training and availability of support services)

The j variables X_{ji} measure the personal characteristics of sample member i and T_i indicates whether the sample member is a treatment or control group member.

Inclusion of the interactions of X_{ji} and S_{ki} with T_i allows the estimated impacts to vary with individual and site characteristics, thereby capturing that portion of the cross-site variation in impacts explained by these factors rather than by variations in the experimental program. The interaction of P_{mi} with treatment status allows us to test whether impacts vary with program characteristics, holding constant individual and site characteristics. The coefficients q_m measure this variation, and the significance tests on these coefficients provide a measure of the confidence we can have that program impacts truly vary with each program characteristic—again holding constant individual and site characteristics. (X_{ji}, S_{ki}, and P_{mi} are also included in the impact equation without interactions to capture any variation in the outcome with these characteristics that are common to both the treatment and the control group members.)

Suppose, for example, that we have found (by estimating an impact model such as that in Equation 6.7, with sites as the subgroups) that the impact of an experimental training program varies across sites. On the basis of our knowledge of the experimental programs at the various sites, we might hypothesize that the more successful programs had larger impacts because they provided more intensive training or because they provided better support services for the trainees. Without further tests, however, we could not rule out the alternative explanations that the participants in the successful sites were better able to take advantage of the training because of their personal characteristics or because the local labor market was particularly favorable for graduates of this type of training program.[16]

To test these hypotheses, we would estimate a regression equation of the form shown in Equation 6.8. The X_{ji} variables would include such personal characteristics as education and work experience that might influence the individual's ability to benefit from training. The S_{ki} variables would include such site characteristics as the unemployment rate and the rate of growth of employment, which might affect the returns to training in the local labor market. Finally, the P_{mi} variables would include programmatic features that might influence the program's effectiveness. These could include the length of the training course, the percentage of the training staff with recent private-sector experience in the skills being taught, or the amount spent on supportive services per trainee.

If the coefficient of one or more of the P_{mi} variables in this model is significantly different from zero, then (subject to the qualifications discussed in the following section), we can be reasonably sure that variation in this program feature affects program impacts. Policymakers can use this information to improve the effectiveness of the program.

Limitations on Our Ability to
Explain Cross-Site Variations in Impact

The model described in the previous section is subject to several important qualifications. First, it is important to note that the estimate of variation in impact with program characteristics provided by this model is essentially nonexperimental. The variation in program characteristics we observe is natural variation and may therefore be correlated with other unobserved factors that affect the outcomes of interest. If so, the variation in impacts across sites may be due to these unobserved factors rather than to the program. That is, our estimates of the influence of program features on impacts are potentially subject to selection bias. We cannot, therefore, have the same confidence in them that we have in the overall impact estimates, which are fully experimental. For this reason, if testing alternative program features is an important objective of the research, the experimenter should consider designs of the type discussed in Chapter 3 in which multiple program variants are implemented at the same site (to hold site effects constant) and participants are randomly assigned to alternative variants (to eliminate systematic differences in participant characteristics across treatments).

The second important limitation of this model is that the number of program features that can be tested is limited by the number of sites. If we were to include in the impact model as many program features as there are sites, the model would explain the variation in impact across sites perfectly— not because we have found the real explanation for cross-site differences but because we have provided a different explanation for the level of impacts at each site. In effect, the number of observations available to estimate the effect of any variable that does not vary within a site is equal to the number of sites. Also, it is a general proposition in econometrics that one must have more observations than the number of coefficients to be estimated. Therefore, the maximum number of site-level variables (i.e., both site and program characteristics) that can be included in the equation is one less than the number of sites.

This is often a severe limitation. Most experimental programs are implemented at a relatively small number of sites: It is unusual for evaluations to include more than 10 sites. In contrast, the experimental sites and programs can differ in literally hundreds of ways. Thus, the analyst is faced with the problem of choosing a small number of site and program characteristics to be tested from among the large number that could potentially affect program impacts. It is important to note that the limit on the number of variables that can be tested includes both site characteristics and program features. Because it is generally important to control for at least a few site characteristics, the number of program features that can be tested will usually be quite small.

Nor can one increase the number of program features analyzed by estimating the impact model repeatedly, testing different sets of site-level characteristics seriatim. Such fishing invalidates the significance tests associated with the impact estimates. If enough characteristics are tested, one can be sure of finding some effects that are significantly different from zero by chance alone.[17]

Moreover, both the number of site-level variables that can be included in the impact model and the power of the impact model to detect the effects of site-level factors, including program characteristics, depend on the number of *degrees of freedom* available to model these variables: This number is equal to the number of sites minus one. The number of site-level variables in the model cannot exceed this number (e.g., if there are 10 sites, at most 9 site-level variables can be included in the model). Moreover, within this constraint, the more site-level variables that are included, the less power the model will have to detect variation in impact with site characteristics.

Given these stringent limitations on the number of site-level variables that can be tested rigorously, it is perhaps understandable that, as noted previously, many analysts simply assume that differences in site-specific impacts are caused by whatever differences in the program seem most salient to the researcher. In an experiment with only three or four sites, it is generally relatively easy to find some program characteristic that correlates with the differences in impacts across sites without any formal analysis. The problem is that there may be many site and program characteristics that correlate with these differences and, with a small number of sites, there is no way to choose from among them the real cause of variations in impact.

The correct conclusion to be drawn in such cases is that the experiment is simply not capable of providing an explanation for the variation in impacts across sites. The lesson to be drawn for experimental design is that, if policymakers are interested in the effects of program variants, either the experimental program should be implemented in a large number of sites or, preferably, the experiment should be explicitly designed to compare alternative program designs within the same locality.

Dealing With Potential Biases

Properly implemented and analyzed, experiments provide unbiased estimates of the impact of the experimental program. Like all other forms of research, however, in practice experiments are subject to a variety of imperfections that require attention at the analysis stage. In this section, I discuss several of the most common problems that can create bias in the experimental estimates: control group members who receive the experimental treatment ("crossovers"), differences in random assignment ratios across sites or over time, missing follow-up data, and inferring the effects of a permanent program from a limited-duration experiment. The discussion of these problems is necessarily brief, intended more as an introduction to the issues involved than as a comprehensive treatment of the problems and their solutions.

Crossovers

As noted in Chapter 2, the experimental estimates will be biased if controls receive an amount or type of service that they would not have received in the absence of the experiment. Control group contamination that takes the form of nonexperimental services similar to the experimental treatment is virtually impossible to detect because, in general, we do not know what level of these services controls would have received in the absence of the experiment—this is, after all, the purpose of the control group. We can, however, measure—and in some cases correct for—control group contamination in the form of controls receiving the experimental treatment. Such controls are termed *crossovers*.

Crossovers can occur for a number of reasons, depending on the institutional context of the experiment. A simple example is the case of an individual who applies to a program, is assigned to the control group, and then later reapplies. If the experiment does not adequately monitor for applications by controls, the individual may be randomly assigned again or, if random assignment has ended and the program is ongoing, he or she may simply be admitted to the program.[18] After the fact, it is usually possible to detect such crossovers by matching the experiment's random assignment records against the program's administrative records.

Some analysts simply include crossovers in the treatment group or exclude them from the analysis altogether. Either of these approaches is likely to destroy the comparability of the treatment and control groups, leading to biased impact estimates. Fortunately, in at least some circumstances it is possible to correct for the influence of crossovers on the impact estimates derived from the entire experimental sample, with crossovers included in the control group.

We can correct for the effect of crossovers on the experimental impact estimates if we can assume that the program had the same effect on crossovers that it would have had if they had been assigned to the treatment group (the following derivation is based on Bloom, 1986). Under this assumption, the outcomes of the crossovers can be expected to be the same (on average) as those of a corresponding set of "crossover-like" individuals in the treatment group. Although we cannot identify this latter group, we know that it exists because under random assignment every subgroup of the control group has a matching subgroup in the treatment group. Also, because the average outcomes of the crossovers and the crossover-like subgroup of the treatment group are, under this assumption, the same, the estimated program impact on crossover-like individuals is zero.

We can express the estimated impact on the overall treatment group, I, as a weighted average of the impact on crossover-like individuals, I_c, and the impact on all other treatment group members, I_o:

$$I = cI_c + (1 - c)I_o \qquad [6.9]$$

where c is the proportion of the control group that crossed over. Because, as noted previously, the estimated impact on crossover-like individuals, I_c, is zero, Equation 6.9 reduces to

$$I = (1 - c)I_0 \qquad [6.10]$$

which can be solved for I_0:

$$I_0 = \frac{I}{(I - c)} \qquad [6.11]$$

Thus, a simple adjustment—similar to the no-show adjustment discussed in Chapter 2—is available to remove the effect of crossovers from the impact estimates. Under the maintained assumption, I_0 is an unbiased estimate of the impact of the experimental program on non-crossover-like individuals. Like the no-show adjustment, the crossover adjustment requires no assumption about the nature of the crossovers. In particular, one need not assume that they are similar to the rest of the control group.

As noted previously, however, one does have to assume that the program had the same effect on crossovers as it would have had if they had been assigned to the treatment group (and therefore the same effect as it had on crossover-like members of the treatment group). This is a relatively strong assumption, which will not always be satisfied. Consider, for example, the case of a compensatory education program that lasts for a year. At midyear, through an administrative oversight, some control students are transferred into the classroom of students receiving experimental services. These transfer students are clearly crossovers, but they do not receive the full experimental treatment; therefore, the experimental program probably does not have the same effect on their outcomes it would have had if they had been assigned to the treatment group and had been in the experimental classroom since the beginning of the year.

In such cases of partial treatment, the best that can be done is a sensitivity analysis of the effect of crossovers on the overall impact estimate. Such an analysis is conducted by assuming alternative values of the impact on crossover-like individuals, relative to the rest of the treatment group. Suppose, for example, that we assume that the effect on crossovers was two thirds the effect on non-crossover-like individuals. Substituting $.67I_0$ for I_c in Equation 6.9 yields

$$I = c(.67I_0) + (1 - c)I_0 \qquad [6.12]$$
$$= (1 - .33c)I_o$$

and

$$I_o = \frac{I}{(1 - .33c)} \qquad [6.13]$$

Substitution of other values, ranging from no effect to effects equal to the impact on the rest of the treatment group, will trace out the range of possible effects on non-crossover-like individuals.

It is important to note that the crossover-adjusted estimate of impact applies only to non-crossover-like sample members and not to the entire population randomly assigned. This is an unfortunate but unavoidable limitation of the results: Because we did not observe crossover-like individuals in a true control condition, there is no way to estimate program impacts on their outcomes. This limitation highlights the importance of taking the steps described in Chapter 5 to minimize the likelihood that crossovers will occur.

Variations in the Random Assignment Ratio

For operational reasons, it sometimes becomes necessary to change the random assignment ratio part way through the experiment. For example, in the National JTPA Study staff at some sites encountered great difficulty recruiting a sufficient number of youths both to fill the available program slots and to provide for a control group. To secure the continued participation of these sites in the evaluation, the researchers temporarily changed the random assignment ratio from 1 control for every 2 treatment group members to 1 control for every 3 or 6 treatment group members (depending on the site). This reduced the number of youths the staff at these sites were required to recruit while still allowing them to fill all program slots. It also injected a potential bias into the sample, however.

For example, consider a simple experiment in which 100 sample members are to be assigned to the treatment group in each of two time periods. Suppose that in the first period one control is assigned for every treatment group member, whereas in the second period one control is assigned for every two treatment group members. The resulting sample distribution will be as follows:

	Time Period 1	Time Period 2
Treatment group	100	100
Control group	100	50

In the resulting sample, half of the treatment group is assigned in each period, whereas two thirds of the control group is assigned in the first period and one third in the second period. Thus, the treatment and control groups are not well matched in terms of time of assignment. If outcomes differ systematically over time (e.g., if there are time trends in the outcomes), this confounding of treatment and time of assignment will bias the experimental estimates. A similar bias would occur if different random assignment ratios were used in different sites and outcomes differed systematically across sites.

There are several ways to deal with this potential bias. The simplest is to randomly remove 50 treatment group members from the sample in the second period to equalize the treatment-control ratio in the two periods.[19] (It is important that the sample members to be excluded be selected randomly to preserve the match between the treatment and control groups within the second period.) Although this approach restores the match between the overall treatment and control groups, it is inefficient in that it does not use the available information on the individuals excluded from the sample.[20]

An analytic approach that uses all the available data to estimate unbiased impact estimates when random assignment ratios vary is to estimate the impact of the program within each random assignment "stratum" (i.e., within each subsample assigned under the same random assignment ratio) and then compute the impact on the overall treatment group as the weighted average of the stratum-specific impacts. Because the treatment and control groups within each stratum are well matched, this yields an unbiased impact estimate.

A number of different weighting schemes can be used to obtain the overall impact estimate. For example, weighting the estimated impact in each stratum by the proportion of the total sample in that stratum will yield an unbiased estimate of program impact for the population represented by the total sample. Alternatively, under the assumption that the impacts are the same for all strata, the minimum variance estimate of the overall impact is produced by using weights that are inversely proportional to the variances of the stratum-specific estimates.

Stratum-specific impact estimates can, of course, be obtained by estimating separate regressions for each stratum. Alternatively, under the assumption that the effects of the covariates are the same in all strata, all the stratum-specific impact estimates can be obtained from a single regression of the form

$$Y_i = a + \sum_{j=1}^{j=J} b X_{ji} + \sum_{k=2}^{k=K} c_k S_{ki} + \sum_{k=1}^{k=K} d_k S_{ki} T_i + e_i, \qquad [6.14]$$

where Y_i, X_{ji}, and T_i are, respectively, the outcome of interest, the personal characteristics, and the treatment status of the ith individual, and S_{ki} is a dummy variable that equals 1 if the ith individual is in the kth random assignment ratio stratum and zero otherwise.[21]

The estimated impact in the kth stratum is d_j. The estimated overall impact is the weighted average of these coefficients, as discussed previously. The null hypothesis that the overall impact is zero is tested by computing the F test for the weighted average of the estimated d_j.

Survey Nonresponse

Perhaps the most common departure from the ideal in real-world social experiments is the loss of follow-up data due to survey nonresponse. A typical response rate in a follow-up survey is 70% to 80%. If the experiment relies entirely on survey data to measure outcomes (as most do), outcomes cannot be measured for 20% to 30% of the sample.

If nonrespondents were a random subset of the overall sample, this loss of data would not be great cause for concern. It would reduce the precision of the estimates because of the reduction in sample size, but the sample for whom data are available would still be representative of the overall sample randomly assigned and the treatment and control groups would still be well matched. Thus, the experimental impact estimates would still be unbiased estimates of the program's effects on the population randomly assigned.

Unfortunately, there are usually good reasons to suspect that survey nonrespondents are systematically different from respondents. For example, surveys are less likely to be able to track people who have moved during the follow-up period than those who remain at the same address. In telephone surveys, nonrespondents are more likely to lack telephones or to have unlisted numbers. Also, people who are not employed are easier to locate and interview than those who work several jobs and are seldom home.[22]

Even if the subsample for whom follow-up data are available is not a representative subset of the population randomly assigned, the treatment-control difference in outcomes estimated on the basis of these data may still be an unbiased estimate of the impact of the program on this subset (although not of the impact on the overall population randomly assigned). This will be the case if the nonrespondents in the treatment group do not differ systematically from the nonrespondents in the control group, resulting in respondent subgroups that are still well matched.

In the worst case, nonrespondents in the treatment group differ systematically from those in the control group, resulting in a mismatch between the two groups of respondents. This will be the case when the experimental treatment influences the probability that the sample member will respond to the follow-up survey. If, for example, the experimental program encourages treatment group members to move or increases their employment rate, nonresponse is likely to be higher, and the kinds of individual who respond are likely to be different, in the treatment group than in the control group. In these cases, the experimental impact estimates may well be biased because the subgroups of the treatment and control group for whom outcome data are available are not well matched.

Some relatively simple diagnostics are available to determine whether survey nonresponse is creating any of the problems discussed previously. Some initial indications can be obtained from the survey response rate itself. A low overall response rate (e.g., < 70%) should be viewed as a danger signal. Any substantial difference in response rates between the treatment and control groups is also a warning that the respondents in the two groups may be systematically different.

A direct test for differences between the respondent and nonrespondent groups can be obtained by comparing the baseline characteristics of the two groups. Tests of statistical significance (*t* tests, *F* tests, or chi-square tests, depending on the nature of the characteristic) can be applied to the difference in each baseline characteristic to determine whether the two groups differ by more than one would expect on the basis of sampling error alone. If the number of differences that are significantly different from zero exceeds the number that would be expected by chance, the subgroup for whom follow-up data are available should be regarded as materially different from the population that was randomly assigned. Therefore, the experimental estimates, even if unbiased, may apply to a population that is somewhat different from the one of interest for policy.

Similarly, one can test for differences in baseline characteristics between the respondents in the treatment group and those in the control group. These tests will provide an indication of the degree to which the treatment and control groups are mismatched and, as a result, will provide biased impact estimates, even for the respondent population.

In some cases, it is possible to test directly for differences in impacts between the respondent and nonrespondent groups. This is the case when follow-up data on some outcomes are available from administrative records that cover the entire experimental sample. These data can be used to derive separate impact estimates for those who responded to the follow-up survey and those who did not. If these two estimates are similar, one can be somewhat less concerned about response bias; to the extent that they are significantly different, one's concern is heightened. Of course, the fact that the two groups have similar impacts on the outcomes measured with administrative data does not guarantee that they will have similar impacts on those outcomes that are measured only with follow-up survey data—for which we can never know the impacts on survey nonrespondents. The comparison, however, is at least suggestive, especially if the two outcomes are closely related.

In the AFDC Homemaker-Home Health Aide Demonstrations, for example, earnings over the follow-up period were measured in a telephone survey with a response rate of 66%. Data on welfare benefits from state administrative records were available for the entire sample, however, including the survey nonrespondents. These data were used to derive separate estimates of program impact on welfare benefits for survey respondents and nonrespondents. These estimates showed that in six of the seven demonstration states, survey respondents experienced larger reductions in welfare benefits as a result of the experimental program than did nonrespondents. This suggests that the program-induced earnings gains of respondents were probably also larger than those of nonrespondents because welfare benefits vary inversely with earnings. Thus, although this analysis did not allow direct measurement of the response bias in estimated earnings effects, it did suggest the likely direction of the bias.[23]

None of the tests described previously provide conclusive evidence of bias or lack thereof. Differences in baseline characteristics need not necessarily lead to biased impact estimates, unless the outcomes are sensitive to the characteristics on which the groups differ. It is possible to control for differences in measured characteristics by including these characteristics as covariates in the impact regression.[24] Conversely, the fact that respondents in the treatment and control groups do not differ in their measured characteristics does not guarantee that the impact estimates will be unbiased; the two groups may still differ in unmeasured characteristics. Even when administrative data are available to test directly for response bias in the impact estimates for some outcomes, there is no guarantee that the results of these tests are applicable to the outcomes for which only survey data are available.

The experimenter with incomplete follow-up data is in much the same position as the nonexperimental analyst who wants to determine if a nonexperimental comparison group is well matched to the program group. Although one can conduct a number of tests that give one more or less confidence in the impact estimates, one can never know how well the two groups are matched. Perhaps the most important difference between these two situations is that the experimenter at least knows that the two groups were well matched at the beginning.

The remedies for any mismatch between the two experimental groups are also essentially the same as those available to adjust for differences between a nonexperimental comparison group and the program group. Discussion of the large, complex literature on these econometric techniques far exceeds the scope of this book. Here, I note only that there is little consensus on which, if any, of these techniques are adequate to address the problem. This discouraging conclusion argues strongly for taking every step possible to minimize nonresponse in experimental follow-up surveys.[25]

Duration Bias: Inferring Responses to Permanent Programs From Temporary Experiments

Experiments are performed for a limited time period (usually 1-5 years) defined in advance. In many (perhaps most) cases, the temporary nature of the experimental program does not affect the experience of the program participant. Participants in an experimental training program, for example, receive the entire experimental treatment in a few weeks or months and exit the program. Whether the program continues to enroll other participants does not affect their experience or the impacts of the training on their subsequent outcomes.

In certain situations, however, the response to a temporary program could be quite different from the response that could be expected if the same intervention were adopted on a permanent basis. Consider, for example, an intervention such as the insurance plans provided by the Health Insurance Experiment. These plans decreased the net price of health care to covered families for the period of time they were enrolled in the experiment.[26] This meant that health care was "on sale" during this period of time, creating an incentive to accelerate the purchase of services that they would normally have made later. Obviously, the timing of many health care expenditures is not discretionary. The consumer, however, has a good deal of latitude in the scheduling of some services, such as dental and psychiatric care, the purchase of eyeglasses, preventive services, and elective surgery. If the experimental subjects used this latitude to purchase services during the experimental period, while the price of these services was low, rather than later, their observed consumption during the experimental period would overstate that which could be expected under a permanent program with the same insurance provisions.[27] Such an effect is termed *duration bias*.

The most direct way to deal with this potential bias is to design variation in the length of the intervention into the experiment. In the Health Insurance Experiment, for example, a random subset of families was assigned plans that lasted 5 years rather than the standard 3 years. The responses of families receiving the 3-year treatment were then compared with those of families receiving the 5-year treatment. Because these two sets of families differed only in treatment duration, any significant difference in response between the two sets would be evidence of duration bias in the estimates of the impact of the 3-year treatment.

Of course, even the longer experimental treatment was still a temporary intervention and may itself have been subject to duration bias. The only way to be sure that duration bias has been eliminated would be to implement a treatment of such long duration that it is, for all practical purposes, permanent. To our knowledge, this has been done only once. In the Seattle-Denver Income Maintenance Experiment, a random subsample of approximately 200 families was enrolled in negative income tax plans that were intended to last for 20 years. The responses of families assigned to the 20-year plans were compared with those of families assigned to 3- and 5-year plans to test for duration bias in the latter two groups, which constituted the bulk of the experimental sample.

Unfortunately, maintaining experimental treatments for such a long period of time is very expensive. Moreover, a long-term subsample is useful for research purposes only during the initial period when its responses can be compared with those of the main sample. For these reasons, the 20-year sample in the Seattle-Denver Experiment was terminated after approximately 8 years, with the families given 2 years advance notice, during which time they received fixed monthly payments to help them readjust to the absence of income support. Although early termination of the sample was clearly optimal from a research standpoint, it raised difficult ethical questions about the experiment's obligations to the families.

If variation in duration has not been incorporated into the design of the experiment, duration bias is much more difficult to detect. In some instances, an indication of the existence of duration bias can be obtained by examining the time path of impacts during the experimental period. In the case of the Health Insurance Experiment, for example, one would expect the incentive (and opportunity) to shift expenditures into the experimental period to grow as the family nears the end of its enrollment in the experimental plan. Thus, rising expenditures toward the end of the enrollment period would be an indication of duration bias. This evidence would be stronger if such rising trends in expenditures were most pronounced among the types of health care that are subject to significant consumer discretion.

In the context of the early income maintenance experiments, Metcalf (1974) proposed a method of estimating duration bias that turned on analysis of changes in the family's savings and consumption behavior over time. Arrow (1973) also suggested a method of estimating duration bias using follow-up data collected after the end of the experiment. The reliability (or general applicablility) of these approaches is unclear.

Estimating the Benefits and Costs of an Experimental Program

My discussion has focused on estimating the impacts of an experimental program on its participants. By "impact," I generally mean the effect of the program on one or more behavioral outcomes that represent the objectives of the program. In evaluating a training program, for example, we focus on its impacts on participants' earnings; in evaluating a remedial education program, we focus on the program's effects on student performance.

A finding that the program had its intended effects, however, is not sufficient to justify adoption (or continuation) of the program. To determine whether the program is worthwhile, it is necessary to compare the effects (i.e., the program's *benefits*) with the resources given up to produce them as well as any adverse impacts (i.e., the program's *costs*). In most cases, it is also important to examine the *distributional consequences* of the program (i.e., who bears the costs and who reaps the benefits).

Cost-benefit analysis has given rise to a voluminous literature; I will not attempt even to summarize this complex methodology.[28] Rather, I discuss the relationship between program benefits and costs and the experimental impact estimates. Then, I illustrate this relationship by presenting a conceptual framework for the cost-benefit analysis of a specific experimental evaluation and discussing the measurement of the benefits and costs involved in this evaluation.

Measuring Benefits and Costs in an Experiment

A comprehensive cost-benefit analysis of the experimental program requires an exhaustive measurement of all the impacts of the program (both beneficial and adverse) as well as the resources required to produce them. As has been shown, experiments are ideally suited to performing the first step of this process: The treatment-control difference in outcomes is an unbiased estimate of the impact of the program on any outcome. Thus, we need only anticipate and collect data on all the outcomes affected by the program to obtain the impact estimates required for cost-benefit analysis.

Perhaps less obvious, the resources required to produce these impacts are also appropriately measured by the difference in resources consumed between the treatment and control groups. This is the increase in resource consumption that would occur if the experimental program were adopted on an ongoing basis.

The treatment-control difference in resource consumption may differ from the budgetary cost of the program for several reasons. First, if the experimental program displaces some nonexperimental services, then the net cost to society is the resources required to produce the experimental services less the resources freed up by the displacement of nonexperimental services. Suppose, for example, that the costs of services per participant are as follows:

	Treatment Group ($)	Control Group ($)	Difference ($)
Experimental	1,000	0	1,000
Nonexperimental	200	400	−200
Total	1,200	400	800

If the experimental program pays the full cost of the experimental services, then the budgetary cost of the program is $1,000 per participant. The net cost to society of the experimental program, however, is only $800 per participant—the treatment-control difference in total service costs. This net cost is the sum of the total cost of the experimental program ($1,000 per participant) and the savings that result from displacement of nonexperimental services ($200 per participant).

The second reason that the net cost of the experimental program may differ from its budgetary cost is because the experimental program may not pay the full cost of the services it provides. For example, training programs often refer participants to basic education programs funded by other sources or to community colleges that are subsidized by local taxpayers. The training program may reimburse these organizations for part of the cost of the services they provide (e.g., it may pay the community college tuition). The social cost of the services provided, however, is measured by the full cost of the services and not just the part paid by the training program.

We can consider the portion of the cost of services to the treatment group that is not borne by the experimental program as nonexperimental services. (This interpretation is perhaps most natural in a case in which the experimental program refers participants to another service provider, but it also applies to cases in which the experimental program is subsidized by other funding sources.) In this case, the experimental program increases the consumption of nonexperimental services by its participants rather than displacing nonexperimental services. In the cost framework presented previously, this case might appear as follows:

	Treatment Group ($)	Control Group ($)	Difference ($)
Experimental	1,000	0	1,000
Nonexperimental	800	400	400
Total	1,800	400	1,400

Because of referrals to other service providers or subsidies to the experimental program, in this case the treatment group actually consumes more nonexperimental services than the control group ($800 vs. $400 per participant). As a result, the treatment-control difference in total service costs ($1,400) exceeds the budgetary cost of the experimental program ($1,000).

Critics of social experiments frequently complain that they understate the full effects of the program because controls receive similar services from nonexperimental sources. This argument has some validity if the evaluator examines only the impacts of the program. In a benefit-cost analysis, however, by taking account of the effects of the experimental program on the costs of nonexperimental services, we automatically adjust the cost side of the benefit-cost analysis to conform to the treatment-control service differential that produced the impacts (and therefore the benefits) measured by the experiment.

In the case in which the experimental program displaces nonexperimental services, the treatment-control service differential is less than the full amount of services provided by the program. The estimated impacts are therefore presumably smaller than would be produced by the full amount of services provided by the experimental program. On the cost side, however, we take account of this displacement; as a result, our measure of added social costs is correspondingly smaller than the full budgetary cost of the experimental program. Similarly, when the experimental program causes increased use of nonexperimental services, the treatment-control service differential and the measured social cost of the program are greater than the full amount of the experimental services provided and their budgetary cost. Thus, there is a strong argument for always conducting a complete cost-benefit analysis when either the treatment or control group receives some nonexperimental services.

Illustrative Example: Benefits and Costs of a Training Program

Table 6.5 shows a social accounting framework for the cost-benefit analysis of a training program for low-income workers. The table lists benefits and costs of the program expressed in dollars per participant. The table also indicates the group within society to whom the benefits or costs accrues—the participants, the rest of society, or society as a whole. Because participants

TABLE 6.5 Conceptual Framework for Cost-Benefit Analysis of an Employment and Training Program

| Costs/Benefits | Costs (–) and Benefits (+) From the Perspective of | | |
	Participants	Rest of Society	Society
Costs			
Operational costs of the program	0	–	–
Forgone leisure and home production	–	0	–
Benefits			
Earnings gains	+	0	+
Reduced costs of nonexperimental services	0	+	+
Transfers			
Reduced welfare benefits	–	+	0
Wage subsidies	+	–	0
Net benefits	±	±	±

and the rest of society together constitute society, the values listed under the society column are simply the sum of the values of the participants and rest of society columns. Positive values indicate program benefits; program costs are denoted by negative values. The *net benefit* to each group is the algebraic sum of the program's benefits and costs to that group—that is, the sum of the values in the column corresponding to that group.

The principal costs of the program are shown in Table 6.5. Operational costs include staff salaries, rent, utilities, and all the other administrative and overhead costs necessary to run the experimental program. They also include anything the program pays to other training providers to serve participants in the experimental program. The operational costs of the program are borne by the rest of society (i.e., nonparticipants) and are also a cost to society as a whole. This entry corresponds to the treatment-control difference in the cost of experimental services in the tables presented previously. (Later, effects on the cost of nonexperimental services are considered separately.)

The major cost borne by program participants is forgone leisure and home production as a result of time spent in training and any additional time spent working. We can measure the time participants spend in work or training relatively accurately through program records and follow-up surveys. The time cost to participants is the treatment-control difference in total hours spent performing these activities. Placing a monetary value on this time loss is more difficult both conceptually and empirically. Theoretically, this value is measured by the area under the participant's labor supply curve.[29] In practice, it is often approximated by assigning the participant's wage rate (if known) or the minimum wage to each forgone hour.

The principal benefit of an effective training program is participant earnings gains. Earnings can be measured through follow-up surveys or the employer-reported earnings records maintained by unemployment insurance agencies in each state. The earnings gain attributable to participation in the experimental program is measured by the treatment-control difference in earnings. The principal problem in measuring earnings gains is that, although these gains may continue to accrue throughout the participant's entire working life, the typical evaluation follow-up period lasts only 1 to 3 years. Thus, researchers must either find some way to project these earnings gains beyond the follow-up period or the evaluation runs the risk of understating program benefits—perhaps substantially so.[30]

One way to project earnings impacts beyond the evaluation follow-up period is to estimate the rate of "decay" of the impact on earnings over the follow-up period and then project the rate of decay over the remainder of the participant's working life. If, for example, earnings gains are falling by 10% per year during the evaluation follow-up period, one could project that the impact observed at the end of the follow-up period would continue to decay at this same rate.

Unfortunately, in many evaluations the follow-up period is not long enough to establish a reliable trend in the impact estimates, especially because impacts on earnings are likely to increase during the first part of the follow-up period and only begin to decay toward the end of the follow-up period. Because of this problem, some evaluations have simply used the decay rates estimated in similar studies that have followed the experimental samples for long periods.[31]

Another approach is to perform a "sensitivity analysis" by projecting earnings gains under different rates of decay to examine the sensitivity of the resulting estimates of net benefits to different assumptions about long-term earnings impacts. If, for example, net benefits are positive under all plausible values of the decay rate, for policy purposes it does not really matter what decay rate is used.

Whatever method of projecting future earnings gains is used, it is essential that the future earnings be "discounted" to reflect the fact that a dollar of benefit in the future is not worth a dollar of cost in the present. More generally, because the costs of most social programs are incurred at the outset, whereas their benefits tend to be distributed over long periods of time, costs and benefits must be calculated in "present discounted value" terms to be comparable. Choice of an appropriate discount rate is a complex issue that is beyond the scope of this book.[32]

In addition to the benefits to participants, in cases in which the experimental training displaces similar nonexperimental services, the rest of society enjoys the benefit of reduced costs of nonexperimental services. (If the experimental program increased nonexperimental services, this would be a cost.) As indicated previously, this benefit is measured by the treatment-control difference in the cost of nonexperimental services received by the sample.

The cost of nonexperimental services is one of the most difficult cost-benefit components to measure because these services are often provided by a large number of agencies not directly involved in the experiment. Identifying and gaining the cooperation of these agencies can be an insuperable task. Sometimes, acceptable cost data can be obtained from secondary sources (e.g., other studies that focused on these organizations). In the National JTPA Study, for example, the evaluators were able to obtain data from federal statistical agencies on the cost of education and training at public schools. To collect data on private schools, however, it was necessary to conduct a telephone survey (Orr et al., 1996, Appendixes A and B).

Some program impacts produce benefits to one segment of society that are exactly offset by costs to another segment of society so that the resulting net social benefit is zero. These are known as *transfers*. For example, if increased employment among program participants leads to reduced welfare payments, this represents a cost to participants equal to the loss of welfare benefits and an exactly offsetting benefit to the rest of society in the form of reduced taxes. Similarly, if a training program subsidizes wages in private employment, the benefit to participants is exactly offset by an equal tax cost to nonparticipants. Transfers are measured by the treatment-control difference in the outcome in question (e.g., welfare benefits or wage subsidies). Generally, this is measured for participants, and the offsetting cost or benefit to the rest of society is imputed to be exactly equal (but opposite in sign) to the impact on participants.

As noted earlier, the net benefit of the program to any given social group is the algebraic sum of all costs and benefits to that group. Table 6.5 shows this sum for each group. As with all costs and benefits, the net benefit of the program to society as a whole is the sum of the net benefits to participants and to the rest of society.

Although programs with positive net benefits to society as a whole are generally viewed as worthwhile, it is important to recognize that computation of net social benefits involves a very important assumption: It assumes that a dollar of benefit to any member of society just offsets a dollar of cost to any other member of society. A typical cost-benefit finding is that net benefits to participants are positive, whereas net benefits to the rest of society (which bears the cost of the program) are negative. Under the fundamental assumption underlying the computation of net social benefits, such a program is socially worthwhile as long as the gains enjoyed by the participants exceed the costs borne by the rest of society. Some would question this assumption, arguing that to justify taking resources away from the rest of society to support the program, the gains to participants should substantially exceed the costs to nonparticipants. At a minimum, the analyst has a responsibility to show the distributional consequences of the program (as is done in Table 6.5) so that policymakers can form their own views of its social desirability.

Nonmonetary Benefits and Costs

In the previous illustrative example, we were able to assign a dollar value to each of the major costs and benefits of the program, thereby allowing computation of net benefits to each segment of society in monetary terms. This is not always possible. Some program impacts simply cannot be expressed in monetary terms. For example, some youth programs are intended to promote good citizenship, develop leadership traits, and change youths' attitudes about work and education.

Even when important program impacts cannot be valued in monetary terms, they can often be measured experimentally in nonmonetary terms. For example, sociologists and social psychologists have developed scales that can be used to measure a number of different attitudes. The treatment-control difference in the mean score on such a scale at follow-up is a measure of the program's impact on that attitude.[33] Similarly, even if we cannot assign a dollar value to illnesses prevented or lives saved by a social program, we can at least measure the program's effects as the treatment-control difference in these outcomes, measured in natural units (e.g., sick days and lives lost).

When some program costs or benefits are measured in nonmonetary terms, policymakers must assess these costs and benefits along with net monetary benefits. In the simplest case, when both nonmonetary benefits and net monetary benefits are positive, the conclusion is straightforward: The program is worthwhile, no matter what value we place on the nonmonetary benefits. Positive nonmonetary benefits simply reinforce positive net monetary benefits. Conversely, if both nonmonetary benefits and net monetary benefits are negative, the program is not socially worthwhile.

When nonmonetary benefits are positive and net monetary benefits are negative, policymakers face a trade-off: They must decide how much society is willing to pay to secure the nonmonetary benefits of the program. If, in their judgment, the estimated nonmonetary benefits of the program are worth more than its estimated net monetary cost, then the program is socially worthwhile; if not, it is not. Similarly, if nonmonetary benefits are negative and net monetary benefits are positive, policymakers must decide whether the former outweigh the latter.

In the AFDC Homemaker-Home Health Aide Demonstrations, for example, provision of home care services to elderly and disabled individuals entailed substantial net monetary costs. Although it was originally hoped that the operational costs of providing home care would be offset by reduced use of hospital and nursing home care, these monetary benefits largely failed to materialize. The program, however, did have statistically significant positive impacts on a number of measures of client well-being, such as orientation, ability to communicate, number of activities of daily living in which the client was able to function independently, and self-reported health status. The clients also overwhelmingly said that they enjoyed the companionship and assistance of the aides. In presenting the results of the evaluation, the researchers characterized the net monetary costs of the demonstration program as the price of obtaining these nonmonetary benefits (Orr & Visher, 1987).

It is important to recognize that the value judgments involved in making such trade-offs are the province of policymakers, who have been elected or appointed to interpret society's preferences in such matters. They are not technical decisions that can be made by the analyst.

Costs and Benefits That Cannot Be Measured

Some costs and benefits cannot be meaningfully measured. For example, an important social benefit of programs that successfully place welfare recipients in private-sector jobs is the satisfaction that taxpayers derive from knowing that such individuals are productively employed rather than being dependent on public assistance.[34]

If such costs or benefits are likely to be important program effects, it is important to take note of them in the analysis and, if possible, to indicate their likely direction, even if they cannot be quantified. This serves both to document the limitations of the study and to remind policymakers to take such potential effects into account in assessing the overall costs and benefits of the program.

Notes

1. These coefficients are generally not of interest in program evaluation for two reasons. First, they reflect natural variation in the outcome and not program-induced effects. Second, because of correlations among the covariates and between the covariates and variables not included in the impact model, as measures of the causal effects of these characteristics they are subject to a number of biases. The purpose of the covariates is simply to reduce the sampling variability of the impact estimates.

2. See Chapter 4 for the derivation of the minimum detectable effect.

3. This can be seen from Equation 6.3. The difference-in-means estimator is equivalent to a regression model that includes only the treatment status indicator (i.e., a model with no covariates). As shown in Equation 6.3, under the null hypothesis of no impact such a regression would have an R^2 of zero and the variance of c would be $V(Y_i)(n/n_t n_c)$. Adding sufficient covariates to achieve an R^2 of .20 would reduce the variance of c to $.8V(Y_i)(n/n_t n_c)$.

4. An alternative approach that is sometimes used is to include each time period as a separate observation for each individual in a single regression, with separate treatment status indicators for each time period. Thus, for example, in an experiment with 1,000 sample members and a 24-month follow-up period, the impact model would contain 24 separate treatment status indicators, one for each month, and would be run on 24,000 person-month observations. It must be recognized, however, that the likelihood of serial correlation in the outcomes for each sample member means that the effective sample size is probably smaller than 24,000. Thus, the standard errors produced by ordinary least squares are biased downward, giving the appearance of greater precision than is actually achieved. To obtain unbiased standard errors, one must use a procedure such as two-stage generalized least squares, which corrects for autocorrelation.

5. Because only baseline variables can be used as covariates, and these are the same regardless of the month for which the outcome is analyzed, the right-hand side of the impact equation will be identical for all months of the follow-up period.

6. The earnings shown in Figure 6.1 are regression adjusted—that is, they are the predicted values from a model such as Equation 6.1. Therefore, the impact estimates shown in the figure control for the baseline characteristics of the sample (Enns, Bell, & Flanagan, 1987).

7. This specification assumes that the decay of start-up effects follows a very specific functional form. More complex specifications would allow a more flexible determination of the time path of start-up effects from the data. I use this form here primarily for simplicity of exposition.

8. Nonexperimental techniques are available to attempt to reduce or eliminate these biases. Discussion of these techniques is beyond the scope of this book. Here, I note only that one can never be sure whether such techniques are successful in any particular application because one can never be sure that the assumptions on which they are based hold for particular applications.

9. By "independent," I mean non-overlapping subgroups. If the two subgroups have some members in common, calculation of the standard error of the difference is more complex.

10. The combined model assumes that the functional form of the relationship between the X variables and Y is the same in all subgroups. If this assumption is incorrect, the combined model may not provide more power than separate regressions.

11. These can also be determined with F tests.

12. The expected number of false positives in this case will be slightly less than 2 for two reasons. First, the expected number of false positives is 10% of the subgroups for which the true impact is zero. The 6 subgroups with estimated impacts that are significantly different from zero presumably include some for which the true impact is nonzero. Second, the 14 subgroups for which the estimated impact is not significantly different from zero presumably include some false negatives—that is, subgroups for which the true impact is nonzero—further reducing the base on which the number of expected false positives should be calculated. The number of false negatives will depend on the power of the design; a weak design is less likely to detect nonzero impacts.

13. Neither overall estimated impacts nor any of the estimates for subgroups were significantly different from zero among male or female youth (see Orr et al., 1996).

14. Note that, to facilitate comparison of the estimates across sites, the sites are ordered in descending size of estimated impact within each demographic group. Thus, the estimates in any given row of Table 6.4 may represent different sites for each of the four demographic groups. Impact estimates are given for youth for only 15 sites because no youth were randomly assigned at one site.

15. Differences in impact due to differences in the participant population could, in principle, be useful to policymakers in deciding how to target the program. In most cases, however, this can be addressed more directly through analysis of subgroups defined on the basis of participant characteristics. Only in programs that can be targeted to specific geographic areas would knowledge of variation in impact due to local environmental characteristics be useful in the targeting decision.

16. It should be noted that the participants with the largest impacts need not be those who would do the best in the absence of the experimental program (e.g., the best educated or highest skilled workers or those living where there is the greatest demand for labor). It could be that the program cannot improve the prospects of well-educated, high-skilled workers, or that workers living in areas with booming economies could find just as good a job without the program. Thus, simply comparing the individual and site characteristics of the successful and unsuccessful sites cannot indicate whether these factors are responsible for the observed differences in impacts across sites; only by formally estimating the variation in impact with these characteristics can we make this determination.

17. Fishing may, however, be a good way to generate hypotheses for testing in future experiments, as long as it is recognized that the results obtained from the current data are no more than suggestive.

18. See Chapter 5 for a discussion of the steps that can and should be taken in implementing experiments to protect the integrity of random assignment.

19. Alternatively, one could randomly remove 50 controls from the Period 1 sample.

20. When the number of observations that would be removed under this approach is small relative to the overall sample, it may be worth the loss of information to avoid the added complexity involved in the approach recommended here. This was, in fact, the approach taken in the National JTPA Study, in which 473 treatment group members were randomly excluded from an initial sample of 20,601 individuals (Orr et al., 1996).

21. Note that one of the stratum dummies must be omitted from the covariates if there is a constant term but that all the stratum dummies are included in the set of interactions with treatment.

22. In most household surveys, the overwhelming majority of the nonresponse is attributable to failure to contact the sample member rather than to refusal to be interviewed.

23. See Enns et al. (1987). By assuming that the relationship between earnings gains and welfare benefit reductions (i.e., the benefit reduction rate) was the same for respondents and nonrespondents, the analysts were able to derive an estimate of the bias. These estimates suggested that in five of the seven demonstration states, the bias was < 20%. In the other two states, however, the estimated bias was substantially larger than the experimental effect.

24. Specifically, they should be included both as main effects and as interaction terms with the treatment indicator to allow treatment to vary with differences in these characteristics. The overall impact can then be evaluated on the basis of the estimated coefficients, setting these variables equal to their sample means.

25. See Chapter 5 for a discussion of ways to reduce follow-up survey nonresponse.

26. The change in net price to the family depended on the provisions of the specific plan to which they were assigned compared with those of the insurance they would have had otherwise. In some cases, the net price to the family was actually higher under the experimental plan. The bias described here does not depend on the direction of the change but rather on the fact that it was a temporary change.

27. See Newhouse (1993) for a more complete discussion of these issues in the Health Insurance Experiment. See Metcalf (1974) for a detailed theoretical and empirical analysis of the corresponding incentives in the income maintenance experiments.

28. For an excellent text on the subject, see Boardman, Greenberg, Vining, and Weimer (1996).

29. See Boardman et al. (1996, Chapter 9) for a derivation of the theoretically correct measurement of this value.

30. For a more complete discussion of the issues involved in projecting earnings gains, see Boardman et al. (1996, Chapter 9).

31. In the area of employment and training programs, for example, several studies have followed experimental samples for 5 years or more (Bell, Orr, Blomquist, & Cain, 1995; Couch, 1992; Friedlander & Burtless, 1995; U.S. General Accounting Office, 1996).

32. See Boardman et al. (1996, Chapters 4 and 5) for a detailed discussion of discounting future benefits.

33. Of course, such impact estimates are only as valid as the scales on which they are based.

34. A similar benefit accrues to the (former) welfare recipients themselves. This benefit, however, could arguably be measured in nonmonetary terms using an attitudinal scale. This approach is not available for measuring taxpayer satisfaction because taxpayers would not derive the same satisfaction from a small demonstration project that they would from a large, ongoing program.

References

Arrow, K. J. (1973). *Welfare analysis of changes in health coinsurance rates* (Research Report No. R-1281-OEO). Santa Monica, CA: RAND.

Bell, S. H., Orr, L. L., Blomquist, J. D., & Cain, G. G. (1995). *Program applicants as a comparison group in evaluating training programs.* Kalamazoo, MI: Upjohn Institute for Employment Research.

Bloom, H. (1986). Accounting for cross-overs. In *Data collection and analysis of JTPA evaluation experiments: Technical proposal.* Unpublished manuscript.

Boardman, A. E., Greenberg, D. H., Vining, A. R., & Weimer, D. L. (1996). *Cost-benefit analysis: Concepts and practice.* Upper Saddle River, NJ: Prentice Hall.

Couch, K. (1992). *Long-term effects of the national supported work experiment, and parametric and nonparametric tests of model specification and the estimation of treatment effects.* Unpublished doctoral dissertation, University of Wisconsin-Madison.

Enns, J. H., Bell, S. H., & Flanagan, K. L. (1987). *AFDC Homemaker-Home Health Aide Demonstrations: Trainee employment and earnings.* Bethesda, MD: Abt.

Friedlander, D., & Burtless, G. (1995). *Five years after: The long-term effects of welfare-to-work programs.* New York: Russell Sage.

Metcalf, C. E. (1974). Predicting the effects of permanent programs from a limited duration experiment. *Journal of Human Resources, 9*(4), 530-555.

Newhouse, J. P. (1993). *Free for all? Lessons from the RAND Health Insurance Experiment.* Cambridge, MA: Harvard University Press.

Orr, L. L., Bloom, H. S., Bell, S. H., Doolittle, F., Lin, W., & Cave, G. (1996). *Does job training for the disadvantaged work? Evidence from the National JTPA Study.* Washington, DC: Urban Institute Press.

Orr, L. L., & Visher, M. G. (1987). *AFDC Homemaker-Home Health Aide Demonstrations: Client health and related outcomes.* Washington, DC: Abt.

U.S. General Accounting Office. (1996, March). *Job Training Partnership Act: Long-term earnings and employment outcomes* (GAO/HEHS-96-40). Washington, DC: Author.

Chapter 7

Social Experimentation
and the Policy Process

" As a society, we have been guilty of what can be fairly termed policy corruption. In pursuit of bold visions, we have launched one bold scheme after another without anything like responsible evidence. . . . The problem is not the visions. Americans across the political spectrum want to improve education, reduce violence, eliminate substance abuse, strengthen families, restore traditional values, and increase opportunity for achieving the Dream. The problem is that we know little more now than in the 1960s about how, on a large scale, to achieve these shared objectives. And the reason is a continuing surrender to ignorance. Major public-policy initiatives are routinely advanced, but rarely do we organize to evaluate what works. "

—Richard Darman, Director, U.S.
Office of Management and Budget,
1989-1993 (1996, pp. 116-117)

In this chapter, I consider the relationship of experimental evaluations to the policy process in an effort to provide useful guidance to those who initiate, design, and interpret the results of social experiments. I begin by discussing the ways in which experimental evidence can inform the policy debate and some of the ways in which it can be misused in this debate. Then, I consider the factors that increase, or decrease, the likelihood that experimental evidence will influence policy. Finally, I discuss ways in which experiments can be used more systematically in the policy process.

The Use of Experimental
Evidence in the Policy Process

Most policy decisions are made on the basis of very little reliable information about the likely effects of the proposed policy. Indeed, these effects are often not even central to the policy debate—precisely because reliable evidence is lacking. In public discussions and legislative debates, and even in the internal deliberations of the executive branch, it is often simply assumed that proposed programs will achieve their stated objectives; the political debate then revolves around whether these objectives are worth the cost of the program. Even when the effectiveness of the program becomes an issue, anecdotes and empty rhetoric often pass for evidence.

In this environment, properly designed and executed social experiments can provide a unique, and extremely important, input: clear, convincing, and valid evidence of the impacts of the program on the outcomes it was designed to affect. In some cases, such evidence is sufficient to make the crucial difference in whether a policy is adopted or rejected or a program continued or discontinued. As described in Chapter 1, the Perry Preschool Project, the Manhattan Bail Bond Experiment, the Work-Welfare Experiments, and the National Job Training Partnership Act (JTPA) Study have all had clear, direct impacts on the adoption or continuation of specific policies or (in the case of JTPA) major funding changes for an ongoing program.

It is important to recognize, however, that the development of social policy is better understood as a process rather than as a sequence of discrete "policy decisions." There is seldom a single point at which all the evidence and arguments relevant to a proposed policy are marshaled and a positive or negative decision made. Rather, a large number of actors in the policy process, both government officials and private citizens, engage in an ongoing dialogue in which policy is shaped incrementally, often as a compromise among the various political factions involved. These actors are in turn influenced by a large number of information sources and interested parties, both inside and outside government.

Given the multiplicity of actors, decision points, and information sources in the process, the policy effects of experimental evidence are usually indirect. In many cases, experimental results affect prevailing attitudes and opinions in a policy area. For example, although the Health Insurance Experiment did not lead directly to any specific policy changes, its finding that cost sharing leads to reduced use of medical care without any discernible effects on health status was an important factor in the acceptance of cost sharing as a cost-containment strategy both in public programs and, perhaps more important, in private insurance plans.

Even when the experimental results do not clearly indicate whether a particular policy should be adopted, they can be very useful in clarifying the trade-offs facing policymakers. For example, the labor supply parameters estimated in the income maintenance experiments were incorporated into simulation models that were used to estimate the costs and behavioral effects of a number of welfare reform proposals in the 1970s. Similarly, the medical care demand elasticities derived from the Health Insurance Experiment in the early 1980s are still being used to predict the utilization effects and costs of health insurance policy proposals (Ozanne, 1996; Rivlin, Cutler, & Nichols, 1994). Although such behavioral and cost estimates seldom constitute compelling evidence for or against a particular policy, they improve the information base on which policy decisions are made.

Experimental findings can illuminate policy trade-offs even when the outcomes of interest cannot be measured in monetary terms. The evaluation of the Aid to Families with Dependent Children (AFDC) Homemaker-Home Health Aide Demonstrations, for example, found that the provision of home care to elderly and disabled clients did not result in the hoped-for reductions in hospital and nursing home costs. It did, however, improve the clients' mental functioning and sense of well-being (Orr & Visher, 1987). Thus, policymakers were faced with the decision whether these nonmonetary benefits were worth the cost of the home care services. In this case, although it could not be decisively determined from the experiment whether the program was socially worthwhile, the relevant costs and benefits were more clearly and accurately determined by the experiment than by any other available form of evidence.

Often, the trade-offs delineated by the experimental evidence are between different subgroups of society. An evaluation of youth conservation and service corps, for example, found that the overall monetary benefits of the programs exceeded their costs (Jastrzab, Blomquist, Masker, & Orr, 1997). When benefits and costs were calculated separately for program participants and the rest of society, however, net monetary benefits to participants were found to be positive, whereas the rest of society bore net monetary costs. Again, in this case, it could not be determined conclusively from the experiment whether the program was a worthwhile social investment, but the distributional trade-off involved in the policy decision was clearly quantifiable.

It is important to recognize that, as these examples suggest, the measure of an experiment's social utility is not whether the program being tested is enacted or not—or, indeed, whether any specific change in policy results directly from the experiment. Rather, the measure of an experiment's social value is whether it improves the information on which policy decisions are based. An experiment that convinces policymakers not to adopt a new program that has net social costs is just as valuable as one that convinces them to enact a program with positive social benefits of the same magnitude.[1] Even if the experiment does no more than to confirm the preconceived views of one side in the policy debate, it performs the very useful function of strengthening the evidence that can be used by that side in arguing for (or against) the policy; this will improve the odds that the ultimate decision will be beneficial to society.

Some Potential Misuses
of Experimental Results

The power and credibility of experimental evidence can also be misused in policy debates. One way in which this can occur is through selective use of experimental results. An agency might, for example, attempt to suppress studies that do not support its preconceived policy positions. Fortunately, most social experiments are large and visible enough that it is hard to bury their findings entirely.

A more subtle (and more common) selective use of experimental results occurs when the sponsoring agency publicizes only those experimental findings that support its policy positions. Thus, for example, an agency might disseminate a summary of the research findings that highlights positive impacts but neglects to mention significant adverse effects of the policy tested. An even more insidious selective use of findings sometimes occurs when the experiment estimates impacts on a large number of outcomes and effects are found that are significantly different from zero for only a small proportion of the outcomes analyzed. As discussed in Chapter 6, there is a high risk that these are false-positive results—estimated impacts that are significantly different from zero by chance alone. Focusing on this subset of results may therefore seriously mislead policymakers.

Another common misuse of experimental (and other) research results is to apply them to a policy or target population that is substantially different from those on which the results are based. Some mismatch in this regard is virtually unavoidable: Given the lags involved in planning, implementing, and analyzing an experiment, the exact policy or target population that will be of interest when the results become available can seldom be anticipated. This means that the correspondence between the experimental intervention and population and the policy and population to whom the results are to be applied must be carefully assessed and appropriate caution used in interpreting the policy implications of the results. In some cases, the correspondence will be so weak that it is better simply not to try to apply the experimental results. In cases in which the intervention tested is sufficiently similar to the policy under consideration, but the population on which it was tested is not, it may be possible to simulate the effects on the relevant population through reweighting of the experimental sample or simulation modeling that incorporates the effects found in the experiment.

Even when the experimental results can be taken to be a valid representation of the expected response to the policy of interest, it is important to remember that the fact that the intervention has an impact that is significantly different from zero does not guarantee that the policy is socially beneficial. Only a careful, comprehensive benefit-cost analysis can determine whether the program impacts are sufficient to justify their cost.

The misuse of research results is a natural outgrowth of the nature of the policy process. That process is basically an adversarial one, in which individuals routinely use new information selectively to support preconceived positions rather than objectively weighing the pros and cons of every action. Analysts can counter the effects of this ideology-driven environment in several ways.

First, they can encourage policymakers to distinguish between their ultimate objectives and the means to these objectives. Often, policymakers believe that concern for any particular population or problem is synonymous with support for all existing or proposed programs intended to benefit that population or address that problem. It is important for them to realize that the program is a means to an end, and that if the program is ineffective, it may be worse then useless: Like wearing a copper bracelet as a cure for cancer, it may divert attention and resources away from finding a truly effective solution to the problem. It is in the best interest of both the taxpayers, who fund the program, and the intended beneficiaries to obtain the best possible evidence with which to objectively assess whether the intervention is truly effective and to scrap ineffective interventions. Although this may seem like a truism, ideologically based support for, or opposition to, specific policies is perhaps the greatest obstacle to the effective use of research in the policy process.

A second way that analysts can combat the misuse of research in the policy process is to ensure that, in their own reports, the results are stated as clearly and completely as possible, with all the appropriate caveats, and that they are widely disseminated. This will allow partisans on both sides of the issue to use whatever support the findings provide for their own positions and to challenge the other side's use of the results. In effect, this strategy seeks to use the adversarial nature of the policy process itself to police the misuse of research results. Although this approach has some obvious shortcomings (e.g., subtle caveats about statistical inference are quickly lost in a world of sound bites), in the long run it provides the best hope of raising the informational content of the policy debate and, therefore, leading to better policy decisions.

Factors That Affect the Likelihood That Experimental Results Will Influence Policy

The flip side of the danger that research results will be misused in the policy process is the danger that they will not be used at all. I hasten to add that by "used" I do not necessarily mean "lead to the adoption of a new program." In practice, it is rare that a single study is decisive with respect to any given policy; fortunately, research can play an extremely valuable role even if it does no more than raise the quality of the policy debate. To achieve even this more limited objective, though, the research must be taken into account by the actors in the policy process as they fashion policy.

On the basis of a review of the literature on research utilization, Greenberg and Mandell (1991) suggest that five characteristics of an evaluation will condition the degree to which it will influence policy: its credibility, timeliness, communication and visibility, generalizability, and relevance.[2] In addition, they argue that the utilization of the results will be strongly affected by the policy environment in which they are considered. Each of these factors are considered in turn.

Credibility

It may seem obvious that the more credible a piece of research, the more likely it is to influence decision makers. The credibility of research results depends on a complex interplay of factors, however, not all of which have to do with the scientific quality of the research. This is true in part because policymakers are generally not qualified to judge the scientific quality of research; therefore, they must rely on indirect indicators of the reliability of research evidence—for example, the reputation of the researchers, whether the results are generally accepted within the research community, and whether the results are internally consistent and consistent with the users' own preconceptions and other evidence at their disposal. The complexity of the results is also an important factor; political actors tend to be suspicious of evidence that requires a complicated explanation.[3] Finally, the willingness of a policymaker to give credence to any given set of results will be strongly conditioned by whether doing so would threaten that individual's political self-interest or established policy positions.

Experiments fare well on many, but not all, of these criteria. Perhaps most important, the fact that there is a consensus within the research community that experimental designs produce unbiased impact estimates tends to lead to broad acceptance of the results of experimental studies. Although large, highly visible evaluations such as the income maintenance experiments or the National JTPA Study naturally attract much scrutiny and some criticism in the research community, their results have been much less controversial than those of nonexperimental evaluations in these areas, such as the Comprehensive Employment and Training Act studies discussed in Chapter 1. The results of smaller experiments, such as the evaluations of state welfare-to-work programs, have generally been noncontroversial within the research community.

Experimental results should also fare well in terms of simplicity. The basic experimental method is quite straightforward; comparison of randomly assigned treatment and control groups is a concept that even laypersons can readily grasp. Nevertheless, analysis of multiple treatments, outcomes, population subgroups, or all three can give rise to an imposing array of impact estimates; unless skillfully communicated, such results can give at least the impression of complexity. Later, I discuss communication of experimental results in more detail.

Similarly, experiments should rank high on internal consistency. Properly designed experiments yield results that are in fact internally consistent. The presence of sampling error, however, can sometimes create the appearance of inconsistency among results if careful attention is not given to correct statistical interpretation. For example, an evaluation of a recent employment and training demonstration found that the intervention increased employment rates by a statistically significant 20%, but that the impact on earnings was not significantly different from zero. If one makes the common mistake of interpreting estimated impacts that are not significantly different from zero as if they are zero and estimates impacts that are significantly different from zero as if they are exactly equal to the point estimate, these two results are hard to reconcile. If one takes sampling error into account, however, it becomes clear that there is substantial overlap between the confidence intervals around the two estimates. It could well be that the demonstration did have the same percentage effect on employment and earnings, but the demonstration sample size was simply not large enough to detect the impact on a high-variance outcome such as earnings as significantly different from zero. Alternatively, the impact on earnings may have been smaller than the impact on employment, although it may not necessarily have been zero.

A different source of apparent inconsistency among experimental results arises when multiple tests of the same or similar interventions are conducted by different researchers. For example, this was the case with the income maintenance experiments of the late 1960s and early 1970s. Although these four projects were popularly viewed simply as tests of the negative income tax, they in fact tested very different interventions (not all of which were negative income taxes) with very different populations, used different outcome measures, and presented their results in very different ways.[4] Not surprisingly, even the professional research community had difficulty sorting out the results.

Researchers can exercise much control over their peers' perceptions of the quality of the experiment and its simplicity and internal consistency by following sound methodological practice in its design and interpretation and by presenting the results as clearly and simply as possible. The threat to the credibility of the results over which they have little control is the possibility that the results will conflict with policymakers' preconceptions, policy positions, or self-interest. Also, given the adversarial nature of the policy process, there will almost always be a subset of decision makers for whom the results are unexpected or unwelcome.

Timeliness

Research results can influence policy only if they are available at the time policy actions are being considered. A traditional view of the policy process is that discrete policy actions are considered and taken (or rejected) within narrow "policy windows" defined by political events (Kingdon, 1984). If this view is correct, then social experiments are at a decided disadvantage with regard to timeliness because of their long life spans. As noted in earlier chapters, a typical experiment takes at least 3 to 5 years to complete and can take as long as 15 years from initiation to final report. Clearly, if an experiment is begun when interest in a particular policy issue is high, by the time it is completed the policy window will have long since closed. Attempting to predict which policy issues will be of interest 5 to 15 years in the future is a hazardous business, however; if experiments must anticipate policy windows this far in advance, most will miss the mark and end up being useless.[5]

Fortunately, in reality policy is made in a much more flexible, continuous way than the policy window model would suggest. Most policies and programs evolve over a number of years. For example, "welfare reform" has been a subject of concern in both the federal executive branch and Congress almost continuously for more than 30 years. Although the specific policies and programs proposed and enacted have varied widely during this period, many of the underlying behavioral issues (most notably, how to equip or motivate welfare recipients to work) have been remarkably constant during this period. Much the same could be said of policy with respect to the federal role in health insurance or job training. In such policy areas, experiments focused on fundamental behavioral issues that are central to the effects of policy are highly likely to be relevant no matter when their results become available. Thus, for example, although the income maintenance experiments were conceived as part of the Johnson administration's Great Society and implemented during the Nixon administration, the results were actually used in the formulation of President Carter's welfare reform proposals.

It must also be borne in mind that the results of experimental research can have a relatively long shelf life. As noted earlier, some of the behavioral parameters estimated from the income maintenance and health insurance experiments in the 1970s are still being used in policy simulations today. Thus, even if the policy window is not open at the time the experimental results are released, the results are added to the inventory of knowledge about a particular policy area and are available to be drawn on the next time the policy window is open. Of course, to be useful in subsequent policy rounds, the experiment must address important, fundamental behavioral issues or generic policy approaches that are of continuing interest. A test of a single idiosyncratic policy package is likely to be obsolete by the time it is completed—if only because the champions of that particular approach are likely to have left the government.

Experiments with particularly compelling results may create their own policy windows. That is, policy issues that would not have otherwise been considered may be thrust onto the agenda because of the results of an experiment or set of experiments. The Unemployment Insurance (UI) Self-Employment Demonstrations are an example of this phenomenon. Conducted by the research office of the U.S. Unemployment Insurance Service as part of an effort to find ways to facilitate the reemployment of UI claimants, the demonstrations showed that providing training and financial assistance to claimants to help them start their own businesses was cost-effective from both the claimant's and the government's perspective. These findings led directly to a legislative proposal to allow states to establish such programs. This proposal was enacted into law in 1993; to date, 10 states have adopted enabling legislation for self-employment allowances, and 7 have implemented programs under this provision.[6]

Finally, one type of experiment for which timing is much less an issue is the evaluation of ongoing programs. Because ongoing programs receive legislative scrutiny every year as part of the annual appropriations process, their policy window is virtually always open. Thus, the results will be relevant for policy whenever they become available unless the program has been eliminated or substantially changed while the experiment was in progress. Thus, for example, the final results of the National JTPA Study, which was launched in 1986, did not become available until 1994 but had an almost immediate impact on program policy via the appropriations process.

Communication and Visibility

Research results can be used in the policy process in any of a wide variety of ways or not at all. Whether and how they are communicated will strongly condition the extent to which they are used by policymakers.

In this regard, it is important to note that "policymakers" can include a wide range of actors in both the executive and legislative branches at several different levels of government. Their level of understanding of social science research can vary equally widely—from those with essentially no familiarity (and often little patience) with technical material to those with advanced degrees in social science disciplines. Communicating with such a heterogeneous audience is difficult both in terms of finding channels to reach them effectively and in terms of articulating the message in appropriate terms.

Sometimes, the channels of communication that matter are relatively straightforward, as in the example described previously of the UI Self-Employment Demonstrations. One of these demonstrations was congressionally mandated at the initiative of a congressman with an interest in the policy. Once the results of the experimental tests became available, he sponsored a legislative proposal to enable states to adopt the intervention as an ongoing program. Because the proposal was backed by solid evidence that it would not cost the taxpayers money and was otherwise noncontroversial, the strong backing of a single congressman was sufficient to secure its enactment as federal law.

Usually, the lines of communication between researchers and policymakers are more indirect. In many policy areas, there are established "issue networks" that link researchers, program managers, and policymakers.[7] This is true, for example, in the areas of welfare, employment and training, and youth programs. Members of such networks communicate through such diverse vehicles as professional meetings and conferences, committees and working groups formed to address specific issues, contractual relationships between private research organizations and government agencies, and personal contact, as well as through more formal mechanisms, such as legislative hearings and dissemination of written documents. Professional organizations and public interest groups, such as the Association for Public Policy Analysis and Management, National Governors' Association, and the National Association for Welfare Research and Statistics, play important roles in these networks. Often, research results are widely known within the network long before they are formally published as reports or journal articles. Although top-level policymakers seldom participate directly in such networks, their staffs frequently do; this provides one of the most important channels through which research results flow into the policy process.

The size and long life span of most experiments give them an advantage in gaining visibility within the policy community. In many cases, experiments have been widely discussed within the relevant issue network long before their results are available.

Finally, experimental results are much more likely to be influential if they have an advocate or interpreter who promotes them in the policy community.[8] It is not sufficient simply to publish a report of the findings and expect policymakers to act on them. Someone has to bring the results to the appropriate policymakers' attention, explain how they relate to policies under consideration, and respond to questions and criticisms from both the research and policy communities. Such advocacy usually involves repeated (and repetitive!) presentations in the many forums of the relevant policy network; it may also involve direct communication with high-level government officials or their staffs.

Perhaps the best example in recent years of such advocacy on behalf of research results is the efforts of Judith Gueron in advancing the results of the work-welfare experiments of the early 1980s. Her numerous presentations at conferences and research meetings led to working directly with the chairman and staff of the Senate Subcommittee on Social Security and Family Policy in the drafting of the Family Support Act of 1988, the most important welfare reform legislation of the 1980s. The evidence from these experiments is generally credited with playing a key role in the passage of the main component of the act, the Job Opportunities and Basic Skills (JOBS) program.[9] Certainly, the results were well-known by participants in the legislative process; one observer-participant counted 40 separate references to the studies in the public hearings on the Family Support Act (Haskins, 1991). Although this level of visibility is rare for social science research, it illustrates the impact that experimental research can have if aggressively promoted.

Generalizability

Experiments test specific policies applied to specific populations in specific geographic areas. The utility of the results therefore depends crucially on how similar the specific experimental intervention, target population, and locale are to the policy context within which the results are to be applied. As noted previously, because of the long life span of the typical experiment, experimenters will seldom be able to exactly anticipate the intervention or program population that will be of interest to policymakers when the results become available several years later.

If the experimental sample overlaps the population that is of interest for policy, mismatches in composition can sometimes be addressed by analyzing subgroups of the experimental sample or reweighting the sample to match the policy population.[10] This might be the case, for example, if the results of a particular experimental intervention are available for the overall AFDC caseload in a state, but policy interest focuses on only those women who have been on the rolls for more than 2 years or where the composition of the caseload has changed since the experiment was conducted. In cases in which the experimental sample and the policy population do not overlap (e.g., where the experiment was conducted in a different state), it will be a judgment call whether the experimental results will provide more accurate guidance than the available evidence for a more similar population (e.g., nonexperimental studies of the AFDC population within the state).

In some cases, similar ex post adjustments can be used to address mismatches between the experimental treatment and the policy of interest. If the experimental treatment was defined as variations along a continuous policy dimension (e.g., tax rates or welfare benefit levels) to allow estimation of a behavioral response surface (see Chapter 3), the response to policy parameters not directly tested in the experiment can be inferred by interpolation from the responses to experimental treatments. Thus, for example, the Health Insurance Experiment tested only four coinsurance rates (0, 25, 50, and 100%), but these four rates covered the policy-relevant range, and responses to other rates can be inferred from the responses to these four by interpolation.

Unfortunately, only a minority of public policies can be characterized with continuous numerical parameters. Most experiments involve "black box" treatments—complex, multidimensional interventions whose overall impacts may reflect the effects of any or all their component parts. To some extent, it is possible to decompose such treatments into their component parts at the design stage through the use of factorial designs (see Chapter 3). There are both conceptual and practical limits to the number of separate program components whose effects can be separately identified, however, and one is left with the fact that the components themselves are black boxes. For example, one might break a training program down into classroom training, on-the-job training, and job search assistance. The impacts of, for example, the classroom training component, however, will be the result of a specific combination of curriculum, instructor's skills and background, physical facilities and equipment, program length and intensity, and so on. If the proposed program to which the results of the experiment are to be applied differs in any of these dimensions, one cannot be sure that it would have the same effects as the experimental program.

It is tempting to conclude that, for these reasons, black box experiments will seldom be useful for policy and therefore should be avoided. This is almost certainly an overreaction. Especially in areas in which there is a dearth of reliable research evidence, knowing with some certainty the effects of an intervention similar to the policy of interest may be extremely valuable, even if the two are not identical. Also, in cases in which there is no preexisting "policy of interest," an experiment that demonstrates that a new intervention is cost-effective may generate substantial policy interest in the intervention that was tested. My point is simply that, in deciding whether to launch an experimental test of a complex treatment, one must carefully consider whether this specific combination of policy elements will be of interest to policymakers 5 or 6 years later when the results become available.

One of the most difficult issues of generalizability for experimenters is that of the geographic representativeness of the sample (see Chapter 4). Because experiments generally require direct contact with the sample to administer the treatment and collect data, experimental samples are usually clustered in a small number of geographic locations to keep costs manageable. In contrast, policy interest usually focuses on larger geographic areas, such as an entire state or the nation as a whole. Many environmental factors and participant characteristics that can potentially affect the impact of the experimental treatment vary across geographic areas. Unless the experimental sites were randomly selected from all possible sites in the larger universe, there is no guarantee that these factors, and therefore the experimental impact estimates, will be representative of the larger universe.

For several reasons, experimental sites are usually not randomly selected.[11] Sites are frequently chosen in ways intended to ensure cooperation with the implementation requirements of the experiment. For example, researchers sometimes issue invitations to participate to large numbers of organizations of the type that will be required for the experiment; the location of the organizations that volunteer then determines the experimental sites. Even where researchers have attempted to select a national probability sample of sites, they have not always been successful because of the refusal of organizations at many of the selected sites to accept random assignment of applicants to a no-service control group.[12] Also, in many cases, funding constraints limit the experiment to such a small number of sites that even if they were randomly selected, their representativeness would be questionable.

Researchers sometimes deliberately forgo random selection of sites in favor of studying sites with "interesting" interventions or "best practices." Unfortunately, although this approach may yield information about the effectiveness of these particular approaches, the question of how generalizable these practices are may prevent policymakers from acting on the experimental results.

In contrast, nonexperimental studies are often conducted on nationally representative databases collected for other purposes, such as the Current Population Survey or the decennial census. Until researchers find ways to select more generalizable experimental sites, nonexperimental analyses will often have the advantage regarding this criterion. This does not necessarily mean that the nonexperimental results are more reliable. It does mean, however, that policymakers are sometimes faced with a choice between internally valid experimental evidence that is of questionable external validity (i.e., unbiased estimates for an unrepresentative experimental population) and externally valid nonexperimental results that may not be internally valid (i.e., potentially biased estimates for a representative sample).

Relevance

Research is obviously more likely to influence policy decisions if it is viewed as relevant to the issues that are central to the policy debate. In this regard, experimental research has the advantage that it focuses on behavioral responses to interventions that are within the control of policymakers in contrast to, for example, research that seeks to understand social interactions and behavior without linking them to policy.

Not all behavioral responses to policy interventions are central to the decision to adopt or retain the intervention, however. Some programs are justified on the grounds that they further certain social principles or values, almost without regard to their effects on behavior. Thus, for example, research demonstrating that the Social Security program has adverse effects on the labor supply of older workers is unlikely to convince policymakers to eliminate Social Security. Unless there is a program feature (e.g., Social Security's treatment of earned income) that can be adjusted to mitigate the effects found by the research, such findings are likely to be ignored. In designing experiments, therefore, it is essential to identify the specific policy decision that might be influenced by the experimental results and to assess the importance of the behavioral responses being measured by the experiment to that decision.

The perceived relevance of social research will also depend on its timeliness and generalizability, which were discussed earlier.

The Policy Environment

The likelihood that experimental results (or any other research) will influence policy also depends on the policy environment into which they are injected. As noted previously, research is only one of many factors that enter into policymakers' deliberations. If research is to influence the outcome of these deliberations, the other factors must be sufficiently inconclusive or offsetting for research evidence to tip the balance one way or the other. Moreover, policy decisions to which the research is relevant must be "on the table" or the research must be sufficiently persuasive to convince policymakers to take up these issues. The latter occurs only infrequently.

In a widely accepted view of the policy process, Weiss (1983, p. 221) summarizes the influences on policy as "the interplay of ideology, interests, and information." In Weiss's model, ideology is driven primarily by principles and values, and "interest" is defined primarily in terms of the policymaker's self-interest and not the social interest. Because policymakers' ideologies and the interests they represent are relatively impervious to empirical information, and research is only one of many sources of information on which they rely, it might seem that research is destined to play only a very marginal role in policy. Indeed, one of the major implications that Weiss draws from her model is that the greater the consistency of ideology, interest, and other sources of information, the less influence research is likely to have in the policy process.

A more optimistic view of the process is that ideology and interests set the objectives of policy but not the methods by which these objectives can be achieved. The latter is an empirical issue on which research can shed light. Thus, even when ideology and political interest are agreed on for a particular objective, there is still room for experimental evidence to influence the means chosen to attain the objective.

An example of such a situation is the policy environment in which the results of the National JTPA Study were released. The federal government had large deficits, which both the newly elected Republican Congress and the Clinton administration had sworn to eliminate. In this budget-cutting atmosphere, the response to the experimental results showing that JTPA had virtually no effect on the earnings of youths was to reduce the budget for this component of the program by approximately 80%. The budget for the adult component was left virtually intact, however, largely on the basis of the study's finding that the adult component was cost-effective. Thus, in this case the experiment was able to show policymakers how to achieve their objective of achieving budgetary savings with the least loss to society.

Of course, there are cases in which means as well as ends are dictated by ideology and political interest. At a minimum, however, the existence of credible, relevant experimental evidence, clearly and prominently presented, makes it more difficult to justify approaches that conflict with the evidence.

Using Social Experimentation
More Systematically in the Policy Process

Although one can cite scattered success stories, experimental research must become a more routine part of how government agencies evaluate existing and proposed policies and programs if it is to play a major role in the policy process. Although a few agencies have begun to develop systematic programs of experimental research, many of the experiments that have been conducted to date represent the isolated triumphs of a few persistent individuals over a system that is not attuned to the experimental method. Moreover, the level of resources currently devoted to evaluation overall is an order of magnitude too small to allow systematic examination of the many existing and proposed programs and policies.

In this section, I discuss ways in which experimentation could be used more systematically to enlighten the policy process. Some of the approaches have already been adopted by at least one federal agency; others have yet to be implemented. The following are the overall approaches considered:

♦ Systematic evaluation of ongoing programs
♦ Testing multiple approaches to the same policy objective
♦ Replicating apparently successful interventions
♦ Mandatory testing of new policies

Systematic Evaluation of Ongoing Programs

It is unfortunate but true that we have little hard evidence of the effects of most ongoing public programs. Also, although most government agencies (at least at the federal level) have research and evaluation budgets, few of them use these resources to systematically evaluate the impacts of each of their ongoing programs to determine whether they are meeting their objectives. Rather, research and evaluation activities tend to focus on collecting descriptive data and testing new policy prescriptions.

As noted in previous chapters, the payoff to evaluating ongoing programs can be quite high. If a social program is not producing the benefits to participants that are its raison d'etre, its elimination can save the taxpayers many times the cost of the evaluation required to measure its effects. Moreover, elimination of a program that is not producing the intended benefits for its participants entails little or no loss to these participants. In fact, continuation of an ineffective program may well harm its intended beneficiaries not only because it wastes their time and creates unfulfilled expectations but also because if policymakers assume that the program's objectives are being achieved, they will not initiate a search for more effective approaches. If, however, the program is effective, it is important to establish this fact so that it will not be scaled back or eliminated on the basis of less reliable evidence.

The tendency not to evaluate ongoing programs, in the face of the fairly obvious benefits of doing so, is probably attributable to several factors. First, the top levels of government tend to be preoccupied with justifying new programs and policies rather than reexamining existing ones. Thus, it is easier to obtain resources to test a new idea than to evaluate an ongoing program. Second, experimental evaluations require the exclusion of the control group from the program, which program staff often find more ethically problematic in ongoing programs than in special demonstrations.[13] Third, unlike tests of new policy proposals, evaluation of an ongoing program threatens an existing bureaucracy, whose wages constitute the "taxpayer savings" that would be realized if the program is found to be ineffective. Finally, as noted at the outset of this chapter, many programs are justified on ideological or political grounds, and it is simply assumed that they have their intended effects.

A notable exception to this rule is the evaluation program of the Employment and Training Administration (ETA) of the U.S. Department of Labor. Beginning with the National JTPA Study, which started in 1986, ETA has systematically launched large-scale experimental evaluations of each of its major ongoing employment and training programs—JTPA, the Job Corps, and the Economic Dislocation and Worker Adjustment Assistance program.

The Job Corps evaluation, which is currently under way, is particularly noteworthy because of several novel features designed to address the difficult problems encountered in evaluating ongoing programs (Burghardt et al., 1997). First, the evaluation sample is a random subset of all eligible applicants to the Job Corps in the 48 contiguous states and the District of Columbia; thus, the results will be generalizable to the national program. This was possible because, unlike many federal programs, the Job Corps is administered directly by the federal government rather than through grants to state and local governments. Thus, it was not necessary to obtain the voluntary agreement of local programs to participate in the study.

This allowed the researchers not only to draw a nationally representative sample but also to spread the sample thinly across all 111 local programs rather than concentrating it at a small number of sites, as most previous evaluations had done. This in turn permitted the second notable design feature of the Job Corps evaluation: Only approximately 7% of all eligible applicants were assigned to the control group.[14] The fact that only a small number of controls were drawn from each local Job Corps program substantially reduced the impact of random assignment on local program recruitment requirements and operations as well as diminished the resistance of program staff to the implementation of random assignment.

A limitation shared by all prior experimental evaluations of ongoing programs, including the Job Corps study, is that they have been one-time efforts, providing a "snapshot" measure of program effectiveness at a single point in time. Because programs evolve and change over time—indeed, the problems they are designed to address may change over time—a program that is cost-effective today may not be a few years from now. Therefore, for policy purposes, it would be highly desirable to have a more continuous measure of program effectiveness.[15]

A modified version of the Job Corps evaluation design could provide such a measure. Instead of drawing the sample at a single point in time, one could assign a small proportion of all eligible applicants to a control group on an ongoing basis and continuously collect follow-up data on the outcomes of all program and control group members. Such a design would allow estimation of impacts for each annual cohort of participants and, because it would be an ongoing system, would provide much longer follow-up than is typical of one-time studies. In addition, by pooling samples from consecutive years, one could obtain much more precise impact estimates for the overall sample or samples large enough to yield reliable estimates of program impacts on small subgroups of participants or both. Because data would be collected and analyzed continuously, an ongoing evaluation system would probably also reduce the lag between the program period under study and the time that impact estimates become available. (One would, of course, still have to wait at least 2 years to obtain 2 years of follow-up data.) Finally, short-term impact estimates would be much more informative for policymakers because they could be compared with the short-term impacts of the program on earlier cohorts, for whom longer term impact estimates are available.

Although continuous random assignment has never been implemented in an ongoing program,[16] it is certainly technically feasible from an administrative and implementation standpoint. Even in decentralized programs, random assignment could be conducted as part of the regular intake process using personal computer-based software. It would require only the political will to provide the necessary resources and make random assignment a program requirement.

Testing Multiple Approaches to the Same Policy Objective

As noted earlier, most social experiments have been tests of new programs or policies. Unfortunately, the tendency has been to test only one approach (or class of approaches) at a time rather than a range of alternative approaches to the same problem. As a result, if the tested approach is determined not to be cost-effective, policymakers have no useful guidance regarding how to address the problem. Only by initiating a new test of a different approach, which will take years to complete, can they hope to obtain a workable policy prescription. With seriatim testing of individual programmatic approaches, it could take decades to identify an effective policy intervention. And even when a cost-effective approach is identified, there is no assurance that it is the most cost-effective approach.

A better strategy would be to test a range of alternative policy options simultaneously in a single, integrated research project. This could drastically shorten the time required to identify an effective approach. Properly designed, it would also ensure that the alternatives tested are truly comparable in terms of their participants and the local environment.[17]

In those cases in which multiple interventions have been tested experimentally, the alternatives have usually not been fully comparable. For example, the National JTPA Study estimated impacts on participants' earnings for several different service strategies (Orr et al., 1996). Participants were not randomly assigned to different service strategies, however; rather, program staff selected the strategy deemed most likely to be helpful to the participants.[18] Thus, differences in impact across service strategies may have represented differences in participant characteristics as well as differences in program effectiveness. Similarly, a large number of different interventions intended to help welfare recipients gain employment have been tested during the past 20 years but almost always at different sites so that differences in program effects are confounded with site differences.[19]

These examples reflect the difficulty of implementing random assignment to multiple interventions at the same site, especially within the context of an ongoing program. In the case of the JTPA study, program staff were unwilling to allow random assignment to replace their professional judgment in the assignment of JTPA applicants to alternative service strategies. In the evaluation of welfare-to-work programs, local welfare program staff were generally unwilling to take on the administrative complexities involved in operating two different welfare-to-work programs simultaneously.

These kinds of implementation problems are very real and must be taken into account in designing tests of alternative policy interventions.[20] The returns to overcoming such problems can be substantial, however. By systematically testing multiple alternative interventions in the same setting, policymakers can obtain much more reliable policy guidance more quickly than can be derived from a collection of single-intervention experiments.

Replicating Apparently Successful Interventions

Occasionally, an intervention appears to be quite successful on the basis of evaluation results from a single site or trial. When the evidence of success is based on a random assignment evaluation, policymakers and researchers have tended to accept such results as definitive evidence of program effectiveness. This can lead to a rush to apply whatever program features were believed to be unique to that site on a larger scale. The problem with accepting such evidence at face value is that it may reflect nothing more than the unique local environment within which the test was run or sampling variability in the assignment of the experimental sample.

This is especially true when (as is often the case) the "successful" program occurs at the one site in a multisite experiment at which positive impacts were found. As noted in Chapter 6, one would expect to find impacts that are significantly greater than zero at the .10 level by chance alone at 1 site of 10. Add to this statistical risk of false-positive results the fact that any given intervention is likely to be genuinely more effective in some local environments than in others, and it becomes clear that statistically significant impacts at one site are not necessarily replicable at other sites.

Even when the successful program is not part of a multisite experiment, a kind of selection bias that tends to bring false-positive results to the fore may be at work. If, as one prominent evaluator has suggested, careful evaluation will show most social interventions to be unsuccessful,[21] any program that shows significantly positive results is likely to receive a great deal of attention. By the same token, however, a high proportion of these apparently successful programs are likely to be among the 1 in 10 trials whose statistically significant results reflect only sampling error. If, for example, only 1 of 100 interventions tested was truly effective, more than 90% of the tests with significantly positive results would be false positives! (That is, in 100 trials, we would expect 1 true positive and 10 false positives.)

It is also true that, in social programs, exactly what the intervention was is not always clear. What was implemented in the field may be quite different from the program model specified by those who designed the test. Even those who operate the program in the field may describe the program quite differently than it is actually run. Also, process analysts employed by the evaluator to document program operations may focus on the wrong subset of the thousands of details that comprise even the simplest program.

For all these reasons, it is hazardous to base policy on a single, small-scale test of a new idea, no matter how successful it may appear to be when tested. This is not to say, however, that such results should simply be ignored. Such interventions are, after all, more likely to be successful than totally untested ideas. They should be subjected to further validation, however, before being adopted as policy.

An instructive example of an intervention of this type is the "job club," or self-directed group job search, a technique for helping the unemployed find jobs that was first evaluated in the early 1970s. In a random assignment evaluation of the original job club program at a single site, postprogram employment rates in excess of 90% were recorded for the treatment group in contrast to 55% to 60% employment rates for controls at the same point in time (Azrin, Flores, & Kaplan, 1975). When the same approach was applied to unemployed workers with labor market handicaps, the results were even more dramatic: Employment rates remained at 90% to 95% for the treatment group, but those for control rates were only 20% to 30% (Azrin & Philip, 1979). During the 25 years since the original job club experiment, this approach has been experimentally tested in a wide variety of settings for a broad range of clients; in fact, it may be the most extensively evaluated intervention in the history of social experimentation. Although the impacts of self-directed group job search are often found to be significantly positive, they have frequently been nonexistent and have never been as dramatic as those of the first few studies that brought the technique to the attention of national policymakers. Far from the panacea that they initially appeared to be, job clubs have turned out to be just one more moderately effective tool in the employment and training service kit.

The follow-up studies of the job club approach were, in most cases, undertaken in the context of broader studies and not as conscious replications of the initial study. A more deliberate policy of testing the replicability of promising findings has been pursued by the Department of Labor (DOL) in the case of education and training interventions directed toward youths. This effort grew out of the National JTPA Study's finding that JTPA had essentially no impact on the earnings of youths. In response to this finding, the DOL consulted a wide range of experts in employment and training and youth development in an attempt to identify approaches that might be more effective than traditional JTPA services.

Two promising approaches were identified. The Quantum Opportunities Program (QOP) is a high school mentoring program that had been found to have strong positive effects on a wide range of outcomes, including graduation rates and performance on standardized tests, among disadvantaged students in a small-scale random assignment study in four cities (Hahn, 1994).[22] The Center for Employment Training (CET) is an employment and training service provider whose San Jose, California, center had been the only site of 13 to have significantly positive impacts on the earnings of youths in an experimental test of intensive training programs for youths (Cave, Bos, Doolittle, & Toussaint, 1993). Mindful of the danger that the programs or participant populations involved in these studies may have been atypical, or that the results may have simply been false positives, the DOL elected to replicate these programs at a larger number of sites, and evaluate the replication programs with random assignment, before attempting to implement them on a broader scale. The CET program is being tested at 7 sites, whereas QOP will be replicated at 12.[23]

Mandatory Testing of New Policies

Another way to protect against the risk of ineffective interventions being adopted as ongoing programs is to require that new policies be evaluated experimentally before being implemented on a permanent basis. This is analogous to the Food and Drug Administration requirement that new drugs pass randomized clinical tests of effectiveness before they can be put on the market.

In the context of U.S. social programs, this approach is particularly appropriate in programs for which state or local governments have much policymaking discretion, with federal funding and oversight. In such cases, new programmatic approaches are continually being implemented, usually with little or no evaluation. For example, during the past 20 years, states have adopted a large number of education, employment, and training programs and financial incentives to help welfare recipients become self-sufficient. Many of these new program components required federal waivers of the state's approved plan; in the late 1980s, the U.S. Department of Health and Human Services began to require that these "waiver projects" be rigorously evaluated, usually with random assignment. Not only has this requirement forced states to objectively assess policy changes that were often launched with great political fanfare and overblown promises but also, over the years, a large body of evidence has accumulated with regard to a wide range of interventions.[24] Although this evidence is not as systematic as one might wish, it nevertheless provides valuable guidance to states considering interventions that have been attempted elsewhere.

Notes

1. For a formal model of the value of a social experiment, see Burtless and Orr (1986).

2. See Greenberg and Mandell (1991) for extensive relevant references to the literature on research utilization as well as case studies of utilization of two important sets of experiments, the income maintenance experiments and the work-welfare experiments. The discussion in this chapter of the factors that affect the likelihood that the experimental results will influence policy owes much to Greenberg and Mandell.

3. Quite aside from the credibility of complex evidence, it is also true that results that tell a simple "story" are more easily deployed in the give-and-take of policy debates than those that require detailed explanation to be understood.

4. At the time the experiments were being implemented, a prescient memo from the White House to the Secretary of Health, Education, and Welfare warned of a "cacophony of conflicting results" if too many different income maintenance experiments were launched. The memo was signed by President Nixon but almost certainly written by Daniel Patrick Moynihan, an adviser to Nixon.

5. As one congressional staffer who played a key role in the development of the Family Support Act of 1988 stated, "Finding out whether the [work-welfare] demonstrations worked better than what we had before was important. Having the data in time to help shape and promote our legislative efforts was nothing short of amazing" (Baum, 1991, p. 608).

6. For a detailed description of the use of these experimental results for policy purposes, see Orr, Wandner, Lah, and Benus (1994).

7. For a detailed discussion of this concept, see Heclo (1978).

8. I use the terms *advocate* and *promote* in the neutral sense of vigorously bringing the results to the attention of the research and policy communities and not in the partisan sense of using them to advocate particular policies. In practice, however, it is sometimes difficult to distinguish the two.

9. See Baum (1991) and Haskins (1991) for two views of the role of these projects in the legislative process.

10. Both subsampling and reweighting involve some loss in precision—the former because of the loss of sample size and the latter because, for a given sample size, weighted estimates are less efficient than unweighted estimates. This is another instance of the trade-off between precision and bias noted in previous chapters.

11. Two experiments that were successfully implemented at a nationally representative set of sites are the evaluation of the Food Stamp Employment and Training Program (Puma, Burstein, Merrill, & Silverstein, 1990), which had 53 randomly selected sites, and the Job Corps

evaluation (Burghardt, McConnell, Meckstroth, & Schocet, 1997), which was implemented at all 111 program sites nationwide.

12. See the discussion in Chapter 4 of the experience of the National JTPA Study in this regard.

13. See the discussion of ethical issues in Chapter 1.

14. The 6,000 control group members were excluded from the program for 36 months. Of the 75,000 eligible applicants assigned to the treatment group, only 9,400 were included in the research sample to keep the costs of follow-up data collection manageable. Thus, the treatment-control ratio in the research sample was approximately 3:2.

15. Some programs (e.g., JTPA) have a continuous "performance measurement" system based on the postprogram outcomes of program participants. Because such systems lack control groups, however, they cannot measure the impact of the program on participant outcomes. At best, they measure the relative impacts of different local programs. Also, if outcomes in the absence of the program would vary across local programs, they are not even a reliable measure of relative impact.

16. I am aware of only one serious proposal along these lines. In 1991, the Food and Nutrition Service of the U.S. Department of Agriculture issued for public comment proposed regulations that would have allowed state Food Stamp Employment and Training programs the option of using random assignment to measure program performance on an ongoing basis rather than an outcomes-based performance measurement system ("Proposed Food Stamp Regs Released," 1991). These regulations were not adopted.

17. See the discussion of tests of multiple alternative approaches in Chapter 3.

18. This design was dictated by the objective of measuring the impacts of the program as it existed in the field, including staff discretion to assign participants to the services they deemed most appropriate. Given this objective, the rationale for estimating the impacts of different service strategies was to find out which parts of the program were working well and which were not rather than to compare the service strategies to find out which were the most effective.

19. A partial exception to this pattern is the evaluation of the JOBS program, in which welfare-to-work programs that focused on immediate job search and placement were contrasted with programs that emphasized long-term education and training. At three sites, welfare recipients were randomly assigned to both types of programs. At the remaining four sites, however, only a single program was implemented (Hamilton, Brock, Farrell, Friedlander, & Harknett, 1997).

20. See the discussion of implementation issues in Chapter 5.

21. Peter Rossi's "Iron Law of Evaluation" (1987) states that "when evaluated, the expected value of the effect of a social program is zero."

22. A fifth site was dropped from the evaluation because staff were unable to implement the program.

23. See Maxfield and Schirm (1997) for a description of the background and design of the CET replication study.

24. See Greenberg and Shroder (1997) for descriptions of these evaluations.

References

Azrin, N. H., Flores, T., & Kaplan, S. J. (1975). Job-finding club: A group-assisted program for obtaining employment. *Behavior Research and Therapy, 13,* 17-27.

Azrin, N. H., & Philip, R. A. (1979). The job club method for the job handicapped: A comparative outcome study. *Rehabilitation Counseling Bulletin, 23,* 144-155.

Baum, E. B. (1991). When the witch doctors agree: The Family Support Act and social science research. *Journal of Policy Analysis and Management, 10*(4), 603-615.

Burghardt, J., McConnell, S., Meckstroth, A., & Schocet, P. (1997). *Implementing random assignment: Lessons from the National Job Corps study*. Princeton, NJ: Mathematica Policy Research.

Burtless, G., & Orr, L. L. (1986, Fall). Are classical experiments needed for manpower policy? *Journal of Human Resources, 21*, 606-639.

Cave, G., Bos, H., Doolittle, F., & Toussaint, C. (1993). *JOBSTART: Final report on a program for school dropouts*. New York: Manpower Demonstration Research.

Darman, R. (1996, December 1). Riverboat gambling with government. *New York Times Magazine*, pp. 116-117.

Greenberg, D. H., & Mandell, M. B. (1991). Research utilization in policymaking: A tale of two series (of social experiments). *Journal of Policy Analysis and Management, 10*(4), 633-656.

Greenberg, D. H., & Shroder, M. (1997). *The digest of social experiments* (2nd ed.). Washington, DC: Urban Institute Press.

Hahn, A. (1994). *Evaluation of the Quantum Opportunities Program (QOP): Did the program work?* Waltham, MA: Brandeis University, Center for Human Resources.

Hamilton, G., Brock, T., Farrell, M., Friedlander, D., & Harknett, K. (1997). *Evaluating two welfare-to-work program approaches: Two-year findings on the Labor Force Attachment and Human Capital Development programs in three sites*. Washington, DC: U.S. Department of Health and Human Services/U.S. Department of Education.

Haskins, R. (1991). Congress writes a law: Research and welfare reform. *Journal of Policy Analysis and Management, 10*(4), 616-632.

Heclo, H. (1978). Issue networks and the executive establishment. In A. King (Ed.), *The new American political system*. Washington, DC: American Enterprise Institute.

Jastrzab, J.-A., Blomquist, J., Masker, J., & Orr, L. (1997). *Youth corps: Promising strategies for young people and their communities*. Bethesda, MD: Abt.

Jensen, G. A., & Marlock, R. J. (1994, March/April). Why medical savings accounts deserve another look. *Journal of American Health Policy*, 14-23.

Kingdon, J. W. (1984). *Agendas, alternatives, and public policies*. Boston: Little, Brown.

Maxfield, M., Jr., & Schirm, A. L. (1997). *The Quantum Opportunity Program Demonstration: Year 1 report*. Washington, DC: Mathematica Policy Research.

Orr, L. L., Bloom, H. S., Bell, S. H., Lin, W., Cave, G., & Doolittle, F. (1996). *Does job training for the disadvantaged work? Evidence from the National JTPA Study*. Washington, DC: Urban Institute Press.

Orr, L. L., & Visher, M. G. (1987). *AFDC Homemaker-Home Health Aide Demonstrations: Client health and related outcomes*. Washington, DC: Abt.

Orr, L. L., Wandner, S. A., Lah, D., & Benus, J. M. (1994, October). *The use of evaluation results in employment and training policy: Two case studies*. Unpublished paper presented at the Annual Research Conference of the Association for Public Policy Analysis and Management, Chicago.

Ozanne, L. (1996). How will medical savings accounts affect medical spending? *Inquiry 33*, 225-236.

Proposed Food Stamp Regs Released. (1991, September 18). *Employment and Training Reporter*, p. 27.

Puma, M. J., Burstein, N. R., Merrill, K., & Silverstein, G. (1990). *Evaluation of the Food Stamp Employment and Training program*. Alexandria, VA: U.S. Department of Agriculture, Food and Nutrition Service, Office of Analysis and Evaluation.

Rivlin, A. M., Cutler, D. M., & Nichols. L. M. (1994). Financing estimation and economic effects. *Health Affairs, 13*, 30-49.

Rossi, P. H. (1987). The iron law of evaluation and other metalic rules. In J. Miller & M. Lewis (Eds.), *Research in Social Problems and Public Policy, Vol. 4*. Greenwich, CT: JAI.

Weiss, C. H. (1983). Ideology, interests, and information: The basis of policy positions. In D. Callahan & B. Jennings (Eds.), *Ethics, social science, and policy analysis*. New York: Plenum.

◆ Index

About the Author

Larry L. Orr is Chief Economist and Vice President of Abt Associates. He received a PhD in economics from the Massachusetts Institute of Technology. He has participated in the design of more than 20 major social experiments in the areas of income maintenance, health insurance, home health care, housing, employment and training, community service, and welfare reform. He directed the recently completed National Job Training Partnership Act Study and the evaluation of the Aid to Families with Dependent Children Homemaker-Home Health Aide Demonstrations. He serves on the editorial board of *Evaluation and Program Planning*. Prior to joining Abt, he directed the Office of Technical Analysis, U.S Department of Labor, and the Office of Income Security Policy Research, U.S. Department of Health, Education, and Welfare. In the latter position, he managed the income maintenance experiments and the Panel Study of Income Dynamics, conceived and managed the Health Insurance Experiment, and chaired the working group that developed the initial design for the Survey of Income and Program Participation. He is author of *Does Job Training for the Disadvantaged Work? Evidence From the National JTPA Study, Program Applicants as a Comparison Group in Evaluating Training Programs*, and *Income, Employment, and Urban Residential Location*.

Printed in the United States
84976LV00003B/49-54/A